Few – if any – s[ecret societies have captured the]
imagination as has the notorious Hell-Fire Club of the
18th Century. And it is easy to see why. The combination
of uninhibited sexuality, occult practices and political
conspiracy, all involving some of the greatest aristocratic
figures of the time, is indeed a heady one.

Although several useful, well-researched works of
historical investigation concerning the Hell-Fire Club
have been published over the years, for obvious reasons
there have been very few firsthand inside accounts of its
astonishing activities available to the general reader. Now,
at long last, this deficiency is remedied by the publication
of *Unholy Passions: Erotic Secrets of the Hell-Fire Club*,
the uninhibited intimate memoirs of a young nobleman
who was fortunate enough to be on close terms with the
Club's founder, the charismatic and lusty Sir Francis
Dashwood. Here, then, is the riveting account of the
sexual excesses, magickal rituals and clandestine
conspiracies of probably the most fascinating undercover
organization in British history.

Also in paperback from New English Library

The Pearl: volume 1
The Pearl: volume 2
The Pearl: volume 3
The Pearl Omnibus
The Oyster: volume 1
The Oyster: volume 2
The Oyster: volume 3
The Oyster: volume 4
The Oyster: volume 5
The Oyster: volume 6
The Oyster Omnibus
Rosie – Her Intimate Diaries: volume 1
Rosie – Her Intimate Diaries: volume 2
Rosie – Her Intimate Diaries: volume 3
Rosie – Her Intimate Diaries: volume 4
The Rosie Omnibus
The Black Pearl: volume 1
The Black Pearl: volume 2
The Black Pearl: volume 3
The Ruby: volume 1
The Ruby: volume 2
The Ruby: volume 3
Erotic Memoirs: volume 1
Erotic Memoirs: volume 2
Arena of Lust
The Secret Sutras

Unholy Passions: Erotic Secrets of the Hell-Fire Club

Anonymous

Translated, edited and introduced by
Marcus Ardonne, Ph.D.

NEW ENGLISH LIBRARY
Hodder and Stoughton

Translation and Introduction copyright © 1997
by Marcus Ardonne, Ph.D.

This edition first published in 1997
by Hodder and Stoughton
A division of Hodder Headline PLC

A New English Library paperback

The right of Marcus Ardonne to be identified as the Translator
of the Work has been asserted by him in accordance with the
Copyright, Designs and Patents Act 1988.

10 9 8 7 6 5 4 3 2 1

All rights reserved. No part of this publication may be
reproduced, stored in a retrieval system, or transmitted,
in any form or by any means without the prior written
permission of the publisher, nor be otherwise circulated
in any form of binding or cover other than that in which
it is published and without a similar condition being
imposed on the subsequent purchaser.

All characters in this publication are fictitious
and any resemblance to real persons, living or dead,
is purely coincidental.

British Library Cataloguing in Publication Data

Ardonne, Marcus
Unholy passions
1. English fiction – 20th century
I. Title
823.9'14[F]

ISBN 0 340 66696 X

Typeset by Avon Dataset Ltd, Bidford-on-Avon, Warks
Printed and bound in Great Britain by
Cox & Wyman Ltd, Reading, Berkshire

Hodder and Stoughton
A division of Hodder Headline PLC
338 Euston Road
London NW1 3BH

CONTENTS

Translator's Introduction   vii
Author's Preface   1
Unholy Passions   9

EDITOR'S INTRODUCTION

The academic year was drawing to a close and the long summer vacation lay stretched enticingly before me like a voluptuous high-priced hooker on her back with her legs apart, snatch glistening damply, tweaking her nipples into a state of perky arousal and moaning softly, 'Oh, Ardonne, give it to me hot, give it to me hard.'

I hummed under my breath my own words to the immortal song of the mercifully mortal Sir Cliff as I sorted out my gear for the forthcoming field trip.

'Ardonne's going on his summer holiday,
Looting, shafting for a month or two.
Ardonne's going on his summer holiday,
Plenty rich pickings for me, not you,
For-hor *mee-ee*, fuck *you* . . .'

As Thatcher Professor of Archaeology at St Augustine's College, Cambridge, I realize that I have to be seen to maintain the highest standards of professional conduct at all times and under all circumstances, however difficult those circumstances may on occasion become. So when it comes to selecting my equipment for a field trip – or 'dig' as we academics call it in our arcane jargon – I am always absolutely scrupulous about the quality and appropriateness of the items that are to accompany me. They can, after all, make that crucial difference between success and failure when one is engaged in those painstakingly sensitive procedures that are the distinguishing features of the modern archaeological expedition.

Opening up the large antique chest in which I keep the tools of my trade, I started to make my selection. I pondered briefly on the respective merits of the double-barrelled sawn-off and the Ingram Model 10. Call me a nostalgic old softy – on second thoughts, better not – but I did feel a bit tempted to take along the cut-down shotgun: there's something about the sheer fucking *directness* of the thing that's always appealed strongly to me for some reason. But in these matters you really do have to let your head rule your heart, so it was back in the box for the shotgun and into the suitcase for the Ingram and its accompanying silencer and ammo clips. (Firepower – especially at a cyclic rate of 700 rounds per minute – rules, OK? OK.)

My Randall Model 18 survival knife and S&W Chief's Special Airweight with a box of .38 Special slugs followed the Ingram in short order, along with a couple of stun grenades. For the delicate excavation work in which I expected to be engaged I slung in a few cakes of Semtex plus detonators. For the *really* sensitive close-up stuff I packed an ordinary heavy-duty builder's crowbar.

I walked over to my wall-mounted safe and unlocked it. Bribes are a regular feature of the kind of archaeological quests I undertake so I withdrew a few stacks of dollars, Deutschmarks, Swiss francs and yen, along with various assorted gold coinage and (nothing if not patriotic) a few thou' in shaky old sterling. Reaching further back into the safe, I located my stash of pharmaceutical-grade cocaine and palmed a couple of one-ounce phials, sealing them in layers of protective bubblewrap before adding them to the contents of the suitcase.

I had no worries about Customs, not on the way out or back and certainly not at the point of entry in my destination country. I would be travelling in the private executive jet of my good friend and even better customer Sheikh K—— of the little-known but ludicrously wealthy Gulf kingdom of Z——, and Customs would have no part to play in my journey as a result. Sheikh K—— had commissioned me to excavate – from the high-security Zurich museum in which they had resided for the past seventy years – some priceless bejewelled erotic figurines of the T'ung Dynasty period. After that, it would be on to Africa, South America, the Far East: money and mayhem all the way, just how I like it.

As I mused on the delightful prospect of the coming months, there came a hesitant knock at the door of my apartment. I checked my gold Rolex and saw that the time for the last stage in the 'continual assessment' programme of one of my most difficult students had rolled around.

'Enter!' I called out, a hearty note in my voice.

The door opened to reveal the curvaceous figure of Lady Diana Fitz-Snugleigh in a skimpy summer dress standing on the threshold. Her long, curly auburn hair fell to her shoulders and her silky-smooth, slightly olive skin was a shade or two darker than usual: the lazy cow had obviously been sunbathing during the recent heatwave when she should have been studying.

'Ah, Diana, good to see you. Come on in and come – I mean, close the door after you, please. Thanks.'

Diana did as she was asked. I indicated the guest's chair beside my desk and she sat down in it, what little there was of her dress rising high up her rounded, tanned thighs as she leaned back. As I sat down in my own chair on the other side of the desk, I looked straight up her skirt to where her panties formed a black 'v' at her crotch. Those'll be coming off soon or my name's Barbara Cartland, I thought to myself.

Diana frowned as she looked around the room at the evidence of my packing: the weaponry, the piles of currency. 'Christ, Ardonne, what's going on here? You thinking of taking over the college administration or something? Mounting a coup, perhaps?'

'Mounting *you*, more like, in about – ah, three or four minutes, I'd say. No, university politics don't interest me. Cunt and money do, though. So just mind your own business and get your clothes off. We've got to see to the last stage of your assessment, haven't we?'

'I don't know why I put up with this . . . this *outrageous* treatment. You're—'

'*I* know why. One, you like it. Two, if you don't co-operate at what you'd no doubt call the last fence, your degree results are going to be distinctly disappointing and you're going to have some tough explaining to do to your family. Simple as that. So strip and spread.'

Looking daggers at me, Lady Diana rose to her feet and pulled her minidress over her head in one fluid movement, flinging it with what she presumably thought of as a defiant gesture into a corner of the room. She stood haughtily, shoulders thrown back so that her breasts jutted forward, straining against the vestigial fabric of her black bra. Reaching behind her back, she unclipped the fastener and slid the bra down her arms before balling it up in her hand and throwing it at my head. I battered the wisp of material aside, laughing softly and admiring the way that Diana's full, firm breasts, crowned by dark pink nipples, bounced and jiggled with the motion.

'Like what you see? Getting a good eyeful, are you?' she hissed.

'You bet. Off with your panties, now. But leave your high heels on, OK?'

Diana flushed with renewed anger but did as she was told, peeling her panties down over her beautifully rounded hips and luscious thighs and letting them drop the rest of the way down her trim calves and ankles. Stepping away from them as they lay on the carpet, she kicked them viciously under my desk. I feasted my eyes on her neat auburn pubic bush.

'Now what?' she said. 'As if I need to ask.'

'But you should. If I haven't been able to instil the true spirit of academic enquiry into you by now, then I've failed as a tutor—'

'Bastard! All you've been interested in *instilling* into me is your fucking great prick!'

'True enough, I guess, but one has to go through the motions. Right now, the motions we're going to go through are those of (a) rear-entry copulation, followed by (b) fellatio – the latter being the Big Test for you, Diana, in view of your previous less than wholehearted performance in this area*. Now, if you'd be so kind as to bend over my desk . . .'

Diana turned and did as instructed. The high heels she was still wearing gave a firm line to the backs of her calves and thighs, at the same time as they caused the full globes of her taut young aristocratic arse to thrust up and back and part slightly in a most appealing manner. As I approached this enticing rear elevation, I looked at the pouting pink pussy lips winking at me from within their nest of auburn cunt hair (already moist, I noticed, rather giving the lie to Diana's hostile protestations), and the cute puckered ring of Diana's anus. I felt briefly like the snooker player in the joke who can't decide whether to go for the pink or the brown but I decided – with some regret – that this was a muff-'n-mouth-only occasion for my rod.

Arriving at my position behind Diana, I unzipped swiftly and let Old Purpletop rear up unrestrained, rigid as a poker and

---

* See the Translator's Introduction to *Arena of Lust* by Sextus Propertius (New English Library, 1996).

raring to sink deep into warm, moist, snug cooze. I placed my left hand on the back of Diana's neck, gently but firmly forcing her head down until it rested on the desktop and she was supporting her upper body's weight with her outstretched arms. With my right hand, I guided the bulging tip of my flesh-cannon to the outer lips of her quim, lodging it just inside before transferring my hand around to the front of her crotch. I ran my fingers through the fleecy hair of her Venus mound before sliding my index finger along the front stretch of her crack, parting the slick flesh-folds there and locating the nublet of her clitoris which I proceeded to frig, softly at first and then with an increasing urgency.

Diana gasped, then moaned with mounting arousal. I leant forward gently, pushing the whole length of my stiffly engorged cock deep into her snatch before beginning a circular thrusting motion of my hips that caused my Hampton to swirl around vigorously inside her quim, bringing sensations of sweet stimulation to every nerve ending on the inner surfaces of her slick jellybox. Diana's moans increased in intensity as she began to build towards her climax.

'Mmmmmrrrggghh... gnnaaasssh... heurrggh... aaarrrr...' she gasped. Her hips began to rotate in synchronization with my own movements and at the same time I could feel her legs beginning to buckle at the knees as her orgasm approached inexorably. Luckily the desk supported her weight. I changed my motion to one of straightforward in-and-out thrusting, withdrawing to the tip of my prick at the top of each stroke before savagely plunging its whole length back deep inside Diana's slit, my free-swinging balls banging against the back of her tanned thighs.

Diana suddenly stiffened as her orgasm finally swept over her and she began to buck uncontrollably under me, her cunt muscles spasming and squeezing frantically at my plunging cock. 'Ahhh! In up to the hilt! Shag me senseless! Fuck-a-cock-horse! Want it! Aaaaaaaahhhhh!' She finally slumped forward, breathing as hard as though she'd just run a five-mile race.

I stood back, withdrawing my still-rigid joy prong from Diana's sated snatch, and coughed discreetly.

'Ahem!'

Diana lifted her head slightly from the desktop and looked towards me, her eyes unfocused and bleary with sex.

'Wha'?' she muttered.

'It may have escaped your attention but I deliberately didn't come up you just now. That's because I want the last part of your assessment to be a truly memorable one for you. When I *do* come – in your mouth – in a few minutes, it's going to be the "copious libation" of erotic legend. And your final grading will depend on how much of it you swallow. None of this spitting it out or slyly letting it dribble out of the corners of your mouth when you think I'm not looking. You'll be assessed on how much of it you get down your neck, so to speak. OK?'

Diana did not look best pleased at this. Genteel distaste was apparent in the way that she hung her head slightly and turned down the corners of her mouth. But, as we both knew, she really had no choice in the matter. She raised herself from the desk and came over to me, then sank wordlessly to her knees in front of me. I nudged her full lips with the tip of my tadger, prodding at first gently, then more insistently until she parted them enough for me to get the tip of the old mutton dagger in. Holding her head firmly in my hands, I gradually forced a few more inches in until I sensed that Diana was just on the point of gagging.

'Right, you know what to do now,' I said. 'Just lick and suck as you have before. But *this* time, remember, you damned well *drink* it when it spurts into your precious mouth.'

Diana nodded mutely as best she could with a mouthful of *viande d'Ardonne* and began to swirl her tongue – with no small degree of expertise, it must be admitted – around my cock's glans and the first couple of inches of its shaft. She started to suck – again, reasonably expertly – after a couple of minutes of this. Because I'd held back from coming during our recent fucking session, this stimulation very soon brought me to the brink of discharging my spunkflood but I restrained myself for a few seconds longer as I held onto Diana's head with an ever firmer grip, pushing my prick deeper and deeper into her mouth. Believe it or not, I was actually trying to make things easier for her, figuring that the more of my creamstick I had down her throat at the time I ejaculated, the more spunk I could shoot directly past her tonsils, so bypassing any involuntary gagging reflex she might experience that would imperil her final assessment grading.

'Right, Diana,' I grunted. 'Nearly there. Coming... coming... ah, yes, *thaar she blows! Come on, now, GULP FOR YOUR GRADE!*'

I felt the ever-welcome electric sensation of the tidal rush of sperm racing down my prick's inner tube from my tightening balls to explode out through my knobslit in gush after pulsing gush. My prick leapt and jerked in spasms of sheer ecstasy as it pumped its spunky load past Diana's tongue and down her throat in wave after wave of liquid delight. As I clung to her head, continuing to thrust my rig into her mouth, I glanced down to see her gulping and swallowing frantically in a desperate effort to keep up with my outpourings. As the last lingering sensations of orgasm faded away and my cock ceased to buck around like a spring ram in Diana's mouth, I saw that she had won the race. As she leant back on her heels and my deflating dingus slipped from her kisser, I saw that not a drop dribbled from her mouth and, as she ran her tongue around her lips, I could tell that she was not holding anything back to spit out when I wasn't looking, either.

Ever the gentleman, when all's said and done, I bent to

retrieve Diana's scattered underwear and dress from the floor and handed them to her. 'Well done, Diana,' I said, as she slipped rapidly back into her bra and panties. 'Good effort.'

'That's as may be,' Diana replied. 'But I can't see myself ever getting a taste for the dreadful stuff. I hope *you're* going to be as good as your word.'

'I'm hurt that you should think I wouldn't be. Let me put it this way: one swallow may not make a summer, but in your case . . . it's got you a First!'

Soho in summer may not be to everyone's liking but it sure as hell is to mine. The sex shops, the strip clubs, the walk-up hookers, the ordinary girls in their vestigial minidresses that barely cover their tits and arses, all this in a sweltering atmosphere that makes skin run with sweat, causing those same minidresses to cling even tighter to the curves of the female bodies they clothe . . . if this is global warming, then I'm off to burn down another fucking tree!

With a few hours to kill before Sheikh K——'s private executive jet left Heathrow for Zurich, I was in Soho to look up my lowlife colleague Horby – Hackney Horby – at his 'studio' in one of those side streets off Wardour Street. He'd only rented it recently and I wasn't sure of the exact nature of the business he carried on there. But I was sure it had to be pretty dubious and hence of potential interest to me. So when Horby had suggested I drop by en route to the airport I'd happily agreed.

I found the street concerned and located without any trouble the multi-occupied building in which Horby had his premises. I ran my eye down the listing of occupiers beside the entryphone intercom until I spotted *3rd flr.: Joxy Cinevideo Productions: prop. H. Horby (estab. 1995)*. I did a doubletake at the name of the enterprise before pressing the buzzer.

' 'Orby 'ere – oozat?'

' 'S the Old Bill, you bent cunt. Fuckin' open up.'

'Oh shit, oh fuck, oh sweet bleedin' Jesus Christ...'

'Calm down, Horby, you tosser, it's only me, Ardonne. Anyone'd think you'd got something to hide. Come on, buzz me in.'

'Oh, thank Christ. You shouldn't do that, guv, give a man an 'eart attack one day, you will.'

'The day you get an art attack is the day I start taking it up the arse from Guy the gorilla. Now fucking *come on* and buzz me in.'

The buzzer sounded, the door swung open and in I went. I climbed the three flights of stairs to Horby's 'business' premises to find the man himself already waiting for me on the landing. The moderate wind-up I'd given him over the intercom didn't seem enough to account for the state of nervous agitation he was manifestly in, shifting from one foot to the other and darting anxious glances all around.

'Good to see you, guv, glad you could make it. Come on in, then.' Horby motioned towards a door set in the right-hand wall of the corridor leading off the landing. Another door on the same side looked newer.

'What, renting the whole floor, are you?' I asked.

'Nah, guv, just this side.'

'Where's that other door lead? Fire escape?'

'What door? Oh, that. Nah, just a ... a broom cupboard, yeah.'

We entered a room full of the clutter of the professional photographer-cum-video-maker: cameras on tripods, towering high-power lights, glare reflectors, that kind of thing. The dominating feature, though, was a four-poster bed with an upright rectangular frame set against its foot in the centre of the room. My trained archaeologist's eye noticed short restraining straps attached to each corner of the frame.

'Horby, don't mind me asking, but how did you come to

choose the name you did for your company?' I asked.

'What, Joxy? Oh, I wanted sumfink that might remind people of the old days of cinema, so I thought of, you know, Roxy, then I wanted sumfink that sounded cheerful, so I thought of "jolly", put 'em together, like, and got "Joxy".'

'Why didn't you just call your company "Cunt Cinevideo"?' I said.

'*What?* Why the bleedin' 'ell should I want to do sumfink like that? "Cunt Cinevideo"? What kind of name is that for a respectable family business? Christ, guv, leave it out, will ya?'

'No, Horby, I'm serious. "Joxy" *means* cunt: I'm surprised you didn't know. It's a long-established slang word for vagina, maybe not that much used today but still . . . look in any decent thesaurus of slang and there it is, just after "jellybox" and "jing-jang" and just before "joy-trail". I kid you not.'

Horby looked distinctly crestfallen. 'Ah, fuck it, guv. This is seriously bad news.'

'Yeah, well, I suppose it *is* a bit of a hassle, getting letterhead changed and suchlike, but . . .'

'Nah, guv, you don't understand. I've just diversified into the cheap-toy business, bringing in loads of stuff from China and that. And . . .'

'Don't tell me, let me guess. You wanted a nice kiddy-friendly sounding name for the product that would also convey an element of the colourful East. So you chose . . .'

'Yeah, that's right: Jing-Jang Toys. Oh fuck, I think I'll kill myself.'

'Bit extreme. Actually, Horby, I wouldn't sweat it too much if I were you. I don't think either term is in widespread current use and, anyway, what's the old adage about no such thing as bad publicity? You might even be able to offload Jing-Jang Toys onto some dirty-minded fuckwit who thinks they're sex aids or some such. Think positive!'

'Well, maybe. Look, guv,' Horby's more than usually shifty

expression was back, 'fink you could do me a small favour?'

'Depends. I've got a plane to catch, after all.'

'Well, I've got to nip out for an hour, max, and I wonder if you could look through this old book for me while I'm out and tell me if there's anything interesting in it. I mean, it's been in my family for fucking ever but no cunt's been able to read it for generations because it's written in some sodding foreign language. And in this bloody oldfashioned handwriting, too, all fucking f's where they should be s's and crap like that.' Horby passed over some undistinguished-looking dusty tome with cracked leather binding.

'Once again I'm left speechless by the scope of your literary and historical insight, Horby. OK, I'll see what I can make of it and if you're not back by the time I have to go I'll leave you a note – one you can read, no joined-up writing or crap like that, eh?'

'Be 'elpful, guv, cheers. Oh, 'n one uvver fing: there's this glamour model due round for a photo session sometime soon. If she arrives before I get back, can you, er, make her comfortable, like, give 'er a cuppa or somefink?'

'Or something, I expect. Yeah, sure. Look, Horby, fuck off now, there's a good chap, otherwise there's no way I'm going to get a look at this book of yours before I leave for the airport.'

'OK, guv. See you, then.'

'Yeah, I guess.'

Horby, still in distinctly shifty mode, left the studio, shutting the door behind him. I strained my ears for the sound of his footsteps along the corridor outside as he headed for the stairs but all I heard was the faint sound of another door opening. I shrugged as I sat down on one of the studio chairs and started to leaf through Horby's book.

The 'foreign language' in which it was written turned out to be Latin, but Latin of the formalized English eighteenth-century variety rather than the original Ancient Roman stuff. A quick browse through the brittle pages revealed several mentions of the Horby name – curious, that, I thought – and, most welcome, a whole lot of meaty shafting action. Frequent references to the Hell-Fire Club also aroused my interest.

Before I'd had time to do more than skim the Horby book, there was a knock at the studio door. I got up, walked across the room and flung the door open. A very welcome sight greeted my eyes.

Standing there was as nifty an example of fuckable femaleness as any man could wish for. Her height was the only average thing about her. Her hair was blonde, long, straight and thick, falling in a shimmering cascade over her shoulders and on down her back. Wide blue eyes, a classically pert upturned nose and pouting, full lips that looked as though they'd been made for the prime purpose of sucking cock were her most immediately striking facial features. As my gaze travelled on down her body, I noted a good pair of tits thrusting pertly against the thin material of her T-shirt, a trim waist above nicely-rounded hips, shapely thighs scarcely covered by an abbreviated skirt and long, slender calves tapering down to trim ankles. I raised my eyes to her face again and noticed that the overall effect of a distinctly class act was marred somewhat by the steady rotation of her jaws as she chewed methodically on a wad of gum. I could think of better things to fill her mouth with.

'Joxy?' she asked.

'Yes, please,' I replied.

'Pardon? Is this Mr Horby's place?' Her voice carried the would-be genteel tones of Essex suburbia.

'Yeah, it is. You must be the model he's expecting. Come on in.'

She entered and lowered a large shoulderbag to the floor as I closed the door behind her. Her blue eyes narrowed slightly as she caught sight of the bed and the bondage frame.

'Mr Horby won't be long. He asked me to, er, help you get ready for the photo shoot. I'm Marcus, by the way. What's your name?'

'Pam. You Mr Horby's assistant?'

'Sort of, I guess. You could say we help each other out from time to time. Now, if you'd like to get ready . . .'

'OK. Mr Horby asked me to bring along the usual gear.'

'Forgive my ignorance in these matters, but what might that be, then?'

Pam looked at me curiously. 'Well, you know, skimpy undies, stockings, suspender belt – that sort of thing.'

'Oh, I see. Yes, I'm sure that'll be fine.' (*You bet it will*, I thought).

'Can I get changed behind there, then?' Pam asked, indicating a folding screen against one of the studio walls.

'Yeah, fine.'

Pam hefted her shoulderbag and disappeared behind the screen. As well as the rustling noises of her undressing I became aware of other noises, faint whirring ones, coming from behind a wall opposite the bed-and-frame arrangement. I wandered over and took a look. The wall itself was some kind of plasterboard partition and I realized that it effectively made the studio smaller in floor area than the dimensions of the corridor outside indicated it should be. A suspicion began to form in my mind.

All other thoughts were set aside, though, as Pam emerged from behind the changing screen in her full glamour-model glory. Starting at her high-heeled glossy black shoes, my gaze travelled swiftly up her legs, now sheathed enticingly in sheer seamless black nylon stockings, over the stretched-tight black-lace suspenders that spanned the smooth area of naked thigh-flesh between stocking-tops and pantie-edge, across the skimpy white-lace panties themselves (so close-fitting that I could swear the outline of her cunt-lips was clearly visible through them) and on up across her slender waist, her breasts, the nipples barely concealed by the briefest imaginable white-lace bra. Pam's curvaceous body was superb: firm and taut, it thrust against the token restraints of her minimal underwear in all the right places.

But as I looked higher, I noted a feature that was definitely *not* acceptable. For some reason, Pam had tucked her glorious long blonde hair up under some fuckawful brunette beehive wig! The effect was distinctly disappointing.

'Pam, why the wig?' I asked.

'Oh, I wear it so's people won't recognize me as a glamour model when I'm out with my boyfriend. It was his idea.'

'Well, I'm very sorry but you're going to have to risk being recognized as far as *this* shoot is concerned. Mr Horby was most insistent that the model for the, ah, the Hell-Fire Club photos has to be a long-haired blonde. He won't accept anything other.'

'What's this about a Hell-Fire Club? No one said . . .'

'Nothing to worry about, just a bit of historical make-believe. But, no two ways about it, the wig has to go. So if you'd be so kind . . .'

With visible reluctance, Pam undid the pins that held her wig in place and removed it, letting her long blonde tresses fall free once again. I hoped that this little episode had shown her conclusively who was in charge here.

'Now then, Mr Horby also wants this shoot to be topless, so if you'd be good enough to remove the bra? I assume you have no problem with that? I mean, I suppose your boyfriend knows what your ti–, er breasts look like but no one else is likely to recognize you from that particular feature, are they?'

The sarcasm was lost on Pam as she cheerfully reached behind her back to undo the fastening of her bra. 'Oh, no, I do a lot of topless. Photographers say they're my best feature.'

'I can see why,' I replied as Pam's tits proudly swung into full view. (Personally, I'm more of a legs and arse man, tending to subscribe to the view that, where tits are concerned, more than a handful is a waste, but there was no doubt that Pam's bazoomas were something special: classically firm and rounded, they stood taut and thrusting even without the minimal support of the discarded bra, their perky pink nipples growing erect seemingly of their own accord as I watched.)

Pam blushed prettily at the compliment. 'When's Mr Horby coming back, then?' she asked.

'He should be back by now, actually,' I responded. 'I know he's on a tight schedule today. As a matter of fact, I think we'd better get you into the first of your poses right now so that he can get started as soon as he returns. OK?'

' 'Spose so,' Pam said with some hesitancy.

'Good. Then if you wouldn't mind standing over by the frame . . . yeah, fine . . . and just lift both arms above your head – as if you were surrendering, ha ha . . . good, that's it . . .'

Moving swiftly across the studio floor, I grabbed hold of one of the restraining straps at the top of the frame and wrapped it swiftly round one of Pam's wrists.

' 'Ere, what . . . ?' She tugged uselessly at her bonds as I seized her other wrist and secured it with the second strap at the frame's top. I stepped back to admire the view. Pam's arms were raised and held securely in position, her bare breasts thrusting forward and jiggling slightly with the motions of her useless efforts to free herself. She had clamped her stockinged thighs tightly together, as if by reflex.

'A magnificent sight, worthy of the Hell-Fire Club itself during its finest glory days,' I remarked.

'Bleedin' well untie me! Mr Horby never said nothing about bondage shots! I don't do kinky! Standard fee, 'e said . . .' Pam fulminated.

'Oh, if it's money that's the problem, don't let it be,' I said, moving over to my holdall, taking out a grand in twenties and placing it on a nearby worktop. I turned to face the plasterboard wall. 'I'm sure *Mister* Horby will be happy to reimburse me for any extra payments I make to you, under the circumstances.' I turned back to face Pam and moved across to stand close to her as she wriggled and squirmed in the frame.

' 'S not what I meant!' she said desperately. 'I think there's been a bad misunderstanding here and . . .'

'Oh, I don't think so,' I interrupted. '*My* understanding of the situation is pretty clear. As I see it, I've been lucky enough to have every red-blooded hetero man's dream made flesh handed to me: a real glamour model in classic gear' – I ran one hand slowly up Pam's legs, savouring the feel of the warm thigh-flesh under my fingertips as they passed from the nylon texture of the stocking-tops – 'more or less to do what I want with for a while. No prizes for guessing what *that* might be, either.' I stroked Pam's breasts with my other hand, gently rolling her stiffening nipples between my thumb and forefinger. She jerked and twisted frantically – and uselessly – against her restraining bonds.

'No, please, you've got it all wrong. Just let me loose and—'

'Not as simple as that, Pam, I'm afraid,' I said as I gave her lace-covered cuntal mound a brief squeeze before taking hold of her arse globes in both hands and kneading them rhythmically through the tight material of her panties. 'You see, I *feel*' – here I slid both hands beneath the snug lower edge of the panties until I had two handfuls of smooth, warm and naked bumflesh in my grasp – 'that I have to make a point here on behalf of all other hetero members of my gender, quite apart from taking my own admittedly selfish pleasures with you.' I pulled Pam's barely-covered pubic mound against the bulging crotch of my jeans. She tried once more to pull away until I stuck a middle finger partway up her anus, causing her to gasp and twitch involuntarily forward, bringing her pubic region once more up against my own.

'As a glamour model,' I went on, 'you actually make money out of prickteasing at one remove.' I bent my head and took one of Pam's nipples into my mouth, sucking gently and running my tongue around it. 'Now, I guess most men – me, certainly – are happy enough to be teased like this. It's fun to look at shapely tits and arses and cunts, after all.' I took one hand away from Pam's arse, unzipped my flies and released the engorged length of my rigid cock. I held it in my hand and rubbed it gently against the lacy flimsiness of the material covering her cuntal mound. 'But I've always promised myself that if I ever got a chance to do more than just *look* – well, I'd be a right fucking idiot not to take it, wouldn't I?'

Pam was breathing hard by now, partly in fear and partly, I was pretty certain, from arousal. 'Look,' she gasped, 'it doesn't have to be like this, you know. You're a good-looking feller, you're built like a tank and you've got money—'

'And a Porsche,' I said, sliding the tip of my prick in around the tight edge of Pam's panties and rubbing it slowly through her moistening pubic bush. She tried to keep her thighs clamped tight but I pushed my hand between them, forcing them apart just enough to let me get the bulging end of my chopper up against her actual cunt lips. I bent my knees slightly so that I could nudge my cockhead into the top of her slit, rubbing at her clitoris. Pam twisted and writhed with renewed fervour.

'Ah, no, let me go, no, please don't, oh *please* ... a Porsche? Wow ... no, please, I mean, if you let me go maybe we could go out on a date, get to know each other better ... oh, not like this, not—'

'Pam, sweetheart, I'm about to get to know you pretty well as it is, I do believe. And what's all this about going out on a date? What about your boyfriend? No, I appreciate your friendly gesture, but I think things could get a bit too complicated for me. I'm a man of simple tastes. Sorry.'

Poised as I was at the very entrance to Pam's cooze, I thought for a moment of plunging on in there and then. But I was put off by the thought of a possible friction burn on my prong from the pantie lace – it can happen, believe me – so I stood back slightly and, hooking my thumbs at the edge of Pam's tiny panties, eased them slowly over her shapely arse, her trembling thighs and on down over her long, slender calves and high-heeled shoes. As her blonde pubic bush came into view, I saw with delight that she had trimmed it into a heart shape.

'Nice touch, Pam,' I said, indicating the sculpted pubes with a nod of my head. 'All ready for a visit from Cupid's arrow, are we? More like Cupid's 25-pounder field artillery piece in my case, of course. Well, you've been very generous in the display of your charms so I guess it's only fair I should return the favour.'

I turned to face the plasterboard wall again and knelt swiftly to remove my boots and socks before getting up to unbuckle my belt. I pushed my jeans and underpants down, stepped out of them and, finally, pulled my T-shirt over my head in one quick movement and threw it to one side. Turning back towards the tethered Pam, I saw how round her eyes grew at the sight of my erect tool.

I noticed a lever arrangement at the base of the bondage frame and soon discovered that it allowed the frame to tilt back through ninety degrees. Pam, though still secured by her wrists, now lay on her back on the four-poster's counterpane.

'Bit more civilized like this, eh?' I asked as I knelt straddling her before lowering myself onto her trembling form. I ran my hands over her breasts before moving them on down across her quivering stomach. I then moved one hand underneath her firm young arse, grabbing one luscious flesh-globe and pulling her hips up as I simultaneously shoved the other hand between her stockinged thighs, forcing them apart as prelude to my pork sword's assault on her sweet honeypot.

'I beg you, please, don't *do* this to me,' Pam breathed desperately as I manoeuvred my crotch into position and placed the distended tip of my rock-hard rod against the outer lips of her moist snatch. She made one last frantic attempt to clamp her thighs together. Once more, I forced them apart and, this time, taking hold of each leg behind the knee, pushed them up and back so the fronts of her nylon-sheathed thighs almost pressed against her shoulders. Her blonde pubic hair and pouting pink cunt lips lay delightfully exposed, framed enticingly by her stocking-tops and the black lace of her suspender belt.

I leant forward slightly so that my cockhead just nudged into the portals of Pam's pussy. For a couple of seconds I relished the feel of the grip of the flesh-ring of her cuntal entrance. Then, slowly and steadily, I sank the whole length of my stiff shaft into the slick, snug depths of Pam's quim.

'Ah, no! Stop! Take it out! Get out of me!' Pam shrieked. I'd released my hold on her legs by now, transferring my grip to her wonderfully firm and smooth bum cheeks, and she began to beat frantically on my own buttocks with her kicking heels. This, of course, had the effect of driving me even deeper into her cunt so I wasn't going to complain.

Pam continued to tug frantically at her bonds as I stepped up the pace of my thrusts into her slick snatch, keeping a tight hold on her superb arse globes as I pulled her crotch tightly against my rod-root. (When you're fucking a glamour model, I figured, best make sure you do it right up to the hilt.) She continued for a minute or two with her futile pleading but I noticed after a while that she'd stopped vocalizing and started moaning and gasping. I grinned inwardly, recognizing the signs.

I carried on driving my ramrod into Pam's most intimate flesh-depths as her facial expression underwent some changes, too. As I continued my pounding thrusts, I saw her grit her teeth, lips pulled back in what looked like (but wasn't) a savage snarl, nostrils flaring as her gasps grew deeper and hoarser. Finally, she threw her head back with a harsh yell of mingled ecstasy and outrage. 'Oh, no! Ah! Ah! I've come! I've come! You fucking bastard! *You've made me come!*'

A thousand quid, an orgasm – and she calls me a fucking bastard! No pleasing some people, is there?

'My turn next, then, Pam. You got there ahead of me,' I gritted, still pounding away.

'No! No more! You mustn't come up me! Get out! Get out of me!'

'Sure – when *I've* come.'

Pam went into a frenzy of kicking, bucking, twisting and writhing as she tried to dislodge me from her vanquished snatch. The effect, of course, was to increase my pleasure in the procedure and, soon enough, I felt the familiar welcome build-up of pressure in my balls as they slapped against Pam's silky-smooth buttocks. Then the sperm-tide was once again coursing down the inner length of my cock to explode in pulse after magnificent jetting pulse out through my pricktip, flooding Pam's innermost cunt-depths with a deluge of creamy spunk.

'I come ... in peace ... for all ... mankind,' I gasped.

I got my breath back quickly and withdrew my (still semi-erect) prick from Pam's conquered quim. She lay on the bed, legs splayed, her skin running with sweat, breasts heaving as she too recovered from our recent lusty exertions.

As I bent to tie the laces of my boots, I heard a distinct grunting sound from behind the plasterboard partition. I charged across the room, raised my right foot and kicked a good-sized hole through the flimsy wall. Then, taking a grip on the edges of the hole with both hands, I wrenched hard, bringing the rest of the partition crashing down into the studio. Crouched in the small room – broom cupboard, my arse – thus revealed was a startled Horby, stiff prick in hand, crouching behind a small tripod-mounted videocamera that had obviously been recording through a small opening the goings-on with the bondage frame and the four-poster.

'Well, well, well, what have we here, eh? It's the lurker at the threshold himself, I'll be bound. What *are* you up to, Horby?' I reached out swiftly and grabbed him by one ear, hauling him out of his lair and into the main studio.

'Ouch, guv, leggo,' he whimpered.

'Not till you explain yourself,' I said, giving the ear a savage twist for emphasis.

'*Aaargh!* All right, all right! I was just doin' my job, see? I wanted to tape a steamy bondage-and-fuck show but I couldn't afford no proper porno actors for it—'

'I thought there was government money available for that kind of thing – you know, small-business enterprise allowances or whatever the fuck they're called.'

'Nah, not for the likes of me, guv, I've got to scratch along as best I can —'

'Oh, Jesus, don't Horby,' I growled, twisting his ear again, 'you'll have me in tears of sympathy if you carry on like that.'

'*Ow!* Can't you take it as a compliment, or sumfink? I mean, I knew I could rely on you—'

'Rely on me to fuck the arse off any attractive woman who crosses my path, you mean? Yeah, well, you've got a point there, I guess.' I released Horby's ear with one last tweak for good measure. He retreated to a safe distance, rubbing the mistreated organ and with a hurt expression on his pocky face. 'But you needn't think that's the end of the matter. Since you've involved me in this particular creative project, I'm taking a controlling interest – let's say sixty per cent of gross revenue, shall we? – and also giving *you* a chance (a chance I absolutely insist that you take, incidentally) at screen stardom.'

I opened my holdall and removed another grand in twenties, holding the wad up for Pam to see. 'Pam, Mr Horby, suitably disguised, will shortly be joining you on the bed for another session of rumpy-pumpy—' I disregarded her shrieks of outrage and shock and went on '—and this time it will be me behind the camera. I doubt whether Mr Horby has my kind of staying power in these matters so I should be able to get the tape finished, in rough-cut form, naturally, with time to spare to catch my plane.'

I turned to Horby. 'Right, then, that's two grand for Pam's fees that you'll owe me on top of my agreed cut of the proceeds. I'll throw in the wording of the video-box credits for free: "An Ardonne/Horby Film for Joxy Cinevideo Productions. Starring Marcus Ardonne Ph. D. as himself and 'Hackney' Horby as the Man in the Mask in—" the title's pretty crucial for these things, let me think, yeah, right, got it "—in *Teaser Gets It*." Right, Horby, to work!'

Marcus Ardonne, Ph. D. *Cambridge, December 1996*

PREFACE

'You're the very Devil in disguise, Horby,' a gentleman of acid wit declared to me the other day at White's, 'and you have absolutely no right, sir, still to be living.' It is possible that the Prince Regent was perfectly correct in his observation and certainly one is mildly astonished to find oneself still in being at the age of seventy-one in this year of Our Lord 1800. I did not expect to survive the century, given the somewhat extraordinary and admittedly debauched and dissipated life which I have lived hitherto. However, I could not but think that His Royal Highness, the Prince Regent* was longing equally and eagerly for the death of his father, our poor, mad King George III, a pleasant simpleton presently confined in a madhouse to the great advantage of the further prosperity of the Whig aristocracy, which the Tories and the democrats assail as an oligarchy, and of which I am pleased for my own advantage to be a member.

In point of fact, I doubt if I *will* live for very much longer. In my youth, of course, one was either a three-bottle man or a four-bottle man when it came to pints of port and my later habit of being a six-bottle man will no doubt hasten my demise. Gout is somewhat painful and although only yesterday I tried an Algerian 'port' that my doctor assured me was a fine remedy for the matter, the cure was worse than the disease and,

---

* Finally crowned King George IV in 1820: Ed.

in all honesty, I prefer the gout. My repeated fucking, too, has taken its toll upon my physique: these days I can only manage to fuck my wife twice a month and some whore once a week. Some call me a dirty old man but at least I was a dirty young one first.

The statement of the Prince Regent brought home to me the notion of my imminent mortality, though this did not bother me unduly since I have enjoyed my life hitherto. I have rejoiced in the company of some of the most interesting and ingenious men and of some of the most delectable and lascivious ladies of the century through which I have lived. During my life I have witnessed changes such as my father could never have imagined, even in the most fanciful of nightmares such as might be conjured out of the paintings of Fuseli and that crazed lunatic, William Blake. Revolution has occurred in the American colonies, now called the United States of America, though one wonders how long this spurious Union will last. And revolution has occurred, too, in the former Kingdom of France, now a Republic and one which, under that expert Corsican corporal Napoleon Buonaparte, threatens the civilization and values of yore, the entire fabric of society and the supremacy of Britannia herself.

'And what do you propose to leave your son, eh, Horby?' A chortle emanated from the fat face of the Prince Regent, then his words lifted my stage-coach of thought from the muddy ditch of introspection onto the rucky road of retrospection. The Prince Regent possessed the squinting eyes of a hungry pig. He could not wait to seize the throne with his clumsy trotters so that he could finally pay his many creditors. I was reminded of the wicked jest of John Wilkes, that former Member of Parliament and former Lord Mayor of London – also the former radical cursed by King George III as 'that Devil Wilkes' – who was asked to propose a toast at a dinner where the Prince Regent was present.

UNHOLY PASSIONS

'Here's a long life to his Majesty King George III!' Jack Wilkes cried out, to the discomfiture of the heir to the throne.

'And since when, Mr Wilkes,' the Prince Regent enquired icily, 'have you been so solicitous of the welfare of His Majesty?'

'Ever since I have had the privilege of knowing Your Royal Highness,' Wilkes responded sweetly.

Even so, it was hard to avoid the bugger in White's and I did indeed want my son to enjoy the same leverage I had with the man who might be King. I consequently informed His Royal Highness that my son would receive my entire estate, since he was my only issue. (I omitted to mention a bastard daughter for whom I have provided well.) There was no need to expound either the details of my lands in Hampshire and Gloucestershire or of those in Devonshire brought to me by my wife. Nor, come to that, the prudent investments made upon the Stock Exchange and with Lloyd's and Baring's, nor the trades in tea, silk and spices which my younger brother expedited most capably from Calcutta where, among other things, he is a leading luminary in the British East India Company. My younger sister is happily married to an extravagantly wealthy Nabob in Bengal, who loses no opportunity to assist his brothers-in-law and who, naturally, receives useful British favours in return.

My father certainly provided well for his two sons and one daughter. Equipped only with a nimble brain and ten thousand pounds left to him by my grandfather, a minor trader with the East, he soon built up the family business to a state whereby he was able to participate in the notorious South Sea Bubble of roughly eight years ago. This, the gentle reader may recall, consisted of a fever of speculation with vast sums being invested into utterly worthless companies. Many of these were controlled by my father, a man on excellent terms with Sir Robert Walpole, whom he kept consistently informed of his doings. At precisely the right moment and at the veritable peak of speculation, my father sold all his holdings; as, of course, did Sir Robert Walpole. All shares then plummeted and all companies crashed into a cess-pit of debt. Sir Robert Walpole became Prime Minister and remained so for over fifteen years. My father enjoyed his reward in being created a Baron and proceeded to buy up lands lost through unwise speculation from indebted aristocrats. This was indeed sound progress for a man whose grandfather, a tanner, had been known as ' 'Ackney 'Orby.'

I was born in 1729 and, my mother having died in my infancy, I was largely educated by myself, a nurse, a governess, a tutor and Trinity Hall, a medieval foundation of Cambridge University. My father died in 1748, leaving me, then aged nineteen, a title and a large fortune. These were items I could leave in time to my own son, but I wondered whether I could conceivably leave him more of my *life*.

After my conversation with the Prince Regent, I ordered my carriage to take me to my town house in Pall Mall where I resolved to contemplate the matter over a bottle of port. I decided to dine alone and late, on turtle soup, two capons and a batter pudding for the next course, then a roast sirloin of beef with roasted onions followed by a syrup pudding with raisins and, finally, apples and oranges. Claret, I find, goes better than port with a repast of this nature, though I certainly intended to attack the port and nuts subsequently. A pinch of snuff, flavoured by sandalwood, would certainly stimulate my brain beforehand and afterwards I would contemplate my life and the world generally over a clay pipe of tobacco, which soothes perturbation of the brain. My wife, comfortably ensconced in Gloucestershire, was not expecting my arrival for several days and was no doubt glad of my absence. My brother in Calcutta had also thoughtfully shipped me a quantity of excellent opium, a substance which renders contemplation doubly agreeable, and hashish, which opens the doors of a man's perceptions.

UNHOLY PASSIONS

Prior to my dinner and over several glasses of sherry, I decided that I wanted to write an account of my life for my son. This account would contain the complete truth concerning that confraternity known variously as The Hell-Fire Club, the Monks of Medmenham and the Friars of St Francis of Wycombe. It would encapsulate the truths behind all the scandals and sexuality, politics and religion of our age. Far too much nonsense has already been written about this 'Club of Clubs', yet the facts should be related and the truths must be told. Since I was a member of the allegedly infamous 'Inner Circle' of the 'Unholy Twelve', indeed was one of the Knights of Sir Francis of Wycombe, I am only too well aware of the Secrets.

That is why this work has been written in Latin. My son is unfortunately not of an academic persuasion but this work may conceivably inspire him to learn that Classic tongue. Moreover, although I treasure the fondest memories of my friend, the democrat and demagogue John Wilkes, I still find that his advocacy is increasingly resulting in mob rule manipulated by the knowing ones; and I prefer the élitism of Sir Francis Dashwood, 'Hell-Fire Francis', the late Baron Le Despenser, Premier Baron of England and Our Founder. If I write the history of my life in Latin, it will be available to the cultured and civilized but the gates will have been barred to the barbarians*. Perhaps and peradventure at some date in the future, when humanity is more enlightened, as was the dearest wish of the Club, there may be one who can translate the truth for the lasting benefit of future generations.

Paul Whitehead, the Club Steward, burned all Club papers one day prior to his death in 1774. I noticed that my dear doctor, Benjamin Bates, possibly responsible for keeping me alive so long and himself a fine fellow and Club member, is

---

* *Translator's note*: Not entirely so. Marcus Ardonne.

informing all enquirers that our association consisted of genial gentlemen and 'was mostly unjustly stigmatized by some of the scandalous and sarcastic fabrications of its contemporaries'. Genial gentlemen certainly, and luscious ladies also: it is indeed essential for the truth to be told, for the Club gave me the most exciting and most treasured years of my life. Within its hallowed portals, it held some of the most sacred secrets of humanity – including the precious truth that the Holy Grail can be sought in sex.

Governments rose and fell on account of our machinations: and the European Revolutions and that of America were unintentionally fomented. Dashwood, Sandwich and I – and some other worthy notables – discovered the sexual secrets of the Ancient Philosophers and their expression in behaviour, art, architecture and landscape gardening. Although our influence upon our time was great, it could have been greater yet and so I regret the chances that we may have missed.

Initially, as a boy, I had thought that the only mystery of sex consists in wondering how to get it, wherefore I shall commence my Memoirs with an account of the loss of my virginity. Subsequently, as a wild young man, I fancied that there was nothing more to sex than a jolly good rogering. Later I would learn some secrets of the vast and starry Universe in which we live and move and have our being. Even though I write in Latin, some may accuse me at a later date of betraying sacred secrets. I answer that there is no such betrayal. One could print these sacred secrets in all journals and have them circulated within every coffee-house or tavern and there is barely a personage who would be one whit the wiser. He or she who *would* be wiser and who can understand the recondite is worthy to receive hidden wisdom.

On this particular night, therefore, given my solemn resolve to write of my life and loves and times, I shall meditate upon the matter in peace and quiet, resolved to commence my undertaking on this coming Monday. I take up my pen and write the ensuing note to my butler:

'Sunday, wind and weather permitting, I propose to be drunk. Place a crate of sherry by my bedside and call me the day after tomorrow.'

CHAPTER ONE

At the tender age of fifteen, when I was still, be it said with shame, a virgin, my father entrusted me to the care of my elder cousin, Lady Clarissa, who had married into the aristocracy and whose exceedingly ugly and unpleasant husband had died within two years of the marriage, leaving the bulk of his substantial fortune to her. This is customarily what occurs when a rake of sixty contracts a marriage with a woman of twenty and, judging from what was subsequently rumoured in the clubs and coffee houses, Lady Clarissa simply wore the poor sod out and fucked him to death. She now enjoyed a substantial income and an estate in Surrey, along with a town house in Mayfair which was where I stayed for three months in the glorious summer of 1744, along with my tutor, the elderly, kindly, learned and affable Reverend Aloysius Herbert, an Oxford graduate.

I have nothing other than fond memories of the Reverend Aloysius Herbert, who enjoyed the ancient Greek and Roman Classics more than he enjoyed anything else, save possibly his many glasses of sherry, claret and port. Although he was an astute, patient and inspiring teacher, he liked to retire early to bed, therein as he muttered to himself to study more Catullus, Juvenal, Petronius, Apuleius and other ancient authors who, even in these more enlightened days, might elicit frowns from the brows of the unduly censorious. After the hour of six o'clock, therefore, I was usually left to my own devices.

Lady Clarissa was an enchanting hostess, one gifted with grace of manner, charm and physical beauty. Her voice possessed the teasing softness of a tinkling bell. She declined to have her head shaven and to wear a wig, unlike so many of her contemporaries, since she ensured that her long blonde tresses were washed every day by her maidservants. Her eyes were a stunning azure blue, her mouth a perfect Cupid's bow, her complexion as white as the finest Chinese porcelain. Her evidently fine figure was inevitably adorned by the finest of the silks and satins of the East. Her dresses accentuated her swan-like neck and a devastatingly low cleavage emphasized the healthy heaving and thrusting of her breasts, outlining her firm nipples. The fashions of the time rendered it hard to guess at the beauties of her bottom in its no doubt glorious naked majesty, but she did poise and switch it, causing her skirts to swish and her petticoats to rustle, at virtually every available opportunity. I could at that time essay no estimation of her legs, though I had witnessed more than one man gasp at the sight of her peeping ankle.

In the Summer months, she used to wake up around midday and ring for her maids to attend her in her boudoir. Sometimes a beau would leave the house quietly: sometimes a beau would stay. Guests were received at two o'clock when Milady took her second cup of hot chocolate, which had to be whirred and whisked by the servants according to her precise instructions, and for the hour following her chocolate, in which, it was rumoured, brandywine had been poured liberally, she enjoyed sherry with the large circle of friends and acquaintances she entertained in her boudoir. My tutor and I would be required to attend at three in the afternoon and it was on these occasions that I first made the acquaintanceship of Frederick, Prince of Wales; Sir Francis Dashwood; and the Earl of Sandwich, who were later to play so great a part in my life.

At three-thirty, a magnificent midday repast would be

UNHOLY PASSIONS

served in the dining-room for favoured guests, all dressmakers, jugglers, clowns, dwarfs, actors, aspiring authors and those of no substance, whose talent was purely to amuse, having been dismissed. As we proceeded to eat a magnificent meal, washed down by copious quantities of claret and followed by even more copious quantities of port, the beaux would compete with one another to obtain Milady's attention. Eventually she would select one, rather as though she were choosing a pastry from a platter and popping it into her mouth, biting upon it with her dainty white teeth in an action of the utmost delicacy. Her admirer would then take her to the play, although there were no good plays at that time, owing to the reintroduction of censorship in the theatre by Sir Robert Walpole. One went to the play simply in order to see and be seen.

Afterwards she would return to her town house, either with a beau or with lady companions. In either case, port would be served or sometimes, in the Winter, hot, spiced claret, accompanied by a cold collation of game, poultry, beef and smoked fish. If it was a ladies' evening, these ladies would usually call for their carriages shortly before the hour of midnight, save on the odd occasions when a particularly close friend of Lady Clarissa was invited to spend the night within the boudoir of Milady. No one ever knew what transpired between the hostess and her female guest, though one can guess. On other occasions, a beau would spend the night: so much did I lust after the sight of Milady and after her gentle favours, that I fear I almost entered at these times into a jealous frenzy of adolescent heat.

On one particularly hot evening of Summer, Lady Clarissa returned with her intended beau of the night. Shortly afterwards, I overhead her driving him from her boudoir with oaths and imprecations.

'You are not a gentleman!' she was shrieking. 'You are not

even a man! Kindly leave before I order my servants to give you a sound beating!' A rather bedraggled-looking beau staggered down the staircase with the sad aspect of a wet spaniel. I saw him from my chair in the library, for I had left the door open, where I was busy perusing *The Art of Love* by Ovid. Some moments later, after the front door had slammed fast, I overheard Milady instructing her servants and it was shortly after that I beheld her sweeping into the library, with a rustling of silken blue skirts and a crackling of petticoats. She held a glass of port in her left hand, with its long and elegantly manicured fingernails like scarlet talons, and she swished her blue dress as she seated herself, placing what looked to me like a luscious bottom upon a chair. I noticed the beauty spot upon her right cheek, which accentuated the haughtily angular nature of her face and the power of her shining sapphire eyes. I had tried to hide my book but I fear that she had already discerned the nature of my reading, as she teasingly opened her fan, festooned with the feathers of the male peacock, and coolly regarded me.

'Well, Horby,' she smiled sweetly as she regarded me, 'are you enjoying reading *The Art of Love* by Ovid?' She laughed, a deep, rich, throaty chuckle, as I flushed furiously. Her mouth then turned downwards at the corners. I was lost for words as she continued: 'And do you wish to essay its practice? You are a good boy; come and sit by me.' I obeyed as if in an hypnotic trance, allowing my book to fall to the floor as I nestled at her feet. Clarissa drained her glass of port and called for more. I did nothing as her butler proceeded to serve her and withdraw. Suddenly she bent forward and kissed me full on the lips: I can only compare this experience to being branded by the flaming torch of desire. My prick rose up so stiffly, I feared I might go mad from lust. I shivered as she caressed my hair and mused awhile.

'How I long to suck the sweets of love from your lips,' she

sighed languorously, 'to fondle and caress your youthful yet lordly priapus...' Here she stroked my prick through my breeches and I shuddered with the sheer joy of the sensation, '... Ah! It would be such a sweet delight to feel the thrilling motions of your Mons Priapus and experience its thrusting lunges within me...'

'Yes...' I sighed deliriously.

'I can but sigh,' she responded, 'as I look upon your kind, loving, young face and admire the fine proportions of my darling younger cousin, as evidenced by the flint arrow-head supported by round stones that you seem to have within your britches. Indeed, young sir, you look to have a key of keys, whose burning thrusts might unlock any virgin cabinet.' The strong fingers of her hands grasped my monster through the cloth I wore and John Thomas pulsated at her touch. My blue-veined piccolo stiff as a rolling-pin, I flung myself into Clarissa's arms and she covered me with kisses.

'Ah!' she exclaimed, 'how I have longed for you these three or four days!' Her hands unbuttoned my britches and grasped my ready truncheon. With a gentle effort, she reclined backwards on her chair and raised her skirts and petticoats until I had a full view of her splendid pair of slim, white legs. But what riveted my gaze most were the luscious, pouting lips of Clarissa's cunny, quite vermilion in colour, and slightly gaping open, in a most inviting manner, as her legs were wide apart; her Mons Veneris being covered with a profusion of beautiful, curly fair hair.

I was down on my knees in a moment and I glued my lips to her crack, sucking and kissing furiously, to the infinite delight of Milady, who sighed and wriggled with pleasure, until at last I could no longer restrain myself. But, inexperienced and unaccustomed as I was then, instinct ruled me, for I brought my stiff shaft to the charge and, to Clarissa's open-mouthed astonishment, fairly rammed it right into the gaping crack until it was deep within her belly.

We lay still for a few moments, enjoying the conjunction of our persons until Clarissa heaved up her generous bottom. I responded to this with a powerful plunge and then we commenced a most exciting struggle. Clarissa raised her gorgeous head to see my manly shaft as it worked in and out of her vaginal sheath, glistening with lubricity, while the lips of her quim seemed to cling to it each time I withdrew, as if fearful she might lose my sugar stick; but this did not last long. Our movements grew more and more furious, until at last we both met in a spasmodic embrace, almost fainted in each other's arms . . . and I could feel a profusion of creamy moisture oozing from the depths of Clarissa as we both lay in a lethargy of enjoyment after our encounter of mutual lust.

'Ah, you rogue,' Lady Clarissa sighed, 'but I mean to have a little more now . . . ohh! . . . I *must* have it!' she exclaimed, squeezing me with her arms and gluing her lips to mine as she threw her beautiful legs right over my buttocks and commenced the engagement once more by rapidly heaving her own bottom. Although I considered myself to be a fine, fit, young man, the weight of my body seemed as nothing in our amorous excitement. She fairly drove me on and I was soon as furiously excited as herself. With a profusion of sighs, expressions of pleasure and words of endearment, we soon died away again into a state of short, voluptuous oblivion.

After a time, I withdrew my instrument from her foaming cunny and saw that it was all slimy and glistening with the mingled juices of our lust. Yet what a contrast it now was to its former state, much reduced in size and already drooping its fiery head. Clarissa promptly kneeled on the floor before me, took hold of my limp affair and gave it a most luscious sucking, to my own enormous delight. As soon as Clarissa had done with her sucking kiss, she saw that my instrument was again stiff and ready for renewed joys.

UNHOLY PASSIONS

'There, my boy,' Clarissa teased me, 'I'll leave you like that. Think of me until tomorrow. I couldn't help giving the darling a good suck after the exquisite pleasure he has afforded me: it is like being in heaven for a little while.' With a last kiss on the lips, she dismissed me and, triumphant though I felt, I gained no solace in sleep that night.

It was a fine hot morning in June and soon after a breakfast of eggs, hot bread, bacon, ham, kidneys and ale, followed by a glass of mid-morning sherry, Clarissa led me to her lake. It was obvious that her blood was on the boil, as was mine; and both of us longed to experience further erotic delights. She asked me to unlock the boat-house and thence to give her a row in a nice, broad, comfortable skiff, well-furnished with soft seats and cushions.

'Ah!' Clarissa exclaimed as I sculled away into the water, 'my head aches a little. Let me recline it in your lap.' Throwing off her hat, she stretched herself along a cushion as we glided along the rippling waters, stirred by a warm west wind. She rested her head upon my lap in a languid manner, looking up and enjoying the confusion into which she had thrown me. As I endeavoured to scull, she designedly rested one soft hand upon the lump which I seemed to have in my pocket, as if to support herself a little.

'Do you think, Horby,' she teased me, 'that I have fine legs?' I gulped and nodded assent as she drew her skirts and petticoats up to her knees. 'Don't you think that I ought to wear long dresses, young sir? I am, forsooth, becoming quite unbecomingly immodest, showing my calves so much.' I had hard work to keep on rowing and to recover my composure, for the vivid recollection of my previous, luscious episode with Clarissa was so fresh within my mind that the soft ladylike hand resting on my privates raised an utterance of desire within my feverish blood. I endeavoured to allay it but, little by little, my unruly member began to swell further until I was sure that Clarissa must be feeling it throbbing beneath her hand.

'You're making game of me this morning,' I murmured.

'Yes!' Clarissa responded excitedly with an unusual flush upon her pale face. 'You naughty young man, you shall tell me what I want to know. How do babies come? Is it not out of a curly lot of hair at the base of a woman's belly? I know that is what I have and I have seen you kiss it, sir!' Perspiration stood out upon my brow in great droplets but my lips refused to speak as Clarissa continued in a soft whisper: 'I saw it all last night, Horby dear, and what joy that great purple-headed thing of yours gave me! O! This is the monster you shoved into me so furiously. I must look at it and feel it again . . . how hard it has become under my touch! La! Lalalala! What a wonderful thing! What an engine to secure womanly joy!' With that, she pulled open my britches and let out the rampant tool of lust. She kissed its purple velvety head, saying: 'What a sweet yet hard thing it is to the touch! Oh! I must caress it a little.'

Here touches were like fire to my senses; speechless with rapture and surprise, I silently submitted to the whim of the wilful lady yet her delicate fingering was so exciting that I could not restrain myself. The sperm boiled up from my balls and spurted through my penis all over her hands and face.

'Ah!' Lady Clarissa shouted delightedly. 'That is just what I wanted to see from you.' She licked away the sperm from her cheeks and her hands. 'Now kiss my quim.' I was too infatuated with Clarissa to refuse so delightful a request and began with a serious of long, lascivious licks upon her cunny. 'How nice to feel your lovely tongue there,' she murmured dreamily. 'How beautifully it tickles and warms me all over . . . oh, but don't leave off just as it seems better than ever, my darling . . . O! Gently, darling . . .' as I licked and kissed her nether button with ardour, imparting a nip to the lips of her quim. 'You mustn't be so impulsive; it's a very dangerous game for one so young. You must – oh! – be careful of – ah! – you look at me or notice me before – uh! – others . . .' And with that she came in a flood of love juice that left her petticoats positively soaking. After a time, I rowed us back to the boat-house.

Clarissa then informed me that she needed some solitude and, in any event, she had to receive, later in the day, an overnight visit from a distant younger cousin. I ate huge quantities of rare cold roast beef, dripping with blood, for my noon repast, then returned to listen to the learned discourse of my tutor, the Reverend Aloysius Herbert, on Ovid and the proper translation of his *Art of Love*. Many called at the house but Lady Clarissa had instructed her servants to state that she was suffering from an attack of indisposition. The house remained quiet, aside from the patient teaching of the goodly Reverend Herbert until we were summoned by bells. Here I refer both to those rung by the servants on account of Clarissa's instructions, which summoned us to her tea-table, and the jingling of horse-brasses which announced the arrival of the carriage of the Hon. Arabella Marchmount. We were distantly related and she was a stunningly beautiful girl, roughly sixteen years of age, with masses of wavy black and glossy hair, high cheek bones, baby-blue eyes and a slender figure. Over tea, which was accompanied by delicate pastries adorned with fruit and chocolate, her behaviour was demure though, for my own part, it nonetheless brought about another erection. Clarissa and Arabella chatted gaily and smiled politely at the demonstrations of wit and learning supplied to them by my tutor.

At length, Clarissa announced that she required a rest and suggested that Arabella might be in need of one also, a proposition to which the latter gave her assent. After the ladies had withdrawn, my tutor asked me if I minded whether we called an end to the lessons for today and as I gave my own glad assent, he withdrew to his rooms with – and zounds! I swear it! – the only bulge in his britches that I had ever noticed. I called to the servants for a sherry and contemplated my situation. My prick was throbbing and I wanted to fuck Clarissa again. Having been initiated into the preliminary mysteries of sex, I also wanted to fuck the nubile Arabella. I therefore crept stealthily up the stairs, hoping to enter Clarissa's boudoir, only to be forestalled by the sight of Arabella rushing with enthusiasm into the boudoir of Milady. Fortunately there were no servants present and so I was enabled to espy that which transpired from a doorway which Arabella had carelessly left open.

'What can I do, Clarissa?' Arabella was saying. 'Are you warm enough? These damp nights can be so chilly.'

'Yes,' said Clarissa, 'that must be what it is. I feel cold and restless. Would you mind getting into bed with me? You will soon make me warm.' Arabella jumped in and Clarissa nestled up to her bosom, as if for warmth but in reality to feel the outlines of her beautiful and no doubt satin-bottomed figure. 'Kiss me, Arabella,' she said. Arabella did so with all too willing alacrity. 'I know that I shall like you.' These words received a loving response. 'What lovely titties you have, Arabella,' Clarissa cooed. 'Let me feel them. Open your nightdress, so I can lay my face against them.'

Arabella was evidently of a loving disposition for she admitted all the familiarities of her elder cousin whose hands, as I watched, began to wander in a most searching manner about her person, feeling the soft, firm skin of her belly and bottom. The touches of Clarissa seemed to fire Arabella's blood and arouse every voluptuous emotion within the sweet girl; she sighed and kissed her hostess again and again.

'What a fine rump!' Clarissa exclaimed, giving out a hard smack. Arabella squealed with delight. 'How delectable your flesh is! Oh! And what is all this silky hair at the nether regions of your belly? My dear, where did it come from?'

'Oh, pray don't, Clarissa, it is so rude . . .'

'We're only girls here,' Clarissa responded softly, 'and there is no harm in touching one another, is there? Just feel me. And I shall feel you.'

'O! Clarissa! You don't know how you make me feel when you touch me there.'

'Does it make you feel better when a man's stiff prick touches you there, darling Arabella?' Clarissa queried as she tickled her younger cousin's hairy crack with her fingers. Arabella gasped with pleasure. 'Softly, my sweet, not so loud or someone may hear you: and, I ask again, do you not obtain pleasure when a strong young man puts that thing of his into your crack . . . ? I am determined to share your joy. Suppose there *was* a man in this house tonight. Suppose,' she stroked Arabella's vagina with brisk alacrity, 'suppose it was Horby!' I stiffened in more ways than one. 'Horby, do stop being such a bore and lurking in doorways,' she called out clearly, to my acute embarrassment, 'and come in here.'

I needed no second encouragement. Casting aside all notions of modesty, I tore away the frontage of my britches, pulling down my drawers to reveal my rampaging and stiffly erect John Thomas as I took a flying leap into the four-poster bed. Clarissa promptly drew its curtains.

'He'll kill me!' Arabella squealed. 'That big thing of his will split me right through.'

'Not at all, my dear,' Clarissa murmured, her fingers flickering over the cunny lips of her younger cousin, 'for you have long been prepared for this particular item.'

In due course I shall vouchsafe a full account of that wonderful night. For the present let it suffice to state that Lady Clarissa's initiation had made of me a rampaging young bull. I spread the ladies upon their backs and proceeded to ram them in turn. Both parted their thighs willingly and gladly so that I was enabled to build up a rhythm, prodding my rod into Clarissa at one stroke and into Arabella with the next, then returning to plunge within Clarissa's comely cunt before returning to a thrilling thrust within the loins of Arabella. We all came simultaneously, uttering screams of delight that might have alarmed the servants had they not been so used to the habits of their mistress.

There was benefit to one and all involved from the twenty-four hours I have described and intend to describe further. Lady Clarissa and the Hon. Arabella became powers in the land. I proceeded to Trinity Hall, Cambridge, where I took my degree without either distinguishing or disgracing myself; moreover, the liberal education I had received gave me that joyous key to the locks of the secret fleshy treasure-chests of ladies. Clarissa ensured that the Reverend Aloysius Herbert was given a comfortable living in a nearby parish where, if his learned sermons do not delight the locality, they at least win general respect; and if his eager discourse which compares and contrasts the Christian theologians with their pagan predecessors causes the attention of his parishioners to wander, he had nevertheless won their lasting affection by his kindness, his genuine attention to their welfare and his influence upon the Bishop obtained for him by Lady Clarissa Hyde.

For my own part, I thank Clarissa from the bottom of my heart for her introduction to Woman: though one must add cynically, concerning the nature of this subject, that the deeper one probes, the lower it becomes.

CHAPTER TWO

'Hail fellow, well met!' Sir Francis Dashwood cried out as I entered The George & Vulture in Southwark to encounter one of the most extraordinary men of my era, a character whose influence would so affect me. We met in one of the most joyous taverns of London. It was said that this was the site of the actual Tabard Tavern, where Geoffrey Chaucer had set his opening of *The Canterbury Tales*. Certainly it was a flourishing coaching inn, dealing mainly with passengers heading to Kent and Dover for overseas travel in Europe. Others such as myself visited frequently on account of its excellence of fare and the charming eccentricity of the landlord. He was known by the name of Harry Bailey, though whether he was a direct descendant of the Host in Chaucer's *The Canterbury Tales* was not clear.

'An extraordinary rendezvous, sir, is it not?' Sir Francis Dashwood demanded of me and I gave my assent. I happen to have a passion for drinking old English ale whilst seated amidst old English oak furnishings: though here one could also enjoy pints of claret or port, hot mulled wine, brandywine and hot water, or milk punch. All the punches were ladled out from bowls of silver which stood and steamed at the bar and were served in tankards of pewter. There were slices of rare and bloody roast beef with roasted potatoes to eat or else generous slices of ham with freshly baked and buttered cottage loaf. One could also dine on a whole roasted capon stuffed with sausage meat spiced by sage and onion or parsley and thyme – or both – and the beefsteak, kidney and oyster pudding was renowned throughout London as being the finest. However, Sir Francis and I simply chose to take two dozen raw oysters each, accompanied by lemon, pepper and brown bread and butter until further members of the company arrived.

'How I adore oysters!' Sir Francis exclaimed. 'They recall so intimately the juicy cunts of women! The fact that they are so dirt cheap, eaten mainly by the poor and given by others to their cats does not deter me from my enjoyment; no, no, sir! Best value for money in town!' He quaffed his tankard of hot milk punch and instantly shouted for another, which was served with alacrity. At the age of forty-one, he was still a very handsome man, though his face did display the lines of his alleged dissipation and debauchery. His father had been a partner of my own father on a number of business ventures involving trade with India, though my own reason for opening correspondence with Sir Francis in the preceding year had been to do with possible membership of the Clubs he had founded, the Divan and the Dilettanti. We had arranged to meet in order to discuss matters of mutual interest.

'Extraordinary tavern altogether,' Sir Francis continued jovially. 'D'you see that?' I looked out of the window, where his finger was pointing, and discerned in the coaching yard a large and vicious-looking bird that appeared to be alarming some of the passengers awaiting the next stage-coach. 'It is a most notable and extraordinary cock vulture that our landlord purchased at Peckham Fair and he regales all his patrons with tales of this bird's supernatural powers. This cock is, of course, the principal symbol of Baphomet.'

'Sorry . . . ?'

'Heavens! My dear Horby! Or should I say Hell? Baphomet is the twin-sexed deity which the Knight Templar Order was accused of worshipping when the Roman Catholic Church suppressed them in the Middle Ages. These Knights were tortured into giving absurd confessions and then burned at the stake. They had their successors, though...' He looked thoughtful. 'Mr Bailey!' he shouted at the bald, stout, landlord in a rough, good-humoured way, 'do be so kind as to escort my young friend and me to the cellar.' Mr Bailey gladly obliged the request of Sir Francis and so it was that I found myself in a slightly damp room, though warmed by a roaring fire of logs, and seated at an oak table with oaken chairs where places had been laid for six. Above this table hung a curious lamp. It comprised a large globe of crystal, encircled by a serpent of pure gold with its tail in its mouth. There were chains of twisted silver snakes suspended beneath it and crowning the globe was a pair of silver doves' wings.

'A symbol of eternity, eh, Horby?' Sir Francis chortled in his joy. 'One discerns sperm swimming around the egg, no? This is called the "Everlasting Rosicrucian Lamp" for it will never go out and it is named after that curious grouping knows as the Rosicrucians, a confederacy of allegedly super-human beings who sought to enlighten humanity in the early seventeenth century by means of Higher Intelligence, mystical practices and magical rituals. What d'you think of that, then, eh, Horby?'

'I'm very interested in learning more, Dashwood,' I replied truthfully. 'I find wars of Religion to be quite sickening. Frankly, I am a Deist: I believe in a Higher Power but I do not believe in any deity laying down petty rules of allegedly moral conduct. I concur with Shakespeare: "To thine own Self be true".'

'Splendid!' Dashwood roared and called for more milk punch and spiced ale from the smiling buxom wench who waited in attendance upon our requirements. (I might add that on the death of the landlord, Mr Bailey's will directed that the sign of the vulture must needs be added to the sign of King

George outside his inn; and that Sir Francis Dashwood purchased the Everlasting Rosicrucian Lamp for use in his caves of West Wycombe: but more of that anon.) As it was, I was a little nervous on account of the rumours I had heard. It had been said that in this very cellar, Dashwood and his associates had enacted the Black Mass, complete with a naked girl stretched out upon a table with the Sacred Host wedged tightly between her legs for the men to suck, lick and eat. I had heard that the allegedly infamous Philip, Duke of Wharton, a brilliant fellow according to my father but one who loved to outrage social convention and mock Christianity, had founded the original Hell-Fire Club here and had had an enemy run through with a kitchen spit in order to roast him alive*. I mentioned to Dashwood that I had heard many astonishing tales about events that had supposedly taken place in the cellar of The George & Vulture.

'Indeed, my dear Horby,' he replied genially. 'Oh, yes, we're quite a Club here. D'you see that print there?' I looked and saw, hanging on the wall, a print taken from an original work by that superb artist William Hogarth, depicting our present environment and showing five men drinking around our table. It was entitled 'Charity in the Cellar' and was quite exquisitely delineated. I recognized these five men as being Dashwood; the Earl of Sandwich; the poet and satirist, Paul Whitehead; George Bubb-Dodington, one of the leading men in Parliament; and Frederick, Prince of Wales and heir to the throne. 'Fine, is it not? Oh, yes, Hogarth is one of us.'

One of us? What did that mean? I stared at Sir Francis Dashwood, who himself enjoyed a most formidable reputation. He was among the richest men in England and possessed fine land in West Wycombe, Buckinghamshire: apparently he had

---

* *Translator's note:* This rumour was repeated in the 1840s by Thomas de Quincey.

celebrated his father's death by getting drunk on the rarest vintages of port from the cellar. Women found him to be most attractive and on his Grand Tour he had fornicated his way across Europe. He had the staying powers of a stallion and the impetuosity of a bull and, though seldom sober, he was always charmingly tolerant and frank, even though he allegedly far exceeded in licentiousness anything seen since the days of the rakes at the court of Charles II. I mentioned the matter of the Grand Tour since I was keen to undertake it for the benefit of my own education and would be grateful for further introductions.

'Ah, my dear Horby, you *must* undertake the Grand Tour!' he exclaimed warmly. 'Taste the sweets of all things. And Do What Thou Wilt, as Rabelais informs us in his superlative *Gargantua and Pantagruel*. You know, I pity my poor tutor. He was Roman Catholic who tried to convert me by taking me to the Sistine Chapel at the Vatican back in 1728. There he urged upon me the virtues of penitence and exhorted me to emulate the example of the monks before us, who were publicly flagellating themselves. I noticed that the whips of the monks were softly innocuous and I was utterly disgusted by this sham and hypocrisy. I could not help but respond by surreptitiously entering the Chapel on Good Friday, disguised in a long cloak from which I produced a bull-whip to lash the kneeling penitents with vengeful savagery. "The Devil! The Devil!" they screeched as they ran. Unfortunately, this practical joke aroused the ire of the Inquisition and would have caused a serious diplomatic incident had I not had the sense to leave Rome with my excruciatingly embarrassed tutor.

'I hadn't done with the Romanists yet, oh no, Horby,' Dashwood continued animatedly. 'Disguised as the sick and allegedly absent Cardinal Ottoboni, I attended the funeral of Pope Clement XII in 1730 and some Italian Duke reported: "Never in my life have I witness anything so mad and so original." Oh! I learned so much during my various travels in Italy! You wish to join my Club of the Dilettanti, Horby? Hah! Young Horace Walpole, offended at his conspicuous lack of election to membership, declares: "The nominal qualification is having been in Italy; and the real one, having been drunk." Possibly so: so get drunk first, young man, then go to Italy and I'll put you up for membership. Oh, and then do give us a donation, there's a good fellow, for Sir Joshua Reynolds and the Royal Academy of Art he is endeavouring to establish*.

'I've had such a glorious education,' Dashwood declared. 'Paris, all of Italy, oh, and St Petersburg, where I disguised myself as King Charles XII of Sweden and enjoyed a glorious two-week affair with the Russian Tsarina, Anna. Ah! What a lady! Greece? A beautiful country! The same is true of Turkey, which inspired me to found the Divan Club.'

'That would interest me,' I said.

'I am glad of your interest, sir,' Dashwood responded, 'though you would first have to visit Turkey. Unfortunately the Divan Club has expired, possibly owing to an excess of opium, with only three members present three years ago. However, I can furnish you with letters of introduction to the Sultan.' I nodded my eager thanks and meanwhile pondered the nature of my host. He was a member of White's, the most exclusive club in England. His noted interest in Science had made of him a Fellow of the Royal Society; and recently he had received an honorary Doctorate of Law from Oxford University. It was said that his private library contained some of the most esoteric, recondite and forbidden works to be found in all of Europe, which he had collected while upon his travels. Having entered Politics, he was an Independent Member of Parliament

---

* *Translator's note:* The Dilettanti Society still exists today, still practises a curious initiation ceremony concocted by Dashwood, and celebrated a jubilee in 1983.

for New Romney, where his endeavours on the part of his constituents secured his continuous re-election. His blunt speaking, without care or concern for the pressure of his peers, on occasion caused a stir in Parliament, for he championed unpopular causes if he believed them to be right, and impressed some while outraging others. His use of obscene language in his speeches occasionally appalled some of his more timid colleagues. Dashwood was in the unique position of being able to say and do whatever he thought fit without fear of reprisal. He did not appear to care how unpopular he might become, providing that he was acting in accordance with his own code of honour. In 1747, he had published his 'An Address to the Gentlemen, Clergy and Freeholders of Great Britain', resolutely stating:

'Man has a natural right to be free . . . by Freedom is not nor can be meant that every Individual should act as he lists, and according as he is swayed by his own Passions, Vices, or Infirmities: but Freedom is a Right every man has to *do what he will* with his own . . .' Dashwood had actually put his own will into practical action, being an active member of Parliamentary committees responsible for the repair and building of roads and bridges, the establishment of toll-booths throughout the kingdom and for the details and dull though essential matters of drainage and coastal navigation. He was responsible for having a new road built from High Wycombe to West Wycombe, thus giving needed and appreciated employment to able-bodied men in his constituency; and he did this at his own expense. Today I look back on Dashwood's years of untiring Parliamentary service and recall his ultimately successful endeavours to set up a Territorial Army and his reorganization of the British postal service. Nor was he, in my opinion, as bad a Chancellor of the Exchequer in later years, under the allegedly notorious 'Hell-Fire Ministry', as his enemies have claimed.

At the time I first made the personal acquaintanceship of Dashwood, he was married to Lady Sarah Ellys, which marriage had brought him houses in Hanover Square, Mayfair, and in Ealing. Gossip in the coffee houses and taverns led one to conclude that Sir Francis was unfailingly kind to his wife while continuing to womanize relentlessly. Gossip also had it that his travels and arcane studies, meetings with remarkable men and purchases of unhallowed books had made of him a master of sinister and esoteric arts. I was not surprised when he asked me to describe my first initiation into the mysteries of sex and told him all as he chuckled and then laughed uproariously.

'Ha! Ha! Ho! Ho! Oh, my dear Horby!' he exclaimed. 'What a wonderful introduction to the matter, sir! Now, I have only one complaint about your excellent tale. Damn it, sir, you have not finished the bloody thing!'

'I shall oblige you gladly, sir,' I retorted. 'There is in fact little to state about the remainder of the evening I described for we were all somewhat fatigued. Nevertheless, as I composed myself for sleep in a delightfully huge four-poster bed with Lady Clarissa Hyde and the Hon. Arabella Marchmount, I noticed that the ladies were indulging in every variety of kissing and tickling and that Arabella learned from Clarissa nearly all the mysterious particulars in connection with Venus and the rites of Sappho before they fell asleep in each other's arms.

'On the following fine day,' I continued, 'we walked through Clarissa's park and, finding a thick copse at its further end, sat down in a little grassy spot where we were secure from observation.

' "John Horby, darling," said Arabella , "or should I call you John Thomas?" She giggled. " You have made me happy by making a woman out of me. Now I want to do it again after a different fashion. I shall soon make you so lustful that you cannot help yourself." With these words she unbuttoned my britches and her cool, long fingers were soon handling my thick, stiff pego as I gasped. "What a lovely dear it is! How I long to feel its juices spouting within my belly! Ah! The heavenly bliss I know you will make me feel . . . let me lay over you."

'I was unable to resist her caresses, being already almost at spending point, and so she knelt over my face as I lay on my back, her intention being that I might first lubricate her little cunny with my tongue. This operation titillated and excited the young girl so that she amorously pressed herself upon my mouth as she faced towards my stiff cock, which she never left hold of all the while until I spent in ecstasy and she felt the shuddering pleasures of her own emission.

' "Ohh . . . splendid . . ." Clarissa murmured. Her hand was deep within her petticoats and her pale white face was flushing a furious and excited pink. "Now's the time, Arabella, dear," she murmured again, somewhat dreamily. "My own affair is *so* well lubricated by this lubricious sight and your pussy is also ready. But do be careful. If Horby gets over you, he might be too violent and so injure you. The best way is for you to straddle over him and direct the head of his prick to your quim and then keep pressing down upon it."

' "You shall see my determination," Arabella responded, as she began to act upon Clarissa's suggestion. And, fitting the head of my pego into her slit, she soon pressed down so as to take in and quite cover the first inch of it. The problem was that my young cock was very big and her young cunt was very small. For an instant, the pain of stretching and distention seemed almost too much for her but she gave me a sudden downward plunge of her body, which, although she almost appeared to faint, got in at least three more inches.

' "What a plucky girl you are, my dear Arabella," Clarissa commented delightedly while she continued to masturbate quite furiously, as the rustling of her petticoats and silken dress testified only too loudly and clearly. "As soon as you can bear it, raise yourself up a little and come down again with all your force. That root is so well planted by Horby that the next good thrust should complete his possession of your lovely charms." I took hold of Arabella's gorgeous white buttocks so as to render all possible assistance to this charmingly grave girl. Clenching her pearly-white teeth firmly and momentarily shutting her sparkling eyes of azure, Arabella essayed another desperate plunge upon my spear of lust and at last she was fairly impaled upon the shaft of my affair.

'Arabella squealed as Clarissa sighed, then Arabella shuddered as her hair whipped my face, and she withdrew for two-thirds of the way up my cock. I glued my lips to hers and gently thrust in the rest of my prick, gradually inserting it until is was three-fourths in; then, without pressing further yet, I commenced to move slowly and carefully. The lubricity soon increased and I could feel the tight, loving contractions of her vagina, which speedily brought me to a crisis once more; and, with a sudden thrust, I plunged in up to the hilt and shot my very essence into her innermost recesses of cunt as I almost fainted with the excess of my emotions.

'We lay motionless, enjoying each other's mutual pleasures until I withdrew and, taking a fine silk handkerchief, wiped the juices of love first from the lips of her cunny, then off my own weapon, declaring, as I put the stained *mouchoir* in my pocket, that I would keep it forever in remembrance of the charms Arabella had so lovingly surrendered to me.

'As Arabella lay back upon the grass in a delicious languor, life returned to my prick, growing yet again at the sight of the beautifully flushed Clarissa. I flung myself upon her, tearing the thin silk from her heaving bosom, and my hands explored every part of her body. She could feel my rampant cock pressed between our naked bellies and we were in a burning heat of excitement. Clarissa had obviously determined to let me do just as I liked; my fingers once more explored her crack and rubbed her little clitoris. I ensured that my right leg got between her silken thighs and I heard her sigh as I gently placed the head of my instrument within her quim. She was evidently so excited that her sudden emission wetted my cock all over with a creamy spend.

'My advancing cock pushed forward with a sudden thrust that elicited a shriek, whether of pleasure or pain I no longer knew or cared, though certainly her arms clung about my body and kept me close to the mark. Then that damn sexy bitch exclaimed:

' "Oh! Oh! How you hurt!" as she tried to push my body away from her. "Oh! For shame, don't! Oh! Let me go, Horby, how can you?!" And then her efforts seemed to be exhausted and she lay at my mercy as I ruthlessly pushed my advantage and stopped her mouth with kisses. She was lost to the pleasures of lust. Taking every possible advantage, I continued to thrust with thrilling energy until she could not help but gasp and respond with delicious thrusts of her own, moving her bottom to meet each returning insertion of my exciting weapon. Within a number of rapturous moments, we both swam in a mutual flood of bliss and, after a spasmodic storm of sighs, kisses and tender hugging pressure upon one another's bodies, we lay together in a state of lazy enjoyment upon the grass . . .'

'Ha! Ha! An excellent introduction to sex for a young man!' Dashwood cried out. 'More oysters,' he muttered to the maid as he chewed his last one and swallowed the juices from the half-shell with relish. 'Can't understand these fools who just swallow 'em,' he added. 'Myself, I love that moment when you bite into the oyster that you are eating alive, and you experience its life passing into you and the taste of the sea from which all life came. So, young Horby, was that your finest fuck? Or do you have more to tell me?'

'Dashwood,' I replied, 'it was very fine indeed, and I was thereby primed for future occasions, for which I am most grateful to the ladies involved.'

'Yes, delectable and charming, aren't they, Clarissa and Arabella,' Sir Francis murmured fondly as more oysters were served. It was obvious that he had enjoyed a most intimate acquaintanceship with both ladies. 'Indeed, it was Clarissa who strongly urged upon me the necessity of my meeting your good self. I have profound respect for her judgement of men; and the same is true of young Arabella. More brown bread, Horby? Essential with shell-fish, I find. And – since my friends and colleagues are invariably late – more salacious stories?'

'Sir Francis,' I responded, 'surely it would only be fair at this juncture to request one from your own good self.'

'Very well, sir,' he replied, 'I shall tell you a tale of Turkey.'

CHAPTER THREE

'It really was jolly good visiting Turkey,' Sir Francis Dashwood declared, 'a country with which my father had long enjoyed a profitable business connection or series of such. I enjoyed thoroughly the smoking of opium with the Sultan. Unfortunately, opium usually diminishes the sexual drive, in my experience; though it is a different matter altogether when the finest quality of hashish is mixed with it. I had such a rampaging erection on this occasion that I would gladly have drilled a hole in a wall and stuck my pego right within there. The Sultan was amused by my discomfiture, made all too evident by my fashionably tight britches.

' "Sir Francis," he told me, "this particular concoction always affects every man in the same way. Now, my dear sir, I have delightful Turkish ladies, not from my own harem, of course, but available only to my most honoured guests. My good Vizier here, Mustapha, will conduct you to them."

'Mustapha, a tall, lean and fierce-looking man with a thick black moustache, led me through the Palace, past fountains and into a room painted in pink where I saw a dozen females enveloped in a white drapery which covered them from head to foot. Desperate though I was to have a fuck, this was not immediately an appetizing prospect. Yet the instant that I stepped up to the female nearest me, she cast her covering behind her. So did the others and I feasted my eyes upon a picture of voluptuousness greater than I had ever dreamt of.

'There stood before me twelve gorgeous females, all perfectly naked, that I think could not be excelled in any other harem in the East. There was a languishing, olive-eyed beauty ravished from the isles of Greece. There was a voluptuous lady from the Caucasus. Africa had yielded up two sable beauties to satiate the lusts of the Sultan. There were two Cypriot women with their dark, flowing tresses, eyes of piercing black and skin of dazzling gold, contrasting with the deep carnation of their lips, the tawny nipples of their breasts and the jet-black, bushy hair that surmounted their cunts.

'I minutely scrutinized each one separately, going over their respective claims to beauty with the eye of a connoisseur. Oh! How I feasted my sight on the row of lovely, luscious cunts that ran around the room. I could look, feel and touch them all, stroking down the bushy hair that surrounded their notches. Indeed I became so excited from the handling of so many cunts that I put my arm around the waist of one charming little creature, who by her looks was assuredly most lascivious, and led her into a small side-apartment where, presenting her with a fine gold chain that I wore beneath my vestments, I laid her down upon a pile of cushions and gave her to experience the most ecstatic pleasure before I got off her. I gave her some time to recover from the confusion I had thrown her into, ere we returned to the apartment in which the women were now standing. They took no notice of our absence other than to raise their heads so as to look at the chain that I had hung around the neck of Laylah.

'I marched her to one side and picked out another, a young African girl who was also called Laylah and who was the most voluptuously formed female I had ever seen and who assured me that she was better fitted for enjoying the pleasures of lust than any female I had ever before possessed. Her hair was cunningly knotted and as black as a raven's wing, her breasts were full and large with nipples as hard as ivory. Her waist was slender, whilst her hips were spread out to a width I had never before seen. Her thighs of a largeness to put to shame any woman I had ever lain with. I gave her, possibly for the first time in her life, knowledge of the difference between lying in an old goat of a Turk's arms and being fucked well by a young and lively Englishman.

'Now Mustapha proceeded to present me with a delectable golden-skinned beauty from Cyprus whose name was also Laylah. Oh! What charms, what beauty met my fiery gaze! I burned with desire to enjoy her. I lavished my eager kisses on every part of her body. I fastened my lips to hers. I sucked the rosy nipples of her breasts. The pouting and imploring lips of her cunt received my fullest attention. What charms I could see all down her neck and voluptuously rounded bosom, having just under my eyes her dazzling golden skin and blue-black hair streaming down in three long plaits along her back; then there were the lovely delicate hands that caressed my cock.

'My manly weapon arose again in all its renewed vigour. This Laylah suddenly dropped backwards at full length, her eyes closed, her sensual smile of enjoyment on her lips, somewhat apart, with one knee bent upwards as she sighed and sobbed with pleasure, accompanying this orchestration with a writhing of her beautiful long legs. I am but a mortal man and however much I might have wished to enjoy and prolong this sight, it was impossible for me to restrain my own emotions. As the ecstatic moment arrived, I directed my swollen, excited member deep within her quim, so that its tip penetrated her womb, which I showered with a goodly stream of sperm.

'As I was recovering from this enraptured spasm, this Laylah left the room and Mustapha entered with a slender, dusky maiden, partly wrapped in a white shawl.

' "A prisoner of war, Sir Francis," he informed me with a wicked grin, "and an Arabian princess."

' "Ah! Ah!" the girl shrieked out, hiding her face in her shawl. "Help! A man! A man!" Mustapha responded by giving her a vigorous kick in the arse.

' "You may scream," he sneered, "but who's to help you?" She sprang for the doorway and attempted to flee but he dexterously caught hold of the tail of her shawl and as she endeavoured to effect her futile bid to escape, he pulled her shawl over her head so that she was quite uncovered, her arms helpless, whilst every part of her beautiful body from the waist downwards was fully exposed.

'What a sight met my gaze! She had a splendid swelling mound, all covered with black, glossy, curly hair that adorned her beautiful, satin-smooth belly: and as Mustapha whirled her around, I saw her rounded bottom, quite out of proportion to her slender waist, but so exciting to behold and replete with the possibilities of voluptuous pleasures.

' "Ah!" she shrieked out, "how shameful! Oh! Let me go or your life will pay the forfeit!"

' "Ha! Ha!" he laughed as he flicked a leather strap in the air. Mastering her struggles, he forced her towards the wall from which, I suddenly noticed, cuffs and chains were hanging; and he clipped these cuffs around her wrists. "Will you indeed spare my life, my lady?" he chuckled as he gloated over her involuntary display of naked flesh. With that, he inflicted a furious lash upon her bottom, raising a welt, and repeated it again and again until she was dancing with pain, waving her well-striped bottom, begging and crying for mercy and promising anything she could think of to be released.

' "Oh!" she screamed. "Oh! Allah! Have mercy! Deliver me from this demon!"

' "Cry away to Allah!" Mustapha laughed cruelly. "You ought to be one of the *houris* in the Prophet's Paradise. A wanton woman such as you would be properly employed there. And, tell me," he smiled with sadistic glee, "what was that instrument our soldiers found in your little bag?" He lashed her hard and she danced and squealed.

' "Oh! Mercy! It is only a French dildo." '

' "Oh?" He brandished it in the air and I could see an artificial penis bound in shining black leather, of at least two inches in breadth and nine in length. "A dildo? What's that for? Speak up!" He gave her another furious lash.

' "Oh! *Oh!* We ladies use it to excite ourselves when our men do not . . . if you only knew who I am!"

' "Indeed, Madam," Mustapha responded. "Pray tell me. Perhaps then I may show you some respect . . ."

' "I am an Arabian Princess!" the beauty shrieked.

' "Oh, indeed? Ha!" Mustapha laughed. "Then you should take it as being an honour and a privilege to be fucked by an Englishman. Step forward, Sir Francis."

'I did so all too eagerly. My rod first caressed her lashed hips and thighs as my hand stroked her mount. Mustapha's flogging had made her red bottom twitch, giving me a most luscious and voluptuous sight, for she was one of those rare women who are splendidly furnished with an enlarged clitoris and prominent pouting lips to her cunny which, as they grasped at the firm tool I had inserted, drew out and receded, as her vagina clung to and gripped the stout shaft of my stiff penis. "A penis tense rather than penitence," is what I always say and so I rejoiced in her unintentionally lascivious series of vaginal squeezes. Her lashed bottom felt delightfully hot in my grasping hands.

'I amused myself by rubbing my pego against her clitoris and all around the gaping luscious mouth of her vermilion gap. My fingers meanwhile pinched and nipped her ripely roseate nipples and my touch seemed to electrify her, causing her to scream with delight.

' "Oh, *oh, ohh*!!! You make me come! How hot I am! Great heavens! Allah! Allah!" And the hot bitch spent with such profusion that it poured all over my prick.

'It was an extraordinary orgasm that I enjoyed, Horby, one of those whereby a man feels that he is uniting with the Universe. Literally, I saw stars. Afterwards, as I withdrew, she sagged and sobbed in her chains. I asked Mustapha if the Sultan could have mercy upon this delightful girl.

' "Only if the ransom is paid," he replied impassively. The sum of money demanded was not in fact too onerous and so I paid it, thus setting free the Arabian Princess who was, incidentally, also called Laylah and who gave me a beautiful kiss upon the lips once she was released from her chains. Of course, I am by inclination all chivalry but I admit that sometimes my motives are mixed. Upon Laylah's arrival within the bosom of her parental home – wherein it was said that, as a gentleman, I had resolutely declined to take her virginity – the family business and all its associates quintupled their volume of trade with the Arab world.

'It was a grand night,' Sir Francis said enthusiastically, 'and by the end of it, I had fucked a dozen women. Hell's teeth!' he exclaimed irritably, 'these days and in middle age I can only manage half a dozen!'

At that point, I stared at Dashwood and saw something extraordinary. It may well have been a trick of the light, yet I fancied that I saw a halo above his head. Just as I was pondering this matter, a face inserted itself within that halo but this was no hallucination: I recognized John Montague, Earl of Sandwich. Perhaps the most curious aspect of this vision was that our finest artist (in my opinion) William Hogarth captured precisely the vision I had seen in his engraving, 'Sir Francis Dashwood at his Devotions'. There he is depicted worshipping Venus as the beaky-nosed Sandwich peers through the halo above his head.

Many detested Sandwich though I did not, knowing him only slightly at that time. Certainly he was furiously hard-working and able, and his formidable talents at administration had brought him to the post of First Lord of the Admiralty at the tender age of thirty-one. His endeavours to cleanse the docks of corruption had made him many enemies. I had been told that he had accomplished little, that he walked as if he were trying to go down both sides of the street at once, that he was mean to his mistresses and treacherous to his friends, that he could never lose the smell of brimstone, that no man had ever carried the art of seduction to so enormous a height; and that being as mischievous as a monkey and as lecherous as a goat, he was fast becoming the most universally disliked man in England. I recall Horace Walpole saying to me in later years:

'It is uncommon for a heart to be tainted so young...' He sighed. 'For there is an inveteracy, a darkness, a design and cunning in his character which stamp him as a very unamiable young man.'

Sandwich was affable enough, though, upon his entry this particular evening. It was hard to believe that this slim, elegant man was he whom John Wilkes, a later friend of mine, would call 'the most abandoned man of his age' and of whom another friend, our greatest poet of the century, Charles Churchill, would write:

'Search East, search Hell, the Devil cannot find
An agent like Lothario to his mind.'

Admittedly his cadaverous face possessed an expression of slow arrogance. I was aware that his speeches in Parliament had been termed 'Awkward, loose and detached – as awkward as his attitudes, as detached as his thoughts and as loose as his morals'. Nevertheless, on this particular night, Sandwich greeted Dashwood warmly and was courteous in his greetings to me.

'Cunts?' Dashwood enquired of his friends. 'Or perhaps you might presently prefer oysters?'

'Thank you, my dear sir, but no, thank you,' Sandwich responded. 'Just bring me a slice of rare and bloody beef wedged betwixt two slices of bread.' Dashwood laughed uproariously and did so. It was brought promptly and as Sandwich chewed upon it with flagrantly open greed, I reflected that the repast he had invented might well become a national dish – which, of course, in our days it has become. I also reflected, thinking of the man's unpopularity, that there are two sides to a Sandwich.

Writing with hindsight, today one sees that Sandwich encouraged Captain Cook's voyages of exploration, which led to the discovery of Australia: and the Sandwich Islands are named after him. Throughout his life he always needed more money but no one could bribe him. Whatever his vices, he refused requests for patronage and was never personally corrupt. He bore his own unpopularity with a cold shrug of his shoulders and despised those who sought to cultivate popular favour, having as he had a cynical contempt for Democracy, which he dismissed as mere 'mob rule'.

'So how's it going, Dashwood?' he enquired in his sharp tenor voice. 'Still bandying jests with peasants?' He drank liberally from his pewter pint of port.

'Sandwich, when *will* you learn that one can learn wisdom from a street-sweeper?' Dashwood expostulated with mild irritability.

'I can learn,' Sandwich retorted acidly, 'how to sweep a street.'

'And that is what I intend to do,' Dashwood answered. 'I intend to sweep the streets of politics, religion and the vexed question of sex.'

'How so?' Sandwich queried. 'Is this another one of your mad schemes? And incidentally, tell me more about this young

UNHOLY PASSIONS

man.' He flicked a finger to indicate me.

'Insufficient imagination, that's your trouble, Sandwich,' Dashwood grumbled, albeit genially as he quaffed more hot milk punch. 'I want to set up a grouping of the best and brightest in Great Britain. Young Horby here is a man of talent and I would like young men and women of his generation and possessing his accomplishments to be one with us. Though first, my dear sir,' he stared directly into my eyes and I felt that his gaze was burning through my brain, 'you must go on the Grand Tour and visit Paris, Italy and Turkey. Then you may be ready for the reception of the wisdom that I am prepared to present.'

'Sir: I am interested,' I replied, 'but what is the nature of the wisdom to which you refer?'

'My travels,' Sir Francis replied, 'have vouchsafed me the good fortune of receiving the wisdom of the East from the lips of holy men. My exploration of Venice resulted in my return with many arcane and esoteric works forbidden by the Inquisition and excoriated by the Index of Prohibited Books issued by the Roman Catholic Church – which, gentlemen, I trust we treat with the contempt it so richly deserves.' Sandwich and I nodded eager assent. 'Now tell me, have either one of you read that wonderful work, *Gargantua & Pantagruel* by Rabelais?'

'Obviously,' said Sandwich as I nodded. 'But nobody seems to know what the hell the bloody thing means.'

'Why, it's obvious, you bloody fool!' Dashwood roared at his friend. 'The search for the bottle in the fifth volume results in the Oracle from the High Priestess of the Bottle and that Oracle is TRINC. Therefore, we should eat, drink and be merry in order to enjoy a state of *ecstasy* in which the truths about human beings and their place in Nature may be apprehended with rapture. The best way to do this, I think, is to establish a community of the finest kindred spirits in the realm, all dedicated to a realization of this vision, and as our model, we take from Rabelais his Abbey of Thelema, an Abbey of Will, whereby our motto shall be DO WHAT THOU WILT.'

'That will is all very well, Francis,' Sandwich said, 'but can it be done? You know how I despise those members of the so-called *Knowing Ones* who declare: "Yes, that's all very well in practice: but how will it work in theory?" Have you any ideas?' He coughed. 'Any practice?'

'Plenty,' Dashwood responded, 'perhaps too much of the horn of plenty, sir. I am in the process of securing a lease upon Medmenham Abbey, situated comfortably upon an island in the Thames. Since it is my belief that architecture affects the minds of all who encounter it, I shall spend at least two years of money, time and energy on making my Abbey of Thelema a place of the utmost felicity. There will be the finest buildings and Temples, works of painting and sculpture that will make even the strongest man shiver with delight, a library before which the most dry of scholars will drool, and meat, drink and ladies such as have rarely made maids and men rejoice so unashamedly. I am taking a vision from a book, my dear sirs, the book of Rabelais, and I intend to make of it a living reality.'

'May God be with you,' Sandwich murmured.

'My Lord of Sandwich,' Dashwood fumed, 'do I detect a slight trace of sarcasm in your attitude? I assure you that all will be in order by 1751. And there we shall celebrate rites more suited to pagan groves than to Christian churches. There will be an outer order, which will celebrate good and plain pagan rites, the rites of the Man and the Woman conjoined before the eyes of God and Goddess. There will be meat, drink and sex in the most comfortable of circumstances and the possibility of learning more. For the Inner Order, there will be all this and, in addition, the use of ceremonial Magick to promote an expansion of mind and body and spirit.'

'A splendid vision indeed, sir,' Sandwich commented, 'though I wonder, with all respect, what will come of it.'

'The regeneration of Great Britain, sir!' Dashwood exclaimed warmly. 'By sex and religious ceremonies, our men and women will become enlightened and this will enable all of us to change the nature of present circumstances by means of Politics. Presently, we endure a corrupt system, let us face it. King George II cannot last longer than ten years. Fortunately, Frederick, Prince of Wales, who will be of the company tonight, is in agreement with nearly all of my ideas. I have urged upon him the study of Bolingbroke's *The Patriot King*, urging him further, when he comes to the throne, to use the power of the monarchy to govern on behalf of *all*.'

'Sir,' Sandwich murmured, 'in order for this to be done, you will assuredly require a most capable executive.'

'I have one, sir,' Dashwood replied warmly as his eyes flicked upwards to discern the entry of a slender man whose face was an admixture of the weasel, the stoat and the ferret. 'Allow me to present to you my excellent Steward, Paul Whitehead.'

CHAPTER FOUR

'May I (can worse disgrace on Manhood fall?)
Be born a Whitehead and baptized a Paul?'

So wrote my later friend Charles Churchill and the pleasant Robert Lloyd, another poet, called Whitehead 'learned in lechery, a sedulous and patient seducer and a veritable troubadour of blasphemy.' For myself, I must state that I never had any occasion to quarrel with him, even if the nature of his conversation was by turns desultory, vociferous and profane. He was aged thirty-nine as he walked down the steps to the cellar of the tavern that evening and I was well aware of his reputation. He was not a particularly good poet, having had little education, but he had undeniable talent as a composer of satirical verses. Having begun his literary career as one who hurled invective against the ruling Whig Establishment, his temper had been dampened by a spell in debtors' prison, and his talents had been hired by both Frederick, Prince of Wales and Sir Francis Dashwood. I would wish to put myself on record in stating that his loyalty, once hired, was absolute. He was the hackney coachman of political writing; and, as it would turn out, a highly efficient financial administrator. Indeed, without the practical skills of Whitehead, methinks that Dashwood could not have realized his vision.

Whitehead had first come to public attention by organizing a travesty of the Freemasons' Annual March, recruiting a parade of tramps and beggars dressed in mock-Masonic regalia. The Masons had responded by purchasing his satirical services. As I would in time realize, Whitehead as Steward, through his administrative efficiency, made possible the gatherings of both the Monks of Medmenham and the Friars of St Francis of Wycombe. Supervising the collection of subscriptions, all matters of beds, food and drink, in short, all details of the logistics that so bored Dashwood, this man with a face that was both complacent and crafty made himself indispensable. Charles Churchill did not like him and wrote:

> 'Whilst Womanhood in the habit of a nun
> At Med'nam lies, by backward monks undone;
> A nation's reckoning, like an alehouse score
> Which Paul the Aged chalks behind the door.'

Well: I must admit that in the days of the future Medmenham Monks, Paul Whitehead used to scrawl on a blackboard the numbers of how many tarts we had fucked and of how many bottles we had drunk and then pursue us assiduously with bills for same. His attention to his own finances no doubt resulted in his ability to write, shortly before his death:

> 'Safe in the harbour of my Twickenham bower
> From all the wrecks of State and Storms of Power
> No wreaths I court, no subsidies I claim;
> Too rich for want, too indolent for fame.'

Myself, I shall not forget a visit I once paid to this 'Twickenham bower' at the time that Whitehead had been appointed Deputy Treasurer of the Chamber at £800 a year during the so-called Hell-Fire Ministry of 1761–62 concerning which I shall tell the unvarnished truth. Whitehead's wife was a wealthy half-wit to whom he was unfailingly kind. I recall

UNHOLY PASSIONS

how she suddenly pointed at the valley below the Twickenham estate which her money had brought him and said:

'Look, dear, there are cows.'

'Yes, my dear,' Whitehead replied with every appearance of interest, 'there are indeed cows. But they are very nice cows.'

'Milk punch, sir?' Dashwood enquired of him and when Whitehead gave his assent, he served him generously from the steaming bowl. Just as he was doing so, we were joined by the fat and wheezing George Bubb-Dodington, a Member of Parliament since the age of twenty-four and now, being in his fifties and still wearing a spaniel wig, probably our leading Parliamentary 'fixer'. Everybody has joked about this fat man.

'Bubb is his name and bubbies doth he chase,
This swollen bullfrog with lascivious face,'

wrote Charles Churchill. Admittedly, his body and double-chinned face *were* as gross as his conversation on occasion. He liked to write indecent verse and obscene Latin inscriptions: William Hogarth portrayed him well enough in his classic visual satire of our political life 'Chairing the Member', for Bubb had no compunction concerning the use of bribery, yet his understanding of the levers that move politics had led him to the heart of public affairs.

Having inherited well and married fortunately, Bubb enjoyed a life of luxury. No one could fault the generosity of his hospitality, which I enjoyed when I later visited one of his many houses, this one having a magnificent view over the River Thames. However, his home here was a monstrosity of purple and orange silks, topped off by too much gilt wood. His fortune was as bottomless as his taste. Everyone loved to laugh at him; and in clubs, countless stories were told at his expense.

'Oh!' Bubb exclaimed breathlessly to a noted courtesan, 'if only I had you in a dark wood!'

47

'What would you do there that you can't do 'ere?' she responded tartly. 'Rob me?'

On another occasion which at that point lay ahead in the future, Bubb bowed to Queen Charlotte, wife of our future George III. Unfortunately, he was brought up short by a loud *riiiip* in his satin britches. Yet there was rather more to this man than mere comedy.

In Parliament he spoke for Liberty, all the while having fifty members indebted to him and therefore obliged to vote with him as he chose. That excellent French philosopher, Voltaire, has written that it was Bubb-Dodington who gave him the finest understanding of the English political system, so my friend could hardly have been the 'Silly-Bubb' that his enemies allege. He was certainly a good man of business. For example, he had invested just a few hundred pounds in Vauxhall Pleasure Gardens and then he sold his half-share for £4,000 when he discerned that Ranaleigh Pleasure Gardens would become popular. He had lent, it was known, £6,000 to the Prince of Wales for his purchase of Carlton House, meanwhile securing his investment by taking out an insurance policy upon the Prince's life. He was a very astute politician and businessman and also a discerning patron of the arts. Those he assisted included Edward Young, author of the exquisite *Night Thoughts*; James Thomson, author of *The Seasons*, the extraordinary *The Castle of Indolence* and *Rule Britannia*; and Henry Fielding, author of *Tom Jones* who dedicated his *Jonathan Wild* to Bubb. One jealous and neglected poet complained:

'While with your Dodington retir'd you sit
Charmed with his flowing burgundy and wit . . .'

In fact, Bubb's wit was not often very witty but in his house his feeblest pun could arouse laughter in the poets who were fed at his table. As was his habit, he joined our table with a pint of burgundy and a story.

'I have just come from seeing the Prime Minister,' he informed us loftily, as if he was the only man who ever did so. 'I do hope that he has the sense to take my advice. He wanted a secret committee, did His Grace the Duke of Newcastle, to amend the Ten Commandments simply by deleting the word "not". I disagreed, remarking that obligatory adultery would ruin its popularity.' We all laughed and slapped the table.

'Newcastle is an idiot,' Sandwich said. 'In the recent war, I endeavoured to persuade him of the need to defend Annapolis. He rushed about shouting: "Defend Annapolis certainly! To be sure, Annapolis must be defended! At all costs, defend Annapolis!" Then I overhead him whispering to a servant: "Pray, where *is* Annapolis?" What is needed is a change of Government.'

'For our ends,' Dashwood added.

'Quite so,' Sandwich smiled.

'I have no objection in principle,' I murmured.

'My dear sir,' said Bubb-Dodington, 'I find that whenever a man says that he has no objection in principle, it follows that he has not the slightest intention of putting the matter into practice.'

'That depends,' I replied to the then Treasurer of the Navy, 'upon what the practice is.'

'Practice?' Bubb chortled. 'Yesterday I also was received most kindly by the Prince of Wales, who informed me that he desired my services upon any terms I cared to name and by any title as might please me. He,' Bubb gazed at us with smug self-satisfaction, 'has put the principal direction of his affairs into my hands. He then continued to say that he would provide for my friends, whom he knows I value more than myself, and, my dear Sir Francis, he has you in mind as being an eminently suitable Treasurer of the Navy.'

'Leading to your elevation to the post of Prime Minister-in-waiting, by any chance?' Sandwich enquired. Bubb smiled. 'So you will become the unofficial leader of an unofficial opposition?' Bubb smiled again. 'Have you any hirelings from the Press to advance your cause?'

'Certainly,' Bubb-Dodington replied lazily, relishing every loose drip of a syllable. 'I am founding a paper to be called *The Champion*, with Henry Fielding as its Editor. I am also in the process of commissioning a good author, James Ralph, to write *A History of England 1600–1715*, its purpose being to show a gross betrayal of the Glorious Revolution of 1688 and the necessity for a Patriot King such as Frederick, surrounded by loyal and able Ministers.'

'Fine work, sir,' Sandwich said. 'After all and as we know, to be Treasurer of the Navy is an interesting and rewarding appointment. The task, a banking job in effect, is to raise money in the City for the upkeep of the Navy and, in the normal way of politics, a proportion of the money flowing through the Treasurer's office somehow finds its way into the Treasurer's private account.'

'I hope, sir,' Bubb replied, 'that under a new regime you would be only too happy to continue in your present post as First Lord of the Admiralty.'

'Enough politics!' Dashwood cried out, and promptly burst into verse:

'We have no idle prating
Of either whig or tory;
But each agrees
To live at ease
And sing or tell a story.

'We're always men of pleasure
Despising pride and party;

While knaves and fools
Prescribe us rules,
We are sincere and hearty.'

'So; come, sirs and let us disport ourselves!' he roared like a lion. 'Young Horby and I have been telling tales of our finest fucks. My dear Sandwich, stop carping for once, as is your wont, and tell us a tale! And charge your glasses gentlemen!'

'Oh, very well, Dashwood,' Sandwich responded. 'All of you are no doubt aware of my various predilections. It has been said that I enjoy the corruption of innocence. I deplore this accusation on the grounds that it is perfectly true. There is no such thing as innocence, gentlemen. No one is innocent. Now, on one occasion I found myself in Rome and being entertained most hospitably by an Italian Countess whose name was Sophia. During the drinks and the dinner, she continuously tempted and teased me by rustling her petticoats, swirling her skirt, exhibiting an almost indecently exposed but finely turned ankle: and at times even allowing her dress and petticoats to ride up so as to expose the delights of her olive-skinned calves. Whenever she arose to admonish the servants or on some other pretext, she made a point of switching her hips so as to make me wonder about her bottom and, if you will pardon the pun, my prick could not stand it. Now, I think it is Cervantes in *Don Quixote* who states, "Between a woman's Yes and a woman's No, I would not care to put a point of a pin." It is curious, is it not, the psychology of Woman? Show me, sirs, a man who understands it and I will show you a conceited liar. Therefore, when the guests had left the dining-room and the servants had withdrawn, I launched myself at the Countess Sophia like a firework rocket and tumbled her upon her Persian carpet.

' "Let me inspect your wanton crack," I cried, "for you were never a modest woman to have behaved as you have."

' "Oh, pity me!" she shrieked. "Let me go now! Do have mercy!" Yet she did not call for the servants.

' "You bitch!" I turned her on her front, whipped up her dress and petticoats and proceeded to spank her delectable bottom rather hard with the flat of my palm. It was a delicious sensation and I delighted in seeing her rounded bum cheeks redden, blush and twitch on account of my hard ministrations: smack! *smack!*

' "Oh! *O!*" she sobbed as her long, slender legs writhed and twisted in the air and the soft bottom to which I had imparted an immodest crimson flush proceeded to switch and squirm. "Mercy!" she squalled. "*Mercy!* Oh, it hurts and stings so much! I have been a chaste woman all my life . . . ow!" *Smack!* "Oh, you bastard!"

' "Hah!" I exclaimed with a resounding spank, and I continued my spanking with every word I spoke: "Chaste, chaste, chaste, eh? Oh, indeed, after what I have seen. So let us make haste, haste, haste." As I smacked her, the Countess Sophia kicked about and squirmed in pain, sobbing and screaming for mercy as the gorgeous bum cheeks I was turning from crimson to scarlet continued to heave and writhe as her pretty face flushed vermilion with the deepest shame: or was it pleasure? "Oh!" she squealed. "Finish me!"

'My excitement was now at its highest. I threw myself upon her.

' "I am dying," I laughed, "for want of your bottom-hole!" Turning her over and throwing her legs over my shoulders, I first plunged my bursting instrument into her cunny, so as to lubricate it. Then, turning her over again, I presented the empurpled head of my rock-hard penis to her dark brown fundament and, thrusting furiously, soon gained an insertion.

' "Oh! *O!* You'll split me!" she screamed. "Not there! Don't touch me there! Ah! I would never allow even my husband to do that . . . *Never!*" Myself, I find that when a wife dislikes her husband, one gains such extraordinary pleasure in the fuck with her, or in this instance, the buggery. "What shame..." she sighed. "What filthiness!" she exclaimed. I responded by using her glossy, long, black hair to lash her back, pushing on and on to complete possession. I had thought of resting momentarily after my exertions but the nervous contractions of her fundamental canal were too exciting. I spent a stream of my essence into her bowels which she met involuntarily with a heave of her soft, rounded bottom. With both of us temporarily exhausted, we remained quite still for some few minutes, affording me added pleasure as I caused my distended instrument to respond to the contracting pleasures of her anus.

' "Are you finished now, you wanton?" I jeered as I withdrew from her body with a noise something like the drawing of a cork, so tightly was the muscle of her bottom contracted around my still enflamed affair. "Ah! Ha! How tightly you hold! Haven't you had enough? Ha! I shall take a love token from you, just to remember your pussy whenever I look at it." So saying, I seized the knife which I always carry about my person in the eventuality of required self-defence and cut away a good lock of the fine long, black curly hair which adorned her quim.

' "Oh! Ah! Help! Oh, do have mercy! My God!" she sobbed. "I shall never be able to take a bath; my chambermaids will discern that it is all gone! Oh, oh, pity me!" she screamed but I continued to cut away, enjoying her screams and sobbings until the mouth of her crack had been well shaven.

' "You lying woman," I chuckled. "I've made a nice *Contessa* of a pussy for you and now I'll really finish you off."

' "Pray be merciful!" the Countess Sophia squealed. "Oh! What more misery can you inflict?"

'I promptly prodded my pego within her (all too

welcoming) cunt. "That will keep out the cold," I murmured. "Be a pity for an Italian Countess to catch cold." Her legs were wide open, showing the mauve lip and clitoris of her pussy all smeared with manly spunk. Gathering my strength, I proceeded to thrust so deep into her cunny that the tip of my pego reached the outer lips of her womb until it was fairly sticking in the entrance. The lady was by now almost unconscious, moaning and sighing, incapable of any efforts to save herself.

'I could not resist uttering a brutal laugh as I shoved and rammed my pego in and out of her crack, and rapidly so, time after time, my belly slapping against hers. "There is nothing like exercise for keeping out the cold," I muttered. I enjoyed the spectacle of her tearful, pitiable looks as she sobbed and moaned in her exhausted state. "Ha! A little nourishment will revive you, my dear."

'I withdrew my prick from her cunt and, moving it swiftly over her trembling belly and across her firm breasts, plunged it deep within her gaping mouth. As her soft, luscious lips closed upon it, I shot more spasms of sperm down the throat of that swan-like neck. She choked, gasped and fell back in a lifeless swoon. This climactic action had finished her. So, leaving her to recover as best she could, I took her pubic hair for onanistic purposes and retired from the scene.'

This story of Sandwich's was greeted with acclaim: and Dashwood then asked Paul Whitehead to tell us a tale.

'Well, gentlemen,' Whitehead began, 'I shall first give you my rhyme upon English women:

'She loves a prick, long, thick and firm.
And she'll wriggle and pant till you madly fill
Her bang full of glowing sperm.
You may frig and gamahauche and try every plan,
But fair fucking's the pride of an Englishman.'

'Hallelujah!' we all shouted.

'One of my greatest friends is Bubb here,' Paul Whitehead continued as Bubb nodded his acquiescence, 'and on one occasion we were at his beautiful home, La Trappe, in Hammersmith.'

'Indeed,' said Bubb. 'All of you gentlemen must come there, though Dashwood and Sandwich have come and gone on many a joyous occasion. Young Horby, you must come there too. I have had this villa restored at *vast* expense with a stucco front, a balustrade, a pillared Temple of Venus, a bathing hut, and a bugle-shaped pattern of white stones on my sloping lawn arranged so as to form my family crest. It was all designed by a most fashionable Italian but I fear that one does forget names. As for the interior...'

'Indeed, sir,' Sandwich interrupted him, 'I am familiar with your interior. One recalls garish frescoes filled with pink-bottomed cherubs, tapestries, antiques, gilt, a marble chimney-piece from which fake stalactites droop, an eighty-five-foot-long sculpture gallery and its crystal roof supported by seventeen-foot pillars of Italian marble, which marble also adorns the floor.'

'Certainly, Sandwich,' Bubb-Dodington replied proudly, 'though some visitors think that this gallery ought to be on the ground floor.'

'There is no need to worry, Bubb,' Sandwich answered with a cruel smile. 'Given its weight, it soon will be.'

'Hah! I always appreciate the wit of your hit, sir,' Bubb retorted with dignity. 'Have you not enjoyed goodly times there? I refer to the place as *My Convent*. Nothing succeeds like excess. But allow our estimable Mr Whitehead to continue with his story.'

'I was there,' said Whitehead, 'on a glorious evening with Bubb and two luscious beauties, Carol and Jane, drinking port and discussing matters of sex after a hearty dinner. My own little lady, blonde Carol, warmly defending the practice of gamahauching, as I did, proposed its practice. Laying Carol down on the couch and parting her beautiful legs, I displayed to the company a cleft that an angel would think it a new joy to lick and suck. Soon the four of us were engaged in an amorous orgy and Bubb, who despite his fat, can certainly boast of a magnificent priapus, took pretty little angel eyes Jane in his arms and gave her what you may call an "Exhibition Fuck". His balls knocked against the entrance of her lovely quim and at last when she wriggled and panted and at length hugged him into a spend, he poured such a libation into her that we could see it overflow and they lay mutually entranced until we revived them with some glorious wine. Meanwhile I fucked the arse off my dame.

'Then we went in for a game of Blind Man's Buff, all being stripped naked and armed with birches. We all scampered about the room, cutting right and left, and endeavouring to land some smart blows upon each other's glowing posteriors until, thoroughly exhausted, we embraced and sank to the floor.'

'Persian carpets upon Italian marble, mind,' said Bubb-Dodington. 'Anyway, I proposed a second round, though after some more wine, naturally. Personally, I cannot bear the endeavours of those who wish upon us temperance, health and chastity. One should be either a three-bottle man or a four-bottle man: five is acceptable, six even praiseworthy, though eight in a day might be considered immoderate.'

'On this round,' Whitehead resumed his story, 'the ladies were blindfolded and a prize would be given to the lady who caught me. Oh, it was jolly good fun to see the girls running about naked and the slipping of their hands down to the proper place to feel if it was a man they held; but they kept giving me such hard slaps upon my bottom that I tried to run out of the room. At this point, one of the girls picked up my walking-

UNHOLY PASSIONS

cane that stood in a corner and made a lunge at me. That she-devil must have looked! Oh! The tip of the cane entered my fundament as it was turned to her and as she withdrew it, the ferrule was left behind, in a manner of speaking, and there it remains, and every time I sigh . . .'

'Every time you *what*?' Dashwood queried.

'Well, every time I fart, if you like, the ferrule whistles and the dogs follow me and I can't help it.'

'Then don't diet windily,' said Dashwood.

'My joke, sir,' Whitehead returned with a wicked leer. 'Meanwhile, I was enchanted with the light flowing hair of Carol, her airy step and her slender figure, delighting in the lovely swell of her bosom, and the creamy whiteness of her face. In fact, she delighted in exposing a delectable pair of creamy shoulders, and her two glowing breasts, small for her size, but round and seemingly polished as marble. If my priapus had been before excited, it was now delirious. Carol offered no resistance. What a joy it was to feel her round breasts, to pinch her roseate nipples and to fire her with my wanton touches and the hot burning kisses that I printed on her lips. I allowed my very own splendid staff of lust to display itself fully before her.

' "Oh, Paul, how it had *grown* since Blind Man's Buff," she giggled mischievously as she took it within her delicate hand.

' "Yes," I replied, and I fear I can never resist a pun: "I have heard my John Thomas *groan* for a taste of your darling cunny. Come, let me feel how it is getting on." As I spoke, I slid my hand betwixt her satin-smooth thighs and felt her cunt, moist and mossy, tickled her clitoris and aroused all her warming passions. We abandoned ourselves to all that our impassioned natures could suggest. Kneeling down, I opened wide the legs of Carol and pressed my hot lips to her creamy cunt, and gamahauched her until she spent in delirious pleasure. And then, when all my feelings were working up to such a pitch of excitement that I could no longer contain myself, I laid her supple form over a love-seat and, getting into her from behind, thrust my prick to the very hilt within her sopping cunt. One, two, three thrusts – and as I clasped her to me with a convulsive thrill, I poured out my manly balm in an ecstasy of enjoyment.'

'Hi, hi! Stop that, you infernal scoundrels!' a voice roared. 'Oh, you dirty rascals!'

In a sudden, bewildered burst of alarm, we looked round to see a man dressed in a coat of white cloth faced with blue satin, embroidered with silver. His hat was laced with silver and garnished with a white feather. He was tall and graceful, his limbs finely proportioned, his countenance open and majestic, his eyes full of sweetness and vivacity, his teeth regular and his pouting lips of the complexion of the damask rose. It was as though he were born for love and inspired it wherever he appeared. I knew him slightly and he was not a niggard of his wit, since he liberally returned it to others: and he had a flow of gallantry for which many ladies of this land can vouch from their own experience.

We all arose to welcome warmly His Royal Highness, Frederick, Prince of Wales and heir to the throne.

CHAPTER FIVE

It is no easy task to be Prince of Wales. One is born to be King but there is not much to do apart from wait until one's father dies in order to fulfil one's function. At the age of forty-two, he continued to upset his father King George II, who according to Bubb called him 'an arrogant coxcomb', and his mother Queen Caroline who, again according to Bubb, declared: 'My dear first-born is the greatest ass and the greatest liar and the greatest *canaille* and the greatest beast in the whole world and I heartily wish he was out of it!' 'That booby, Fritz!' his father stormed, especially annoyed by his son's extravagant patronage of poets and painters. 'I hate *b*oets and *b*ainters!' King George II had snarled.

Myself, I have never been especially happy with the Hanoverians upon the throne. King George I was a bigoted murderer; King George II a bigoted bore and boor. Intelligence was somewhat lacking and they appeared to have married Queens even more stupid than they themselves were, producing children they hated and who hated them in return. What a Royal Family! It has lost all its dignity. We all know that the Hanoverians were shipped over after the death of Queen Anne, last of the Stuarts and a much under-rated monarch, to be puppets for the Whig oligarchy. Though I benefit from this regime, I then inclined more towards the Tory policy whereby, with the King leading the way, the fortunate in society have a duty of care and obligation towards the less fortunate. Bonnie Prince Charlie of the Stuart line (*Editor's note:* the line from which the present Princess Diana is descended) had endeavoured to take England just four years before but his incompetent generalship had led inevitably to a series of ignominious defeats: we were stuck with the Hanoverians; and Frederick seemed to be the best among them.

His sexual success with actresses and opera singers was legendary, though in 1736 he had obeyed his father's wishes in marrying so as to produce an heir, the wife being the pleasant Princess Augusta of Saxe-Gotha, who was then aged seventeen. She gave him five sons and two daughters, though this had not prevented Frederick from fornicating further. He liked sex, he liked women and women, on account of this, liked him. As far as men were concerned, he was an affable, generous, good-natured person who liked to play the cello, sing French songs and recruit his friends into the performance of amateur theatrical entertainment. At the time that I knew him, his quarrels with the King had intensified. George II had ordered him out of St James's Palace and the allowance which he gave his son, a mere £50,000 a year, was just half of what George himself had received when he had been Prince of Wales.

Be that as it may, he nevertheless held court at his town house in Leicester Square and in the country at Cliveden House, by the Thames near Marlow, in total opposition to that of his father and mother. 'I hope in God I shall never see the monster's face again,' his mother had declared after the birth of Frederick's first son. Her wish was granted since she died without any reconciliation back in 1737. For his part, Frederick had taken to cultivating both the London Mob and the élite.

He had won over the former by giving beef and beer to the poor and by personally assisting in the fighting of fires. 'Crown him!' the London Mob had roared. He had also

UNHOLY PASSIONS

become the first British Royal Freemason within the hallowed portals of United Grand Lodge.

'I am,' he told us upon this evening, 'accelerating my endeavours to become the principal focus of the Opposition.' Taking a deep drink of his pint of port, he muttered in an undertone: '*und* zo where are the women ... ?'

'Later, possibly, sire ... ?' his aide and ally Bubb suggested. Between them Prince Frederick and Bubb-Dodington controlled over one hundred seats in the House of Commons.

'Yes, let us speak of Politics!' Frederick proclaimed. 'I think, as Lord Bolingbroke says, that the Glorious Revolution of 1688 has been betrayed and that those who think so should support a future monarch eager and willing to restore its formerly promised glory. My intention is to dismiss this entire, useless Whig government and appoint another.'

'Bravo!' shouted Dashwood who, being an Independent and one of a hundred and fifty such, was neither Whig nor Tory. 'Your Royal Highness, I well recall your party at Cliveden just four years ago, when the guns of the Young Pretender, Bonnie Prince Charlie, were pounding the Hanoverian defence of Carlisle, and you, sire, gave us an iced cake to represent its fortifications and hired some nubile young girls to smash it to bits by hurling little cannon-balls.' Frederick shouted with laughter.

'On another occasion,' Sandwich added acidly, and he could afford to do so since he was First Lord of the Admiralty under the Whigs, 'Your Royal Highness forced his guests to go gardening in wild, wet February weather, then rewarded us with cold food and your own rendition of Shakespeare's *Macbeth*. Are these enthusiastic eccentricities of Your Royal Highness absolutely essential?'

'Don't misunderstand me, Sandwich,' Prince Frederick replied. 'I intend for the future to abolish all distinctions of party. Government will be by the best and the brightest but always *for* the people.' He adjusted his silver silken stockings. 'Your friend, Bubb-Dodington here, *my* friend also, will make a splendid First Lord of the Treasury.' Bubb drank deeply to that and nodded enthusiastic assent as all of his five chins wobbled in accord. 'For his deputy I propose that excellent fellow, John Stuart, third Earl of Bute. I first met him two years ago at a race meeting in Egham, Surrey. Rain forced me to take shelter in a tent and we needed a fourth to make up a game of whist. He proceeded to delight us with his skills at conversation and the playing of his cards. Later he delighted me by his arrangement at Cliveden of his amateur dramatics.'

'Ah, yes, young Bute,' Sandwich murmured, pondering his own gleaming footwear. 'Pleasant, certainly, but perhaps a little vain. I hear on good authority that the ladies lust after him most lasciviously.'

'*I* hear on good authority,' Dashwood drawled as he signalled for his fourth bottle, 'that he is so vain that one of his greatest pleasures is to walk by the River Thames, all the while admiring the beauty of the neighbouring calves, being his own.'

'Oh, that man owns to an athletic pair of legs,' said Sandwich. 'I told him so and he did fain agree with me.'

'*I*,' said Bubb-Dodington, 'hear on good authority, according to the fashionable intelligence, that Lord Bute declares the wife of Your Royal Highness to be the most beautiful lady of the Kingdom.'

'She is indeed, sir,' Frederick responded warmly as Sandwich muttered: 'Flattery will get you everywhere, Bubb.' 'And she concurs fully with my opinion that Lord Bute will be appointed a Lord of the Bedchamber.' Dashwood and Sandwich glanced at one another. 'The splendidly able Bubb-Dodington here is henceforth appointed Treasurer of the Chambers.' Bubb beamed broadly and, at £2,000 a year for doing next to nothing, one could discern why. 'We need effective opposition.'

'Your Royal Highness, opposition for its own sake is futile,' Bubb returned earnestly. 'What is needed is to establish a programme to which every right-thinking person in and out of Parliament can happily subscribe, based upon principles which only the notoriously corrupt would not cheerfully support. In this way the opposition obtains a moral superiority over the government.'

'I agree,' Dashwood declared. 'I want a Patriot King who appoints his Ministers on merit rather than taking on tired old hacks whose sole qualifications consist of blind party loyalty and saying: "Oh, my dear Lord! Your shoes, with all respect, are not looking quite as shiny as perhaps they should be, sir, though I would not wish to venture any criticism. Would you allow me the privilege, kind sir, of licking them clean, if you please?" '

'I have to see these dreadful, wretched petitioners every day,' Sandwich sighed, 'and when they speak to me like that, I simply kick 'em in the teeth.'

'Gentlemen,' the Prince stated solemnly, 'I want only the best men to govern my future kingdom. A palmist I visited recently informed me that my reign would be most glorious. Sir Francis,' he gazed earnestly at Dashwood, 'it is said that you are an expert on that most recondite sacred subject of High Magick.' (The Prince pronounced it as though it were indeed spelled with a 'k'.) 'It is heard that your collection of arcane books within your library, selected from the choicest items of the Orient, Europe and the Middle East, purchased in Paris and in Venice, contains the enshrined magical secrets of the Ancient Wisdom.'

'Yes,' Dashwood answered simply.

'Sir Francis,' Bubb leaned forward confidentially so as to explain, 'wishes to create the most exclusive Club for the celebrations of Magick and Religion and Politics and Life that has ever existed since ancient times. We wish to help you realize the vision of The Patriot King. Your Royal Highness, will you help us to realize the vision of a Club dedicated to religious truth and artistic beauty, with the method of science and the aim of religion, all to be brought forth into politics so as to enflame the spirit of the people?'

'Nobly put, sir!' Frederick cried out. 'Of course I give my glad and royal assent! All I ask is that Sir Francis here vouchsafes me some instruction in these magical mysteries.'

'Gladly.' Dashwood inclined his head.

'It'll be a Hell-Fire Club, one trusts,' the Prince said eagerly, clearly enthused by the idea, 'and one of the sort that my father had outlawed in the 1720s, eh? Ah, yes! Naked virgins on the altar and plenty of wine and blasphemy, sirs! How I could do with that!'

'It is not *quite* like that, sire,' Bubb-Dodington came in hastily. 'Though of course,' he looked lecherous, 'one trusts that there will be plenty of naked virgins, ha ha! Meanwhile I am sure that Sir Francis here can teach you all about the secret, sacred, *inner* rituals.'

'Naturally,' said Dashwood; 'Come tomorrow.' And I wondered if I could, it being that the subject of the conversation was new to me. 'We have then six, which forms the Holy Hexagram, making of the matter an appropriate start. Now we need another seven to make thirteen and a Devil's Dozen. Whom shall we have, gentlemen? I propose my own doctor, Dr Benjamin Bates, a man most learned in Masonry. Any objections? Motion carried. I propose Lord Bute if he be in agreement with us: ah! I see you all agree. Any other nominations?'

'Sir Henry Vansittart,' said Bubb, 'for then we'll have the India connection. He is a surprisingly popular and efficient Governor of Bengal.'

'Quite right, Bubb. Good, so we all agree. Another nomination?'

'George Selwyn,' said Sandwich. 'He is a reliable Member

of Parliament and possibly the man of greatest wit during this presently benighted era. I was the victim of his morbid wit only the other day. He wrote me a letter of condolence upon the death of my uncle who recently died at sea, by drowning, and who had been accused of sodomy; Selwyn said how sorry he was that my relative had gone to the bottom. It is said that he likes to copulate with corpses at midnight in graveyards and he frequently attends public executions. Forsooth, he would not miss a hanging at Tyburn for the World. If you want the finest seat at a hanging, just be a friend of George Selwyn.'

'Always been a pleasant but strange sort of fellow,' Bubb-Dodington murmured. 'But most amiable, so let us have him. Let us also have the handsome Thomas Potter, son of the Archbishop of Canterbury. That'll get the Church of England rolling in the aisles.' I smiled at the mention of that notorious debauchee.

'We'll need a good woman,' Dashwood stated, 'and I propose my dear friend, Lady Mary Wortley Montague.' Loud cheers assented to this proposition, for Lady Mary was renowned as the most lascivious, most travelled and most intelligent woman in England. 'Finally,' said Sir Francis, 'I would like to nominate my dear young friend, Frank Duffield, who had kindly leased me the island of Medmenham and who has also come to me in quest of magical instruction.' All agreed. 'We shall want an Outer Order too, gentlemen. I shall approach Mrs Hayes to ensure that her brothel supplies us with only the finest of girls. Their presence will enable us to compound literature, paganism, art, architecture, Templarism, Freemasonry, Rosicrucianism, Hindoo Tantricism and all Hermetic Renaissance influences into powerful shot that will go flying from our cannon. To the Christians, sex is evil. To the many, sex is natural. To the few, sex is sacred. For our sociable celebrations, therefore, I recommend my cousin, the squire Sir Thomas Stapleton; Mr John Clarke, to handle all legal matters; John Tucker MP, you know him, Bubb, I think he's your Navy office cashier; Sir John Dashwood-King, my half-brother and a decent chap; oh, and Dr Thomas Thompson who does valuable work for Great Britain . . .'

'Yes, Sir Francis,' Bubb came in, 'he tells all the World that he is working for the British Secret Service.'

'And no one believes him,' Dashwood retorted. 'That is why he is such an effective agent. All with me so far? Ah, yes, must have Sir William Stanhope, Chesterfield's brother; and Henry Vansittart's two brothers, Arthur and Robert, for they're decent chaps. Good. Any objection to the Earl of Orford, you know, Horace Walpole's elder brother . . . ?'

'Yes,' said Sandwich. 'He is so silly a man that even a fish-wife would consider him feeble-minded but as long as he cannot enter inner proceedings, one doubts if he will spoil things. Let us also have my favourite artist, William Hogarth: and the Duke of Kingston, the Marquis of Granby; Joseph Banks, the nation's leading scientist, who I predict will become President of the Royal Society if I have anything to do with it; and Lord March.'

'Old Q?' Bubb queried. 'I thought he only liked horses and girls, in that order. He seemed somewhat jaded when I went to see him the other day. "What is there to make of the Thames?" he sighed wearily as he gazed out of his bow-windowed villa at Richmond; "I am quite tired of it – there it goes, flow, flow, flow, always the same . . ." Still, I suppose he could be quite useful to us in the House of Lords . . . hmmm.'

'All agreed, I think,' Dashwood muttered briskly as he waved a hand for his fifth pint of port. 'And for our leading ladies, let us invite Francis, Countess Vane, my dear friend . . .' There were gasps since she was renowned as being the most salacious lady in the Kingdom and her beauty was past compare. 'Ah, and Lady Betty Germain;' there were gasps again as we all thought of her beauty and lascivious reputation. 'She is presently in possession of the Aztec Mexican "scrying stone" of the Elizabethan magus Dr John Dee, and this may assist us with our magical rites. Lady Clarissa Hyde and her pretty younger cousin, the Hon. Arabella Marchmount . . . does anyone have any objections . . . ?' I certainly did not and nor did any other man. 'Any other nominations?'

'Miss Fanny Murray,' Sandwich pronounced. This was the voluptuous and celebrated courtesan whom Sandwich had taken as his mistress. All of us gave unqualified assent to his proposal.

'Now, sire,' Dashwood smiled at Prince Frederick, 'since we are all in concord, we proceed to the custom whereby it is your turn to tell us a bawdy story about a good fuck. Don't be modest, Your Royal Highness, you're among friends here, I can tell you!'

'It is a pleasure to be among you, sirs,' said Prince Frederick.

'We are honoured by your company, sire,' Sir Francis responded, 'and in your honour, I have ordered a gargantuan pie filled with birds. By your side, to accompany it, you will be served potted larks and marmalade with buttered toasted bread. As you break open the pie crust, you will see the birds in thick dark gravy, ladled by copious quantities of burgundy. There are old capons and young chickens, crisply roasted duck, goose, grouse, partridge, pigeon, pheasant, quail: and the turkey-bird, especially imported from the American Colonies. With this pie there will be also roasted potatoes and chestnuts accompanied by fresh peas, a favourite dish of King Henry VIII whose dissolution of the monasteries we all abhor. Then, plum pudding and whipped cream. Ah!' Dashwood burst into song.

'Sing a song of sixpence
A pocketful of Rye . . .'

'And Rye,' the Prince commented wryly, '*is* in your pocket, sir, you being the Honourable Member for nearby New Romney, is it not?' Dashwood nodded his head and continued to sing:

> 'Four and twenty blackbirds
> Baked in a pie.'

'So you control twenty-four votes in the House of Commons . . . ?' the Prince of Wales queried. Dashwood nodded again, then recommenced his singing that was lusty rather than skilful.

> 'When the pie was opened
> The birds began to sing.
> Wasn't that a tasty dish
> To set before the king?'

'I think that I am with you so far, sir,' Prince Frederick murmured.

'Splendid, sire,' Dashwood bellowed. 'One does hope so.' He proceeded to slash the pie-crust in one swift move of his knife and thence to help the happy guests with a ladle, murmuring that the servants would assist us in the carving of our birds. 'Pie, pie, glorious pie!' Dashwood sang out. 'More pie, Horby?'

'Oho! Not I.'

'No pie? But why?' Dashwood and I both burst out laughing as he served me with a magnificent plate of delicious birds. For a time there was nothing other than the satisfying sounds of guzzling and then the Prince of Wales addressed us.

'Gentlemen,' he began, 'it is now Pudding Time, an expression used to denote the most felicitous time of the evening. I believe that this expression is also used to express the satisfaction of the people with the accession of my Hanoverian family.

UNHOLY PASSIONS

The people of England called the time of my grandfather, King George I, also Elector of Hanover, Pudding Time.' With that said, the Prince of Wales commenced his tales.

CHAPTER SIX

'Ah! what fond memories!' Frederick, Prince of Wales sighed. 'Let us take Lady Barbara, for example: what a voluptuous blonde termagant she was! I gladly accepted her invitation, extended to Bubb here and myself on one occasion, to visit her town house in the region of Hyde Park. Servants escorted us into a tastefully furnished little room. A pianoforte stood in one corner, other musical instruments were about the room, there were splendid pictures of voluptuous scenes adorning the walls and two glorious couches that seemed fit for seraphs to recline upon stood ready for our attentions. Barbara received us graciously with sherry and introduced us to her friend Henrietta, a slender brunette. After some courteous conversation, Lady Barbara, never one to mince her words, said:

' "Frankly, Your Royal Highness, I am dying for a fuck and I shall take great pleasure in feeling you operate if you are up to the task. I hope and trust that you are in good form. Henrietta, my dear fried here, is similarly so disposed and one trusts that Bubb is up to the matter, for if men cannot fuck and fuck well, pray tell me, what on earth is the use of them?"

' "I trust," Bubb declared, "that faced with the delectable prospect of you delicious ladies we shall be invigorated by the very sight of the matter." It took but a little time for us to undress these two lovely ladies and lay them at full length upon the soft couches. I was on Barbara instantly and had my prick buried to the hilt within her luscious cunt.

' "Go to it, sire," Bubb urged me. "Give it to her. This young lady has some good stuff to spend, I know, for she sucked my prick most delightfully three times only Tuesday last." At this instant, Lady Barbara pulled away from me, seized a birch standing in the corner and laid it smartly across Bubb's arse.

' "There now!" she snarled as she swished him, "you are getting slow but I shall warm you up, I warrant!" Swish! Swish! *Swish!* Barbara suited the actions to the words, visibly quickening the sexual strokes of Bubb and soon a shiver took their bodies and Henrietta and he melted together within a glorious spend.

' "Oh, poor Fritz, look at his prick," Henrietta muttered, turning around as Bubb slid off her and certainly noticing the state of my prick, which was in a most painful state of excitement. Barbara responded by dropping quietly to her knees and, taking my stiff penis between her ruby lips, soon sucked it into a state of rapture while Henrietta looked on, highly amused by the look of gratified pleasure which soon enough spread over my countenance as I came within milady's deep throat. After that, I gave her a jolly rogering.

'The earlier days of my sexuality were not quite as pleasurable. During my adolescence, my father and mother placed me in the hands of a governess, Millicent, and her assistant, Sarah. Millicent was a delectable and willowy brunette and Sarah was a buxom blonde. For a short period, they were also responsible for the education of my distant cousin, Charlotte, a strikingly good-looking girl possessed of a magnificent head of flaming red hair. I was also absolutely obsessed by the way in which she switched her bottom. Soon enough I managed to inveigle my way into her bedroom at night and endeavoured to seduce her. But although this exquisite young lady felt so good to the touch, she declined my offer to take her maidenhead on the grounds that she wished to marry well and did not wish to bear children before that happy occasion.

' "No, not there, Charlotte," I endeavoured to explain to her. "My love, you have another maidenhead I mean to take tonight. The normal way of doing only leads to getting a lot of children and surely my quiver is potentially full of enough of them. No, no, it will be the French style for us, do you understand? I mean to get into your bottom," I added, with evident excitement.

' "What a nasty idea!" Charlotte, who was only eighteen, retorted.

' "But I must and I will, Charlotte," I returned. "There are so many different ways of 'doing it'. Why, we can suck each other and fuck – ah! You start at the vulgar word – but it is fuck – fuck – fuck! – that's the name for it. We fuck within beautiful bottoms, under armpits, between the bubbies – another name for titties – anywhere and everywhere. It is all the same to a man, all what is called CUNT, a word, I am sure, which you have seen somewhere, written on shutters, doors or even on the pavement – a deliciously vulgar word, Charlotte, but the universal toast of men when they meet in company, I assure you, Madam!"

' "Why Frederick, are you mad," she replied. "I will not learn your filthy ways!"

' "Don't drive me to extremities, Charlotte," I responded. "I may be rough, for I am determined to put my prick into your arse, now and at once!" I tried to turn her over.

' "Frederick, Frederick, for shame!" she shrieked. "Millicent and Sarah will hear your disgusting language. You will never abuse me this way!" Hiding her face in her hands, Charlotte began to sob.

' "But I will," I answered coldly, "and you may blubber like a child. Your tears only urge me on. If you resist, I shall smack and beat you until you are obedient."

'Charlotte struggled with me but a woman's strength is soon exhausted and at last I got her face down on the bed, with her bottom on the edge and her feet on the floor. Then, giving the girl a tremendously painful smack upon her bum, I spread her legs wide apart, opened the cheeks of that so glorious bottom, anointed the head of my bursting prick with spittle, also the tight brown hole I was about to attack; and then I pushed on to the assault of her virgin fortress. I could hear her moan as the head of my stiff pego gradually forced its way within her sphincter muscle.

' "Ah!" she shrieked, "it's *pricking*! Oh . . . oh! You'll rend me, Frederick . . . oh, pray . . . Ah . . . *aargh!* O! . . . ohh . . ."

'At last I was in and, having rested a moment or two, I then began the motions of my buggery. Presently I could tell by the wriggling of her bottom that she was enjoying the matter. My hands were busy frigging her quim in front. How excited we became, each of us seeming to spend at the same moment, but I kept my place and the second finish was so marvellous that both of us screamed loudly in the frenzy of emission. As Charlotte actually fainted away, I fell exhausted upon her senseless body. Unfortunately, that was how we were found by our Governess, Millicent, who summoned us sternly to her drawing-room.

' "Now, sir," she declared fiercely, "what to do? I must decide for myself. Frederick, you must submit to a good whipping for this or else I shall write to your father and mother and send Charlotte home disgraced in the morning and you will have to promise to marry her, sir! You bad boy, I am determined both to punish you and to make you offer her all the reparation in your power."

'Charlotte began to cry and begged Millicent not to be too hard, as I had not hurt her much and in fact had quite delighted her ravished senses.

' "Upon my word!" Millicent stormed, "the girl is as bad as

the boy! Charlotte, this could not have happened if you had not been too complaisant and given way in weakness to the rudeness of Frederick." Quite unmindful of my condition, I started up and clasped Charlotte around her neck, kissing her most lovingly. "You impudent fellow!" Millicent shrieked. "Why, now I see you raising her dress and petticoats, stroking her belly... and passing your hand over her mossy mound!"

' "What a pity, Millicent," I answered slowly and deliberately, "that you are my governess or I would give you the same pleasure as I have given Charlotte." Here I unbuttoned my britches and laid bare my thick and throbbing thruster. "Still, I will submit to your chastisement, however hard it may be, and I promise that I may consider that my love here may become my future wife."

' "You scandalous fellow!" Millicent expostulated. "How dare you insult my modesty so in exposing your manhood to my sight! But I *will* punish you and avenge both myself and Charlotte. You are my prisoner so just march into the other room next door. I've got a tickler there that I brought home from school," she lisped, "little thinking that I should so soon have a use for it."

I was marched to the next room which featured a fourposter bed, often used by Millicent whenever the household had retired for the night. Millicent ordered Charlotte to tie my hands to the bedposts and then to secure my ankles with strong twine. Sarah now entered the room, brandishing a rod of birch.

' "Lower the britches of Frederick, yes, young master Frederick and pin up his shirt to his shoulders," Millicent coldly commanded Charlotte and Sarah, who gladly obeyed her every word. "I will see," Millicent laughed cruelly, "if I can't at least draw a few drops of the impudent blue blood out of the posterior of His Royal Highness, which blood Charlotte may wipe off with her handkerchief as a souvenir of the outrage she has so easily forgiven." With a flourish, Millicent brought down the bunch of springy twigs with a thundering whack on my bottom. The effect was startling since I was only anticipating some playful fun.

' "Ah!" I cried out. "Madam Millicent! My God . . . you'll cut the skin . . . !"

' "Hah!" Millicent exclaimed with a smile of satisfaction. "Did you think I was going to play with you? You have soon found out your mistake, young sir! Will you? Will you again take such outrageous liberties with a young lady charge of mine?"

'She cut me quite half-a-dozen times in rapid succession as she thus lectured me and, as the mirrors held before me and behind me by Charlotte and Sarah showed, her each blow was leaving long red lines to marks its visitation.

' "Your birching, Millicent," Sarah enthused, "is suffusing his fair bottom all over with a peach-like bloom."

' "You she-devil!" I shouted. Finding myself to be quite helpless, I had been grinding my teeth and biting my lips in fruitless rage. "Ah! Do you mean to skin my bum? Be careful or I will take a rare revenge some day and before long."

' "Ooooh!" Millicent squealed delightedly as she switched her hips and swished her petticoats. "You show temper, do you?" she added with great calmness and determination. Yet this was accompanied by a most excited twinkle in her eyes. "I will keep you there." *Swish!* "So you mean to be revenged on me for doing a simple act of justice, sire?" *Swish!* "I shall cut away at your impudent bottom . . ." *Swish!* ". . . until you fairly beg my pardon . . . uuh!" *Swish!* ". . . uh . . . O! . . . and promise to forgo all such wicked revengefulness."

'I, her victim, writhed in agony and rage but her blows only increased in force, beginning to raise great, fiery weals all over my buttocks.

' "Ah! Hah!" Millicent cried out her cruel glee. "How do you like it, Your Royal Highness? Shall I put a little more steam into my blows?" *Swish!* I struggled desperately to get loose but the bitches had secured me too well for that. I admit that there were tears of shame and mortification standing in the corners of my eyes but I was still obstinate.

' "Look!" Sarah shouted gleefully. "I can observe a very perceptible rising in his manly instrument ... oh! look again ... beneath his belly it is standing out in a rampant state of erection."

' "Look at the fellow!" Millicent snorted with assumed fury of indignation. "How he is insulting me by exhibition of his lustful weapon!" She waved her rod of birch in the air. *Swish!* My bottom jerked upwards and writhed, this delighting the ladies. "Oh! You are beginning to feel properly, are you?" *Swish!* How my bottom was glowing! "Are you sincerely penitent?" *Swish!* "Beg my pardon at once, young sir, for the way you have insulted me." *Swish!* "And young Charlotte!" *Swish!*

' "Oh!" I screamed. "Dear Madam Millicent! Miss Sarah! Stop! Please stop! I will, I will beg your pardon." *Swish!* "Oh, I can't help my pego sticking up as it does."

' "Down, sir!" Millicent snapped, eyes flashing. "Down, sir! Your master is ashamed of you," she teased as she playfully whisked my pego with her rod. I was in agony. My writhing contortions were excruciating in the extreme and I groaned:

' "Oh! Oh, Millicent ... my governess, let me down. Upon my word, I will do anything you order. O! Ah! You make me do it ..." I shut my eyes as quite a jet of jism shot from my virile member.

Millicent dried her rod.

' "Girls," she commanded, "kindly untie the culprit, who appears terribly crestfallen. Now, sir," she addressed me, "get down on your knees and kiss the rod." Without a word, I complied with her command.

' "Oh, Millicent," I said at last, "the last few moments have been so heavenly. All sensation of pain has been blotted out. I thank you for punishing me and will always honour Charlotte. I thank Miss Sarah also for her kind attendance." I was then allowed to rise as the ladies gloated over my burning buttocks and rapidly renewed erection. Millicent wiped the drops of blood from my lacerated rump and then I was given some glasses of port and, to my stupification, I was also given something that looked like a sausage skin and sternly instructed to put it over my penis and use it wisely. I was then allowed to sleep with Charlotte, having been pardoned for my insolence to ladies; and we retired as Millicent and Sarah, their amours aroused by the rod, indulged in their favourite touches and appeared to be enjoying a most luscious time of it.

'My prick was throbbing and my bottom was glowing as I clambered into bed with Charlotte.

' "Having enticed me into so much trouble," I said, "you must now suck my prick before I place the prophylactic upon it." I presented the purple, throbbing head to her mouth.

' "No," Charlotte protested, "no! I never can do such a dirty trick. Besides, it is doubly disgusting. You have not even washed since you outraged my bottom and had yours outraged in consequence. Do you never learn your lesson?"

' "No," I replied coldly. "What is what you say to me? *I* am the one who has suffered the birching and were it not for the erotic fervour which the rod arouses, we would not be here now. You've *got* to suck it, so go on, my dear, without all those wry faces, which only add to my fun. It is a rare sport to make you submit to my fancies. Even if I be birched on the morrow, I assert my right, having proposed marriage, to do as I please with every bit of your person, cunt, arse, mouth, bubbies . . . they can all afford me intense pleasure without getting you in the family way. Now go on, and I will fuck your cunt with my fine large thumb. Mind you, you must swallow every last drop of my spending when it comes into your gorgeous mouth."

CHAPTER SEVEN

'The blood is the life,' it is said. Certainly I signed my Pact in my own blood, as did all the others present. I looked forward eagerly to the foundation of the Club, which Sir Francis had assured us would be done within a year and a day. On attaining the age of my majority in 1750, I took my seat in the House of Lords and in my maiden speech, spoke strongly for the abolition of bad traditions and the stout maintenance of the good ones, which speech was quite well received, particularly when I declared that we all had to be stiff in upholding our moral values.

This speech, and my support from the Club Sir Francis Dashwood was constructing, brought me into contact with a man whom they wanted as a member, Thomas Potter, son of the Archbishop of Canterbury, who invited me to accompany him to a prize-fight. I gave my glad assent, knowing that we would see more blood. 'He drank with drunkards, lived with sinners/Herded with infidels for dinners,' I had been told. Yet when I met him at a tavern near Tottenham Court Road to see the Prize-Fight between Jack Broughton and Jack Slack for the bare-knuckle Championship of England, I found myself talking to a handsome, witty and charming man in his thirties, and one most popular with Sir Francis and his friends.

'They call me an evil genius,' Potter informed me over tankards of strong ale. Outside this public house, there was a sign stating: 'DRUNK: for a penny. DEAD DRUNK for twopence: clean straw for nothing.' Obviously the beverage proffered there was gin, which I dislike. 'So do be careful with me, won't you . . . ?' Potter continued with a wicked chuckle. 'I poison all my friends' morals, or so it is said. Married, are you, Horby? No? Ah! No doubt you prefer young women and whores to old women and wives, for toying away hours with little satin-bottoms is vastly preferable to an evening conference with one's mother-in-law...'

I had some inside information from Dashwood and Sandwich upon the background of this man. He had inherited a substantial estate at Aylesbury and become a Member of Parliament. In spite of this, he spent his fortune so fast that he had to marry for more money. He did not give a flying fuck about anyone or anything and there were many who thought his conduct to be scandalous. He was a compulsive womanizer; and he could be mischievous, too. When the Bishop of Warburton sternly defended the morality of the Christian religion in a series of dull pamphlets, Potter had responded by seducing the man's wife.

'Has the Heavenly inspired passion called Lust deserted you?' Potter enquired. I shook my head firmly. 'Then,' Potter drank deeply and called for more, 'I strongly suggest that we watch the fight, then fuck. Fighting and fucking, eh, Horby? That's when two human beings come closest.' I nodded assent, hoping that he would not drag me to other pleasures he enjoyed, such as watching public executions and fornicating in graveyards.

Thomas Potter's handsome face and ready charm had made of him the Secretary to Prince Frederick. In time he would become Paymaster-General and Vice-Treasurer for Ireland. His portrait would be painted by my friend, William Hogarth. On this occasion, I asked after his opinion of Sir Francis Dashwood.

'I know the nothingness into which the genius of a Potter is apt to shrink under a superior influence,' Potter replied wryly with uncharacteristic modesty. 'But you see, Dashwood, damnit, he really does discern the occult significance of sex. In common with him, I do not believe in God as being an old man with a white beard roaring: "Don't argue: do as I say!" It sounds too much like my father. I am persuaded by Dashwood that God is *within* us and Goddess, or as he calls Her, the Bona Dea, the Good Goddess, is of all the Universe *without* us. I am perfectly prepared to essay his experiment whereby, with appropriate ceremonial, the male and the female will be brought together in a way which gives all participants ecstatic consciousness. That will be in the future, but meanwhile, in the present, drink up, sir! We must not be late for the prize-fight. I have a thousand guineas on Jack Broughton. What is your opinion of the renewed sport of Boxing?'

'In our times,' I told Potter as we left the public house and walked towards the booth they called 'the Amphitheatre', 'it is assuredly necessary to know methods of self-defence. In consequence, I have not only taken lessons in pistol-shooting and fencing but also in Boxing from the Champion of England, Jack Broughton.'

'Ah, yes,' Potter murmured as we approached the Amphitheatre, set up in the midst of Covent Garden and surrounded by thick crowds. 'I was always enthused by the descriptions of Boxing in classic texts by Homer and Vigil. It was James Figg who restored the sport on British lines via his booth in Southwark.'

'True,' I replied, 'and he defeated everybody. I believe his portrait has been painted by our mutual friend, William Hogarth.' Potter nodded. 'Figg was actually more skilful with the quarterstaff, the small backsword and the cudgel. Upon his retirement, and having moved his booth to Oxford Road, he left it to his pupil, George Taylor, who was decisively defeated in twenty minutes by Jack Broughton ten years ago.'

'Broughton has been the Champion of England at bare knuckles ever since,' Potter stated correctly. 'No man has come within an inch of beating him. And that is why I am backing him.' He took a pinch of snuff laced with sandalwood and offered some to me. I accepted his offer gladly, since I enjoy snuff. We both sneezed together and wiped our noses upon silk handkerchiefs. 'His patron, the Duke of Cumberland, has placed ten thousand guineas upon the matter. Who is his opponent? Why, Jack Slack, a vulgar butcher from Bristol and little more than a brawler.'

Ushers guided us to seats by the foremost side of the ring. We were quietly informed that we could enjoy any refreshments we chose, including women. 'Put us down for two girls, provided that we get a look at 'em first,' Potter commanded, 'and bring us ale and baked potatoes smothered in butter! Now sir!' he continued for my edificiation, 'Jack Broughton could not see the point of a right-handed man adopting the fencing stance of James Figg and so he stands with his *left* arm extended to block blows and uses his right to knock them out. This technique worked so well against the estimable coachman, George Stevenson, that the latter died.'

'I know,' I replied. 'Broughton was horrified and so constructed the first and proper rules of the sport. Although he allowed wrestling, he banned eye-gouging and any blow below the belt. These days a round ends when a man goes down. He is then allowed thirty seconds to come up to scratch and to toe the line in the centre of the ring. What a wonderful Champion he has been!' I exclaimed. 'The veritable Father of Boxing! He has invented these "mufflers", padded gloves enabling men of our class to practice this excellent sport too. As Broughton has it, these effectually secure his aristocratic patrons from the inconvenience of black eyes, broken jaws and bloody noses. I thoroughly enjoyed the excellence of his tuition.'

'I presume, Horby,' said Potter, 'that you have placed a substantial bet upon Broughton . . . ?'

'No, I have not, sir,' I replied. 'I am sorry to state that our Champion, who has beaten with ease all comers for the past ten years and who has taught me of the Noble Art of Self-Defence, as he has to so many others, whilst turning away all contenders has of late allowed his good fortune to sink him into a period of dissipation. Why, whilst sparring with him the other day, I caught him with both a left and a right which I could never have done were he in his prime. Therefore I shall not bet.'

'But Jack Slack is just a crude Bristol butcher,' Potter protested. 'Ah! The programme begins.'

The programme began with three cock-fights, the third of which had razors tied to the legs of the cocks and, although it was bloody, the matter was not especially edifying. I have never enjoyed the sight of animals being forced to fight one another and, unlike many of my contemporaries, do not enjoy bull-baiting or bear-baiting. There were then some moderately interesting contests of men involving the quarterstaff, the cudgel and the small backsword, the decision being given on first blood.

'The Masters! The Masters!' the crowd cried as Broughton and Slack made their way to the ring. Broughton was indeed a big man but his face looked flushed and a roll of fat drooped over his waist-band. By contrast, Slack looked slim and fit, though somewhat ugly of countenance. Broughton was cheered loudly by his London supporters: Slack was cheered by those who had travelled from Bristol and also by the South Londoners who knew that Jack Slack was the grandson of James Figg.

In truth, I had actually placed a bet of a hundred guineas upon the first round on both first knockdown and first blood, which I won. Slack swung wildly, Broughton blocked the blow with his left and then he clobbered Slack with his right, breaking his nose and drawing blood. Slack came up to scratch nevertheless for the second round. Seeing blood, Broughton lunged at him with his right but Slack avoided this blow and grasped Broughton in a clinch. It was at this moment that Slack's fist came down hard upon Broughton's neck, and Broughton sank to the boards. This was a new punch, later named 'the rabbit punch', and Jack Slack could fairly claim to have invented it.

When Broughton came up to scratch, he now looked clumsy and awkward. Slack promptly punched him hard in his left eye. This eye began to swell as Broughton rushed Slack, who promptly staggered him with another rabbit punch and fell to the floorboards. The following round saw Slack slam a slow and panting Broughton with a right to his right eye, then fall to the boards for a breather the instant that he was touched again. The eyesight of Broughton was damaged as he squinted at Slack in the ensuing round and rushed at him. Slack responded with two short but brutal punches to both of Broughton's blackening eyes, closed with him fast for the wrestling, hit the Champion very hard with a chop to the back of the neck and, upon receiving a hit to the ribs, promptly fell to the floorboards so as to gain respite.

Broughton, panting hard, was in a sorry state for the next round with both eyes swelling tight. Slack smashed him with his right hand to both eyes time and time again, broke his nose and broke his jaw, then clasped him around the body and hammered his neck. Broughton fell crawling upon the floorboards. Although he assured his patron, the Duke of Cumberland, that 'I'm blind but not beat,' Broughton was easy meat for Slack as he staggered out for the next round. The Bristol man they called 'the Knight of the Cleaver' planted his punches deep to the heart, liver and kidneys of the blinded Jack Broughton and, taking him by the shoulders, finished him

UNHOLY PASSIONS

with a final chop to the back of the neck. As Broughton, utterly unconscious, was dragged away, Jack Slack became Champion of England. This match had lasted a mere fourteen minutes.

Being a great follower of the Prize Ring, I should add that the Broughton Rules still govern all contests and that Broughton has since made sensible investments in property. (*Editor's note:* he then became a Yeoman of the Guard and died at the age of eighty-five: a paving stone in Westminster Abbey honours the memory of 'The Father of Boxing'.)

Jack Slack was Champion of England for the next ten years, during which time the Prize Ring degenerated into a foul stew of corruption. It has only been rescued from farce by the worthy Thomas Johnson; Daniel Mendoza, the Jew; Gentleman John Jackson, who has founded the Pugilistic Club to keep the sport honourable and clean; and Jem Belcher, our present excellent bare-knuckle Champion, 'the Napoleon of the Ring', and curiously enough, the grandson of Jack Slack.

'Not too pleased, sir,' Thomas Potter muttered as we entered his carriage, on this occasion a sprightly cabriolet influenced by Italian design. 'Lost a bet. But let us cheer ourselves up with some violence to do with ladies.' He whipped up the horses. 'On for seeing Mrs Hayes in the Haymarket?' I nodded assent and that is where we went. 'Ever heard Prince Frederick's story about Millicent and Sarah? They are presently within the finest brothel in London. Oh, yes, indeed, my dear Horby, they have a comfortable life there, thanks to the Prince of Wales. I hope he is not eventually the Prince of wails, or if he favours flagellation, whales.'

Potter and I were welcomed warmly by the charming Mrs Hayes, who gave us strong milk punch and asked us to take our pick of her beauties.

'I would like Millicent and Sarah, please, for my friend here and myself, Mrs Hayes,' Potter demanded of our hostess. As

Mrs Hayes nodded and left the room, Potter said softly: 'You see, Horby, a former governess to the Prince of Wales can actually make much more money this way for herself and her maid. Why,' he told me, 'they can earn more in a week of sex than in a year of teaching.' Soon enough, Mrs Hayes returned with the willowy brunette, Millicent, and the buxom blonde, Sarah. 'Sarah has on occasion been insolent to me,' Potter declared, 'especially when she thought me to be out of favour with the Prince of Wales: ha! ha! This pert young miss has exhibited no sign of penitence whatsoever and I demand that she be punished. The prize-fight that we witnessed, Horby, has got my blood up. Mrs Hayes, a classic Eton flogging block, please . . .' Mrs Hayes snapped her fingers and instantly a buxom maid brought a flogging block as a second followed her with a bower of birches. Sarah was promptly strapped to the flogging block, which allowed no movement to her arms and legs. 'Ah . . .' Potter surveyed the selection of rods with satisfaction. 'That will do nicely.' He took a pinch of snuff before poising and switching his rod in the air, all the while gloating with satisfaction. 'Just what I need,' he told the bound and hapless Sarah. 'You will be more penitent in the future, I assure you, young Miss. I have a good bramble here with which to implant pain upon your bottom and perhaps you might feel that . . . ? Don't you think, Mrs Hayes and Miss Millicent, that she has too many clothes on?'

'Shall we reduce her to her chemise and drawers so you can administer the supreme penalty?' Mrs Hayes, also known as Lady Charlotte Shawcross, asked. She had been a temporary mistress of the young Prince of Wales, as he had told me, and had since married a man, Sir Joshua, who had bought his way into Parliament by wealth obtained through owning more brothels than anyone else in the kingdom and, by giving money to the Whig ruling establishment, had bought both his Parliamentary seat and his baronetcy.

UNHOLY PASSIONS

'Yes! Yes!' Thomas Potter shouted. He promptly assisted Charlotte and Millicent in stripping Sarah of her petticoats and in the undoing of her stays, thus fully displaying the large, fine, plump globes of her splendid bosom, with their pretty pink nipples.

'Oh!' Sarah shrieked out. 'No! Pray don't! I didn't do it and wouldn't have done such a thing to my worst enemy...'

'Why don't you confess, you wicked creature?' Potter snarled at the bound young lady. 'Don't you think, Madam,' he turned to Charlotte Hayes, 'that she's still got too many things on her? I am,' he gloated over his captive, relishing the sight of naked female flesh, 'not given to cruelty. But this is assuredly a case requiring greater severity than is customary.' Charlotte Hayes responded calmly by ordering Millicent to expose the fine figure of Sarah by lifting up her chemise to her shoulders and exposing her beautiful plump bottom to general view.

'Oh!' Sarah squealed. 'Oh, Madam! Oh, Sir! Have mercy! Would you murder me?'

I observed quite a titter of admiration for her twitching buttocks amongst the two women: moreover, it cannot be denied that Potter and I were smiling, for he was whisking the birch in the air. For my own part, I had originally thought that education was generally conducted with the greatest possible propriety with regard to morals; but had fast discovered that it was only an outward show of decorum. Private arrangements admitted of a variety of very questionable doings, not necessarily conducive to the future morality of the pupils, and this easily accounts for that aristocratic indifference to virtue so prevalent at the present time.

'Mr Potter,' said Lady Charlotte, 'the floor is yours.'

'Thank you.' Potter stepped forward and spoke sternly as the bottom, so pale and smooth, of Sarah continued to writhe and twitch upon the flogging block before a blow had even been struck. She cast down her eyes and blushed furiously. 'How dare you persist in telling so many fibs to Prince Frederick!' Thomas Potter yelled, thwacking her bottom with his birch and causing it to twitch and turn crimson. 'Speak the truth at once and openly withdraw your lies or I will thrash your impudent bottom into ribbons of scarified flesh. You can't deceive me, for we know the effects of the rod and – ah . . .' momentarily he seemed to misplace his thoughts, 'the voluptuous feelings it induces.'

Then we heard the sounds of the birch – *whisk!* – then whack, *whack*, WHACK! as this weapon of chastisement ruthlessly wealed the bottom of its victim. Potter became visibly excited and shivered with a thrilling sensation; each stroke had an energizing effect upon his nerves; the cries and screams of Sarah appeared most delightful to him and all the spectators were in ecstasies of voluptuous emotions. The victim shrieked out in agony, she writhed her bottom about, displaying her lovely figure in a variety of contortions, shifting continually at every scathing touch of the birch.

Charlotte and Millicent at first watched the scene with cool attention but gradually the blood coursed in warm excitement through their veins, mantling their cheeks with a rose-like bloom, as their eyes sparkled with unusual animation. At last and by common impulse, these two ladies seized fine rods of green twigs and formed a triangle around Thomas Potter as he continued to flagellate the victim bound to the block. Both Charlotte and Millicent raised their skirts under their arms so as to leave all exposed from the waist downwards. For a moment, there was a lovely scene of plump white buttocks and thighs, fascinating slender legs encased in silk stockings, pretty garters and attractive elegant high-heeled shoes, set off with jewelled buckles. Above all, there was such an inviting collection of impudent-looking cunnies, hairily bedecked with several shades of colour, black, auburn and light brown.

UNHOLY PASSIONS

Thence all was motion and the birch rods soon put a rosy polish upon Sarah's pretty bum, each lady doing her best to outdo on the girlish bottom in front of her the smarting cuts left by Potter which Sarah felt so acutely. Female laughter, shrieks, and yelps filled the apartment and the ladies' whipping motions were so rapid as to make quite a rainbow – complemented by two excited purple penises – upon the punished bottom.

This luscious scene lasted only a few delicious minutes. Sarah became exhausted, her shrieks declined into squeals and thence changed into sobs and at last she sighed lower and lower, then fairly fainted, with her head hanging helplessly forward and her twitching scarlet bottom a veritable portrait of weals. 'Ohh . . .' Sarah sighed.

'There, ladies,' said Thomas Potter, casting aside his broken and used-up rod, 'let's stop the game and let's all help to bring her round; she'll soon recover; how pretty her roseate bottom looks.'

Sarah was loosed from the flogging block and, by the use of Millicent's large fan, soon showed signs of returning animation. Her eyes opened as she looked around herself in bewilderment.

'Where am I?' she murmured in a low voice. 'What a beautiful dream . . .' She was a little more refreshed by a strong cordial poured down her throat. 'Ah! I remember, my bottom smarts so!' Putting her hand down to feel her own posterior, she suddenly sobbed: 'What a cruel girl Miss Millicent must be if she would make me suffer thus! And the gentlemen gloated over my sufferings! Ah! Let me only handle the tickler over Millicent's bum some day!'

At this, we all burst into a loud laugh and thoroughly enjoyed the sight of Sarah's shame and confusion. If the notorious Thomas Potter was indeed poisoning my morals, I was enjoying every instant of the matter.

CHAPTER EIGHT

A spot of barbaric brutality is most enjoyable, I find, but it is always a pleasure subsequently to seek some delicacy. That was what led me, after taking leave of the engaging Thomas Potter, to take late supper with Lady Clarissa Hyde, at her invitation to her town house in Mayfair. She received me well and, after several glasses of sherry, she ensured that we were both served with a side of ham, cold roast beef still dripping with blood, a pheasant and a venison pie accompanied by all accoutrements and washed down by copious quantities of claret.

Lady Clarissa had, of course, heard of the Club Sir Francis Dashwood intended to found and expressed her whole-hearted approval of the matter; also her approval of the membership, including that of her younger cousin the Hon. Arabella Marchmount who had still not made a marriage and whose education and prospects, Clarissa thought, could be furthered by her participation in clubbable activities, provided that she wore a mask. I nodded my enthusiastic assent.

'It is indeed a fine idea,' she commented as she fluttered her fan with her left hand and drank a glass of port with her right after the repast had been cleared away. 'I hope only that it may succeed.'

'My dear lady,' I replied, 'I also hope for that eventuality. Meanwhile I admire you as a woman of the World who has by her introductions done so much, and in other ways also, to further my education.'

'How you see me!' she exclaimed. 'I used to be so innocent. Even so, I do not regret my life so far. There was a time, though, when I was a virgin. As a young girl,' she sighed and called to the servants for more velvety vintage port, 'I was segregated from boys and disciplined by nuns in the convent to which I was sent. Yet I wondered inwardly how effective their tutelage could be and hoped in vain that it would not be too religious.

'The nuns wore their wimples as though they were still living in the Middle Ages, when all was based upon conditions of homage and service. Much of their lives was spent in the chapel where candles and incense were burning continuously. Each nun wore a ring upon the second finger of her left hand to acknowledge the fact that in a life without sexual intercourse, a life without men, she had consummated a marriage with God: was that true? Or was each nun living a lie? In the early hours of the morning, the cock would crow, boasting of male superiority as he cried out his pleasure. If it were not for the cock, I reflected, our hens would not be capable of laying eggs.

'Our breakfast was always held in silence; there was fresh milk from the udders of cows and goats; porridge with a sprinkling of pepper...'

'Salt, surely?' I interrupted.

'No, dear, pepper, for we are speaking of nuns.. and these delicacies would be followed by Matins and then classes would begin after the sound of the bells from the tower called the campanile. It was considered an honour to pull upon those mighty chords, tassels, *passementerie*, lace and braids with trimmings of gold and silver. Every day the classes were the same; English Grammar, Latin, Greek, Arithmetic, History, Geography, French, Handwriting – especially the importance which calligraphy adds to the epistolary art – needlework, filigree and Bible studies. For our classes we sat upon strong

UNHOLY PASSIONS

oaken benches, which could be painful, since our naked bottoms were soundly birched for the slightest transgression and usually in front of the entire school. I do not know which subsequent punishment after a birching was more excruciating: having to writhe with burning buttocks upon a stiff oaken seat or else to be stood in a corner and be forced to bare my wealed, whaled and punished blazing bottom to one and all.

'Be that as it may, I do not regret the days of my education and somehow still think fondly of our school uniforms, the stiff purple skirts which adorned us in the winter and the crackling white frocks of hot summer days . . . and I acquired the skills to become a lady with a sense of pride in my station tempered by modesty: scrupulously chaste, decorous in manner and conduct . . . oh, do stop laughing Horby! Then I had absolutely no understanding of the extravagance of my class, though one trusts that I may have made up for it since. During my attendance at the convent, and remember that I was only sixteen when I left it, my knowledge of the male was so limited.

' "Beware of the follies of the young swain," the nuns used to warn us. Indeed, we were forbidden to wear shiny shoes lest passing boys and men might discern in them a reflection of our underwear. And so, apart from my somewhat cold and distant father, whom nevertheless, I loved most dearly, since at times he had a tender heart, I had enjoyed no intimacy with members of the opposite sex. I did not know that my father had lost so much of his money on unwise speculations in business and in consequence desired, for the repairing of his fallen fortunes, a dynastic marriage.

'I recall the first time that I met the husband whom my father intended for me, knowing nothing of the dealings between these men. Lord Edward Hyde had been invited to dine at three. He had been alive for three score years and I cannot say that I was attracted to him for his anatomy was so bulbous and nothing that he wore could disguise it.

'At the top of the table there was salmon with fennel sauce to it, melted butter, lemon pickle and soy sauce imported from the Orient; at the bottom, a loin of roasted veal accompanied by kidney beans from the American colonies; in the middle, there was a pigeon pie stuffed with yolks of eggs; and there were dishes of ham and chicken on either side of that, the ham aged and the chicken young and tender. How that symbolized the matter! The wines, cyder, and subsequent currant tart accompanied by melon and gooseberries did little to alleviate my impending anxiety.

'I then had to retire to one of our drawing-rooms with my mother and for a few minutes we sat in silence whilst I waited for an explanation. She responded by slipping into a slumber. I could do little other than pick up and read *The Rape of the Lock* by Alexander Pope, which describes a day at Hampton Court where the late Queen Anne, "whom three Great Realms obey, Does sometimes counsel take, and sometimes tea." They called it "tay" in that age. When my mother finally awoke, being as sleepy as had been stated about Queen Anne, she looked upon what I was reading.

' "Queen Anne," she declared with delight, "gave royal approval to horse racing and established the Ascot races. That kindly gentleman, our guest of today, is a patron of Ascot." That was all she said as she relapsed into somnolence and I reflected that my father owned a stable of horses. At eight o'clock in the evening, we were to reassemble in the dining-room, though it was essential for me to change into a more formal dress. With assistance from my chambermaid, I put on my blue silk dress with a Spitalfields brocade...oh! such a delicate floral design with a lace-edge kerchief of fine Irish linen crossed over and fastened with a golden pin and my mother's sapphire brooch fastening a blue silk bow across my bosom.

'As I re-entered the dining-room, I noticed that the table had been reset, graced by laundered linen and with freshly-wick'd candles in the silver candelabra. My husband-to-be sat across the table from me and he appeared to be unfit for anything other than sleep. He nodded assent to all words I spoke but was otherwise uncommunicative. Following the meal of stuffed brawn from a young calf, cheeses and a negus of hot sweetened wine, I obeyed my father's request to sing a madrigal which father and my intended bridegroom applauded loudly before sinking into snoring slumber. I retired to bed where Lucy, my chambermaid, brought me a mug of hot chocolate topped by a dollop of clotted cream, then lit the logs and coals to heat my bedchamber.

' "He is a good man, Miss, and will render you no harm."

' "Do you think that I should marry him?"

' "Yes, most certainly," was her response, "if you wish to save the future of your family." In consequence I endured a formal ceremony of marriage to a man I neither knew well nor cared for in any especial particular.'

'Were your wedding-bells the bells of hell?' I asked.

'Hell's teeth!' Clarissa laughed. 'Let us move on to my wedding night, the first night that I would sleep together in a bed with a man. He entered the bridal chamber wearing a dark olive silk coat and breeches with a white silk waist-coat, richly embroidered in silver-coloured tones and shades of silk that could neither cover nor disguise the bulge of his midriff: there was a white feather in his hat and a sword by his side. Downstairs, my father had hired some violinists to play music composed by Handel. My husband, Lord Edward Hyde, raised my right gloved hand and kissed me softly upon my wrist prior to lifting my lace veil. He touched the golden ring he had earlier placed upon my finger in the Church, kissed me tenderly upon the lips and caressed my beauty spot upon my left cheek before removing my garters that I had previously untied that they might hang down. The bridesmaids, who had carried me into the bed-chamber, now served us with a good posset, a caudle consisting of hot milk curdled with wine and flavoured with the yolks of eggs, sugar, cinnamon, nutmeg and other assorted spices. The friends of the groom, allegedly brave and chivalrous gentlemen, yes, the gallants so markedly attentive to ladies now received my thrown garters that the bridesmaids arranged in their three-cornered hats. They proceeded to assist my husband's undressing in another room: eventually he reappeared to me, surrounded by all relatives – fathers, mothers, uncles, aunts, brothers, sisters and heaven knows what else – as he climbed into bed with me and they cheered us.

'Finally we were left alone together in a canopied bed surrounded by chenille trimmings. He took me so gently into his arms and I felt the warmth of his body against mine as he kissed me firmly upon the lips. His tongue entered my mouth and he pressed both of his hands upon my bosom and then took each nipple and sucked upon them as a calf would suck upon the udder in order to attain nourishment. I felt a tightening sensation, a pulsation within my lower abdomen and a moisture slowly developing between my thighs.

'He kissed me upon my navel and then his lips descended further with a sudden attack upon my pubes, curls of light hair that tickled upon his nose. He uttered no words of speech as his tongue licked my juices and his mouth swallowed.

' "You taste more delightful than a delectable posset!" he exclaimed. "Ah! The nectar of your honey pot is sweeter than the taste of mead!" His fingers touched all parts of my anatomy from the northern to the southern as an explorer would want to discover and investigate the nether regions of the Earth and perhaps undiscovered territories within the equatorial zone. My long blonde tresses fell down around my shoulders and I teased my husband by covering my face with my hair as a veil. "You tempt, excite, delight and torment me, my darling wife," he sighed. "You flirt and tease as a coquette and arouse my love."

' "My Lord!" I exclaimed, "what delectable words of flattery!" As he entered me with his penis, I felt a strange sensation between my thighs and a slight pain, though not an ache. I felt so naive concerning how to perform with such an obviously sexually experienced gentleman. Ah! and he penetrated deeper against my hymen, the outermost hurdle of the virginal vagina.

'Droplets of blood fell upon the sheets as his semen entered me, gushing out in spurts.

' "There is blood upon the bedding – stains!" I exclaimed. "These discolourations will not be easily removed."

' "Have no worries," he replied, "just lie down next to me." Underneath the eiderdown, lying with my husband, I did not shiver. In the morning we were served another sack-posset and we then retired to separate chambers in order to be prepared for our mid-morning walk. My husband's wig had been powdered and curled with irons, for his skull was bald beneath it, and he wore a black suit and I wore a white silken dress, open gown, girdled with black silk around the waist. Upon my head, I wore a large black hat trimmed with white ribbons and ostrich feathers, with a silk gauze stole around my shoulders.

'I never expected our marriage to be so brief. He had a kindly disposition towards me, though. Every time we made love, I yearned for a child, hoping that I could deliver to him a son. But unfortunately, it was not to be so. Before two years into our marriage, my husband was dead of a stroke. He had had his failures, yet there had been kindness within his heart. Gossip has it that I fucked him to death. I make no comment. What should I resent? He awakened me to potential pleasures . . .

'For his funeral I attended wearing a black mourning dress.

Underneath I wore stockings of cobweb silk and upon the top of each, our name wrought into the weaving. His last will and testament left me with an estate in Surrey, a Mayfair town house, four King Charles spaniels, a set of bells resounding from a harpsichord, called a caulion, which I later learned to pluck so well by the use of quills . . . oh, yes, and a hundred thousand pounds in the Funds. My hair turned quite gold from grief and I had to retire to my bed with an attack of indisposition. Indeed, from now onwards, I *needed* only to see people whom I *wanted* to see. Oh, Horby, I am too young to be a widow! Courage! I thought, courage and you will soon be back upon your feet again.'

'Yes, indeed, Madam, you will be!' I replied enthusiastically as I flung myself upon Clarissa. It was such a thrill for me to whip up her dress and voluminous petticoats and to espy her delectable oyster. Oh! what a wondrous slit it remained after all our time apart!

I divested her of everything until she was in a state of buff, excepting her pretty boots and stockings, which I always think look far sweeter than naked legs and feet. Lady Clarissa was anxious to see the working of my fine prick within her splendid cunt once more. I was in a rampant state of anticipation, so she laid me at full length on my back on a soft, springy couch, then, stretching across my legs, she first bent down her head to kiss and lubricate my twitching cock with her mouth. Next, placing herself right over me, she gradually sheathed my grand instrument within her longing vagina, pressing down upon me with her lips glued to mine as she seemed to enjoy the sensation of possessing it all. I inserted my finger within her gorgeous and voluptuous bottom and Clarissa understood the idea at once. At this instant, something happened which I was not expecting. There was a knock of three-five-three upon the door.

'Let her in,' sighed Clarissa, as if this was an agreed code.

UNHOLY PASSIONS

The door was opened to admit the Hon. Arabella Marchmount, whose petticoats swished lustily as she marched straight to the bed, kissed me lightly and then fell upon Clarissa, brandishing a well-creamed dildo. The two ladies kissed one another with tender sighs of endearment, then Arabella, removing my hand, brought the head of her dildo to the charge against Clarissa's brown-wrinkled bottom-hole, at the same time clasping her other hand around my body to touch the shaft of my thrusting prick, presently involved in stiffly tickling the fine clitoris of our mistress of ceremonies.

This made for a delightful tableau and it excited us all awfully when Clarissa and I at once plunged into a course of delicious fucking. Arabella was as thrilled as either of us as she vigorously dildoed Clarissa's beautiful arse and I slammed in with straight fucking. How both ladies screamed with delight as I came, spending over and over again.

'Ah...!' Clarissa sighed as I withdrew. 'Now,' she squeezed my cock, 'I have got Horby's fine prick in my hand.' We kissed and indulged in every possible caress. 'Oh!' she squealed as she continued to commentate. 'Though it has spent its first force, it is yet throbbing within my grasp as I repeatedly – uh! – draw back the foreskin. No, sir, you shall *not* spend in my hand!' She sank back upon her sofa, then drew me upon her, guiding my affair to her longing quim whilst I clasped her around the body and kissed her nipples more ardently than ever. She rode furiously upon me while a gleeful Arabella tossed her head in frenzied enjoyment as the twirling of her dildo drove Clarissa to an ecstatic distraction by its exciting movements within her bottom. Meanwhile, the Honourable young lady stroked her own delicious vagina. All three of us came together with screams, shouts, squeals, gasps and sighs.

Ten minutes later, no one could possibly have believed that matters of this nature could have taken place as the three of us entered the drawing room to partake of a glass of refreshing late afternoon sherry. 'What would the servants have thought?' a rather stupid and vulgar industrialist asked me only the other day when I related this tale to him, causing him visible relish. I explained to him that servants are paid not to think at all.

'I trust that you will be staying for supper, Horby?' Clarissa smiled at me.

'Thank you, Madam, but I cannot do so, though I may seek to join you later, given your permission.' I looked at the clock. 'I have promised George Selwyn Esquire, MP that I will meet him at White's after which I shall accompany him to a hanging at Tyburn. We also need to discuss various matters of Dashwood's proposed Club in which I gather you ladies have rightly been granted membership.'

'Ooooh, yes!' Arabella exclaimed excitedly. 'And who is to be hanged?' She gulped her glass of sherry. 'I have never been to a hanging before. Is it not rather late in the day?'

'It is a fine June afternoon,' I responded, 'and I am assured by Mr Selwyn that sunset is the finest time to witness a hanging.'

CHAPTER NINE

It was impossible to deter the ladies from their insatiable curiosity even though they fully accepted the fact that White's does not admit women.

'It is quite simple, Horby,' Lady Clarissa declared. 'I shall order my coach-and-six. As you take wine with Mr Selwyn in White's, Arabella and I shall enjoy stirrup cups. Then, since I believe that Mr Selwyn has only a small carriage, we shall ride in mine to the execution.' Arabella looked excited and eager: and I have never known ladies to make themselves ready for departure so swiftly. Soon enough, we were trotting away towards St James's and over an excellent stirrup cup, I was having to explain to my delectable companions the nature of the victim.

'His name is Claude Charay,' I said, 'and he was a highwayman.'

'Claude Charay!' Arabella squealed. 'Why, he robbed me on a stage-coach journey to visit my aunt in Bath – though,' she sighed romantically, 'I cannot honestly state that this experience was entirely unpleasant. He was *such* a gentleman.'

'Yes...' Clarissa sighed patiently as the horses clip-clopped on their way, 'this very coach was robbed when I went to visit my uncle in Brighthelmstone (*Editor's note:* subsequently Brighton) and although he was indeed a gentleman, he was still a thief and robber. Arabella!' she sternly reprimanded her younger cousin, 'let us face the fact that he fucked well while holding us at pistol point, which is exciting, but he still stole our jewels. He has had his day and I shall be glad to see him hanged. Now, Horby, what do you know of Mr Selwyn?'

'He is in his thirties,' I replied, 'an Independent Member of Parliament and accounted amongst the first of the fashionable wits. He was educated at Eton and then at Hertford College, Oxford.'

'Yes,' said Clarissa, 'but then he was expelled for toasting "queer deities" from a chalice which included blood from his own arm in a parody of Christian communion held at a tavern on the High Street, near St Martin's Church.'

'He sounds rather exciting,' Arabella observed.

'Certainly he has a morbid fascination for death and its many modes,' Clarissa responded. 'Some say that in common with my friend Thomas Potter, he likes to fuck corpses in graveyards. His wit is morbid. After the beheading of Lord Lovat for his part in the 1745 rebellion, I distinctly heard him murmur: "My dead Lord Lovat, your Lordship may now rise." "Show Mr Selwyn up," Lord Holland said as he lay upon his death-bed; "If I am alive, I shall be pleased to see him; and if I'm dead, he will be pleased to see me." '

The carriage of the ladies dropped me outside White's and I entered to be greeted by George Selwyn who was sitting with Bubb-Dodington and a certain Lord Grimsby whom I knew only slightly and had always detested. Selwyn was a dandified, somewhat somnolent man with a lazy, drawling manner of speech. Grimsby was one of the most insufferably pompous prigs that I have ever encountered, and he was speaking of his self-proclaimed travels in Abyssinia.

'I only saw one lyre there,' Grimsby lamented.

'Yes, and there's one less since you left the country,' Selwyn retorted.

'Ha! ha! Always a cruel wit, ain'tcha, Selwyn, eh? No

offence taken and none intended, I am sure. But I trust that you will be coming to the opening night of my play, *How She Loved Him*, a sentimental drama? Or will you merely be coming to see me hanged?'

'Oh no, my Lord,' Selwyn drawled, 'I never go to rehearsals.'

'Ah! You and your wit, Selwyn!' Grimsby coughed. 'I must take my leave.' Selwyn took leave of him with the sudden geniality with which one takes leave of a bore.

'Now, sir,' he turned his attention to fat Bubb-Dodington, 'word has it that you are presently involved with Mrs Henderson, that notorious courtesan of South London, in a bid to gather votes as a "man of the people". Why not, sir? With whom should "a man of the people" consort other than with a woman of the people?'

'Selwyn, your wit makes me smile without laughing,' Bubb-Dodington replied, 'though I look forward to our clubbability in the future,' he wheezed as he tossed back another glass of excellent port, such as I too had taken, and his belly threatened to split his waistcoat. 'However, I must tell you that this bore whom you rightly drove out of here tonight, the appalling Lord Grimsby, has inherited a mistress passed to him from his grandfather, thence to the father and now to the son. I tell you, sir, there is nothing new under the sun!'

'Nor under the grandson,' said Selwyn.

I pointed out over our port that two exquisite ladies were waiting for us within their coach and six and that moreover, these would be our Sisters in the Brotherhood and Club that Sir Francis Dashwood had declared his intention of establishing. Both men drank deeply in a toast to the ladies and arose.

'By the way,' said Bubb-Dodington, 'for I shall follow on in my own carriage, where are we going?'

'To the execution at Tyburn of the highwayman, Claude Charay,' I answered.

'Thank you, gentlemen, but no, thank you,' Bubb-Dodington replied. He mopped his sweating brow with a silken handkerchief. 'You have your pleasures but this is not one of mine. I shall go and see,' he glanced at Selwyn, 'Mrs Henderson, lady of the people.'

'I shouldn't bother, Bub,' Selwyn smiled cruelly, 'for as a receiver of the highwayman's stolen goods, she will be at the hanging.'

'I would prefer seeing my wife to seeing that, sir,' Bubb answered, 'but I wish you good cheer.' Bubb was always quite humane.

Selwyn had a servant whom he ordered to drive his cabriolet as he entered Clarissa's coach, where he proceeded to delight the ladies with his exquisite manners.

'Is it true, Mr Selwyn,' Arabella asked him, 'that you regularly go to see the chopping of men's heads?'

'Nay, my dear ladies, I make amends,' Selwyn replied, 'for I go only to see them sewn on again.' I did not laugh: but the ladies did, I do not know why.

The sun, a disc of deep yellow ochre, was beginning to set as our carriage arrived at Tyburn, by the Marble Arch. We all alighted and strolled along through the minor attractions. Two men had sat all day in the stocks, their crime as proclaimed by placards having been breaking into houses and stealing goods. Their faces could barely be recognized beneath the stains of rotten eggs and rotting vegetables that had been hurled at them all day. Many just pointed at them and laughed. In vain they endeavoured with their free hands to wipe this filth from their faces since a showman, who had bought a licence from the local municipal authority, was selling rotten eggs and tomatoes and offering a prize of a guinea to anyone who could hit one of the prisoners precisely upon the tip of the nose. The rascals kept ducking and the showman was making a good profit until Arabella purchased her tomato and hit the criminal

UNHOLY PASSIONS

smack in his face beyond all reasonable doubt. The large crowd applauded her.

We proceeded to the pillory. Here there were two men being punished for two rather different crimes. Members of the London Mob were yelling and jeering at one who was there for the rape of a woman; the other was there for criticizing the Royal Family in journalistic satires. The latter was obviously popular with the London Mob since his face was unmarked and strong men were on patrol to ensure that not even one little piece of egg or vegetable reached his face. The rapist was not as fortunate. Although a notice urged the spectators not to throw stones, they had obviously done so to start with, and his bruised and bleeding mangled features were a sorry ruin of the human face. Since he had not been sentenced to the death penalty, officials were now ensuring that stones were not being thrown any longer but the throwing of rotten eggs continued, done entirely and continuously by the women.

'Is this man definitely guilty of rape?' Clarissa enquired of some young tart who was throwing rotten eggs with enthusiasm.

'Oh, yes, Ma'am,' she replied, 'and he has been beating us too.' A tear streamed from her eye. 'Why, he even murdered his kindly wife, my friend Jane, and he should hang for it, but all he gets is the pillory and we cannot even stone the swine. Yet if he had stolen a pocket handkerchief from a gentleman or lady, this rogue would be hanged. He has strangled his wife, me best friend . . .' and she began to cry.

'Take a guinea from me,' Clarissa responded graciously, 'and here is some silver. Now, go and buy some rotten eggs and vegetables. Put stones within your vegetables and smash his ugly foul face to pieces. Meanwhile, leave the man guilty of freedom of speech alone.'

'Thank 'ee, Ma'am,' the girl curtsied. She whispered words to her friends, bought more rotting grenades, sent her children in search of stones and returned to pelting the face of the rapist in the pillory with the utmost alacrity.

We proceeded to the next pillory. Here a woman labelled 'HARLOT AND BROTHEL KEEPER' was about to be whipped with a cat o'nine tails.

'Stop!' Clarissa shouted. 'This is a former servant of mine and I will not permit it.' The fat, balding man, holding the cat leered at her.

'Who the fuck are you to defy the Law?' he sneered.

'Lady Clarissa Hyde, coming to the aid of a very foolish woman. Did you not know that her case is under judicial appeal?'

'I don't give a bleedin' shit 'oo you are,' the man replied, twirling his cat o'nine tails, iron-tipped, with smug satisfaction. 'What I *do* know is that orders is orders and this tart 'ere is to 'ave one hundred strokes.'

To my stupefaction, Clarissa produced a flintlock pistol from her bag and pointed it at his groin.

'Touch her flesh,' she snarled, 'and I shall blow away your balls!'

'YEAH!' yelled the London Mob behind her, led by the girl she had earlier assisted. 'Let's tear that bastard to pieces! Yeah!' They started a song:

'Tear them bastards to pieces!
'Cos they all stink just like cheeses!
They say: "Just a job..."
But two hang for a bob,
They won't be forgiven, by Jesus!'

The London Mob moved in on the man with the cat. He quailed and dropped it.

'Tear him! *Tear him!* TEAR HIM!!!' they roared.

'Enough, good people!' Lady Clarissa cried out. 'I see no

need for violence provided that my foolish former servant Janine be released from the pillory and placed in the custody of Mr George Selwyn, MP and Justice of the Peace here, pending her appeal. *I* shall answer to the authorities for my actions. Now let us go to the hanging!'

'Oh, Clarissa,' Selwyn sighed as the girl was released from the pillory and the Mob loudly cheered Clarissa. 'I don't want this bloody responsibility.'

'It is about time that you had some,' she responded sharply, and led the way to the public execution, followed by the Mob. The man who had held the cat had wisely disappeared. The girl who had been released from her whipping was told brusquely by Lady Clarissa to shut her mouth and behave herself in company.

'I was rather looking forward to seeing a stripping and a good whipping,' Selwyn sighed.

'Oh, never mind,' said Clarissa, 'you will see a good hanging instead, one trusts. As for Janine, I shall have her bound over: you, Janine, should never have stolen my silver spoons and left my service thinking that you would not be caught, you little fool. One more mark of dishonesty and you will be back in the pillory for a whipping, understood?' The girl nodded dumbly. 'Now, let us hope it *is* a good hanging.'

A loud cheer went up from the crowd as a cart brought in the notorious highwayman, Claude Charay. It was said that he had never harmed a lady, though he had killed five men and stolen much from many, including prize possessions from elderly and helpless people. Insofar as I knew, his skill with pistols and the blunderbuss had enabled him to shoot dead two guards, one driver, and two men who had endeavoured to resist his own endeavours to rob them, and I do not think that his gallantry to ladies can conceivably atone for these facts. He stood in the cart with a handsome dignity, his features composed.

'When a man is about to be hanged, sir, it concentrates his mind wonderfully,' some fat, ugly fellow declared loudly just behind me. I paid him little attention since his clothes were falling to bits, but in later years I would know him as 'Dictionary' Johnson, then impoverished but subsequently and rightly renowned as the greatest intelligence, perhaps, of our age. In any event, the magnificently dressed Claude Charay, hands tied behind his back, looked as cool and calm as any man can under these circumstances. He undertook a light step upon the scaffold, surveyed the thousands of spectators below him and commenced his farewell speech.

'Ladies and gentlemen,' he declared, 'I am about to bid you farewell.' The London Mob laughed coarsely. 'I have indeed robbed many men and have killed at least five. In my defence I state that these men were greedy oafs who, in their own way, robbed *you* and who, through their cruel policies, killed your children. Therefore, I am no worse than those who have condemned me.'

'YEAH!' the London Mob roared.

'I have indeed robbed women of their treasures,' the condemned man continued, 'but I think I have given them more pleasure than pain.'

'Yeah!' the women of the Mob shrieked: some of them were crying openly.

'I do not think that my life has been any better or worse than that of anyone else of our time,' said the highwayman, 'and that is what I will say when I go to meet my Maker.' The crowd applauded: and then the hangman placed the noose around his neck.

'Oh, good,' Selwyn murmured softly, like a connoisseur. 'That wasn't a bad farewell speech. And it's Hankin doing the hanging... ah! that will be much better than if it were Sharpsby. Y'see, Sharpsby likes it if they strangle slowly to death and some spectators take delight in the bulging eyes,

UNHOLY PASSIONS

twitches and expiring gasps, not to mention the rope-burns. Oh, a slow one for a bad one is indeed a pretty sight to see and the Mob love it. However, I feel that for this one, Hankin is in order for his skill is to kill at one stroke. He oils his ropes and has told me: "They never even twitch." Now, just watch.'

We did and saw the hangman tighten the noose upon the victim's neck. Then he stepped back and pulled a lever. A trapdoor opened and the condemned man shot through it. There was a *snap*! which those at the front could hear and then the body was left dangling like a lifeless puppet on a string.

'Oooh, Alf!' I heard some witless female idiot exclaim behind me, ' 'e ain't 'alf got a big boner on 'im now.'

'A masterpiece of quick execution for a gentleman,' George Selwyn commented calmly.

'Death is all very well,' Clarissa replied, 'provided that it is quick, but I much prefer sex. Would you care to join us, Mr Selwyn?'

CHAPTER TEN

'There is no part of the world where our sex is treated with so much contempt as in England,' Lady Mary Wortley Montague declared to me indignantly a few days later. 'I do not complain of men having engrossed the government but I think it is the highest injustice that the same studies that raise the character of a man should hurt that of a woman.' I accepted more port from this remarkable elderly lady, renowned for her reputation as the wittiest and most intelligent woman in England, which she had honestly earned. She had been a noted beauty in her younger years and still retained traces of the matter. Her pretty face and delectable figure had made her the toast of the Kit-Kat Club back in the 1720s. 'I suppose you spend most of your time at Clubs, Horby,' she observed. 'What is the point of them?'

'The purpose of a Club,' I replied, 'is to assemble like-minded people, ban bores and to close it to the general public. My social position required me to join White's, Boodles, Pratt's, Brook's, The Sublime Society of Beefstakes and sundry others.'

'Interesting,' said Lady Mary, who was then living in a beautiful Twickenham house with Bubb-Dodington as her neighbour. 'Why did you not also join the Mohocks and/or the Mollies?'

'Quite simple, Madam,' I replied. 'The Mohocks savage elderly night watchmen with weapons and also maim anyone else who is outnumbered and helpless: this is not one of my pleasures. As for the Mollies, this is for men who enjoy wearing the clothing of women, and again, this is not one of my particular pleasures.' She laughed, a rich, deep-throated chuckle. 'I look forward most to the founding of the Club of Sir Francis Dashwood, of which I believe you will be an honoured member.'

'Oh, yes,' Lady Mary sighed, opening her fan and fluttering it with an elegance unlikely to be witnessed among girls half her age. In earlier years, as the wife of a diplomat, she had spent spells in Italy and Turkey, writing interesting books on the art of travel in consequence. After thirty years of marriage, she had separated from her husband and had become a friend of Dashwood. In her earlier years, the poet Alexander Pope had made unwanted sexual advances to her, and when she had politely rejected him, he had savaged her in verse. 'I just hope that Sir Francis does not make the mistakes of the Duke of Wharton. Ah . . .' she sighed softly, 'Philip assembled twenty pretty fellows and, with himself as president, formed them into a committee of gallantry, who called themselves "schemers", and met regularly three times a week for the advancement and enjoyment of every branch of happiness, or as the French might pronounce it: "A penis!" ' She laughed again. 'In my view these schemes should be spread wherever men can sigh and women can wish. Men think and ask: "Why?" Woman dream and ask: "Why not?" ' She sighed and fluttered her fan once more with her left hand while causing her petticoats to rustle with the other. In spite of her advanced years, I could not help myself from feeling lust towards her. 'It is a pity that enemies and debt caused Wharton to flee the country. Francis Dashwood, however, is rather more sensible.' As she kicked up her legs at the thought, I noticed that she was wearing blue stockings and wondered if perhaps the phrase 'blue stocking' came from her.

UNHOLY PASSIONS

'And the Politics?' I queried.

'I cast a wry eye upon it,' she replied. 'Why, a visit to the House of Commons is like going to the theatre. There's a little door to get in and a great crowd without, shoving and thrusting who shall be the foremost. People who knock others with their elbows, disregard a little kick of the shins and still thrust heartily forward are sure of a good place. Even so, as long as Prince Frederick stays alive, this Club may yet do well provided that his ghastly father, the King, dies. My daughter is friendly with Lord Bute, one of us, and he could be the coming man. What is vital is that there are good women in the Club, just as in the days of Wharton.' Suddenly she startled me by ringing a bell and after a moment, a maid escorted two young girls into the room. They could not have been younger than eighteen or older than twenty. 'These are Lizzie and Jane,' Lady Mary announced as I stared at their startling prettiness. Both girls curtsied delicately and awaited orders from their mistress. Lizzie was blonde with a clear, fair skin: Jane had long auburn hair, a pert nose and light freckles. They both were possessed of nubile slim figures. I looked at them and licked my lips.

'Go to the upper drawing room,' Lady Mary commanded them, 'and there you will be served with hot spiced claret. Lord Horby and I will join you in due course.'

'Thank 'ee, Ma'am.' They curtsied and left the room.

'Fancy fucking 'em, Horby?' Lady Mary asked.

'Certainly. Where are they from?'

'The gutter of London,' Lady Mary answered. 'They are orphans who could not bear the cruelty of the orphanage, who ran away and whom, in consequence, I found shivering on the street. I have consequently taken them into my home where they receive excellent food and basic education. In due course they will join the brothel of the excellent Mrs Charlotte Hayes, and there, if they are sensible, they will make a good living. It can be a *very* good living as a celebrated courtesan nowadays and I shall be introducing them into the most excellent circles. But drink up, Horby, for there will be more if you wish it, and let us join these young ladies.'

We proceeded upstairs where young Jane and Lizzie were drinking their hot spiced claret and coolly awaiting us.

There were only two problems concerning their apparent innocence: they had failed to shut a cupboard door in which reposed a full-length looking-glass; and they had failed to hide the pair of silken drawers which one of them had dropped upon the floor.

'What is *this*!' Lady Mary demanded sternly with flashing eyes.

'Please, my Lady, it was Lizzie,' Jane said with a wicked look at her companion.

'Ah, no, you fibber! It was Jane who began it!' retorted the other, looking quite abashed.

'I can guess,' Lady Mary declared, 'pretty well what you two girls were amusing yourselves about. Now, tell me truly, were you looking at each other's private parts in the glass?' This question hit the mark and seeing how shame-faced and blushing they were, she continued with: 'No doubt you were examining to see which one showed most signs of hair on your little pussies. Let me see, Lizzie – and help me, Horby.' I suddenly caught the hem of Lizzie's dress and petticoats and in an instant had her clothes reversed over her fair head so as to cover up her face and expose all the rest of her beautiful slender figure. It was obvious which girl had removed her drawers. 'Why!' Lady Mary squealed delightedly, 'the poor little thing doesn't have a pair of drawers of which to boast.' She tumbled Lizzie over her knee. 'Give her bottom a good slapping, Jane!' Jane was only too pleased to do so and the slaps fairly echoed through the room, mingling with Lizzie's piteous cries to let her go.

My blood was up. The sight of Lizzie's beautiful bum, all flushed and rosy under the sharply administered slaps of Jane and Mary, working in tandem, made me fairly lust to take further liberties. Meanwhile, Mary let the little victim Lizzie go, having whispered something in her ear, and her tearful eyes were brightened in a moment. She darted at Jane, whipped up her dress and petticoats over her head, tore down her drawers with her free hand and then dragged her about the room with her breasts and buttocks fully exposed.

I amused myself by spanking poor Jane's pretty posterior until it turned bright scarlet, regardless of her sobbing and crying for mercy. At last we let her go and I took her on my lap to kiss away the tears. She soon smiled again and nestled herself to my body quite lovingly. This seemed to make Lizzie jealous as she appealed with a flushed face to Mary to kiss her also, which Mary readily did in a most loving manner.

'Oh, my dear lady,' Lizzie sighed, kissing her again and again. 'You don't know how much we both love you and feel for you, having been left alone and unhappy. There is nothing we would not do to bring a smile to your pale face . . .'

'Then we'll sleep together and have a romp on the bed,' I insisted 'Only mind, you be good girls, and never tell of your mistress's doings.' Lady Mary and I took a glass of mulled claret and ordered Lizzie and Jane to do the same. A second and a third glass seemed to open their eyes immensely: the least touch or joke sent them into fits of laughter. They blushed and were visibly excited. In fact, Jane, who had remained on my knee, seemed almost ready to faint with emotion as she caressed my face and chest, the cause being a hand I had managed to slip under her dress, so that two fingers had been tickling and playing with her young, slender slit and gradually working her up to a state of excitement that she was at a loss to comprehend.

'Lizzie . . .' Lady Mary murmured between kisses, 'meet Mrs Charlotte Hayes, a fine friend of the Prince of Wales, and thereby you may secure a promising future, my dear, for I will gladly introduce you. AH! . . .' she exclaimed as Lizzie caressed her breasts, 'there is a good girl. Let us all be naked! I have a *huge* four-poster bed next door, across the way. We shall go there. Throw off every rag, my dear ones, for I want to feel your soft, warm flesh next to mine, to cuddle you and to feel you all over . . .'

'Certainly, Ma'am,' Lizzie replied, 'but may Jane and I first answer a call of Nature?'

A few moments later, Lady Mary and I were reclining in one of her magnificent four-poster beds and awaiting the arrival of her two young and delectable young waifs. For a lady of her years, Mary had surprisingly smooth skin. The servants had placed goblets of port upon our bedside tables and had stoked the coals and logs in the fireplace into a merry blaze. Rain hammered upon the window panes but within the sheets and blankets, we were warm.

'Oh, John Horby, young John,' Lady Mary sighed, 'how I hope to high heaven that Sir Francis will succeed! I hope he will also have Frances Anne Hawes as a member, if you will kindly pardon the pun.'

'Sorry?'

'Oh, you probably know her these days as Frances, Countess Vane.' At that moment, there was a knocking upon the chamber-door. 'Yes,' said Lady Mary and Jane and Lizzie, both naked, lissom and lithe, ran through the doorway and jumped into bed with us. We greeted them with amorous caresses that they eagerly returned. Both Lady Mary and I had fingers in their cracks sooner that it takes to record the matter. 'What darling little quims each one of you has!' Lady Mary squealed delightedly. 'I long to keep you in my bed all night so I can kiss them. What do you think of mine, with its soft, curly hair? Only it's a broken pan, you know, my dears, as I have of course had a husband.'

'Lalala – and was that really so nice, dear lady? Oh, I love you so, do let me look!' Lizzie exclaimed, kneeling between Mary's legs to obtain a better sight of her curiosity, which she first kissed most lovingly and then, parting the hair, put a couple of fingers deep within Mary's vagina. This so tickled and delighted Mary that she leant back upon her pillows and pulled Jane close to her bosom as she hugged and kissed her, having a finger in her little slit inserted as far as it would go. Mary's thighs were now wide open to facilitate inspection.

'How deep my two fingers can go, right up and it is so warm and moist . . .' Lizzie murmured approvingly. 'It makes me feel that I could eat it!' Seconds later, we were all romping on Mary's bed in a state of nature. Mary, Lizzie and Jane laughed, screamed and blushed as I excitedly examined and kissed their respective cunnies. How my tongue revelled around their budding clitorises, in the case of two, and an experienced one in the case of the other one, until they rewarded me with those first emissions which are usually so thick and creamy. How lovingly all three repaid my caresses! Lizzie paid the most ardent attention to my prick, which delighted her more and more every moment, whilst Jane seemed to prefer sucking the bubbies of Mary as I gamahauched her. It was a glorious hour and we all would have welcomed more had it not been for a tap on the door.

'Come . . .' said Mary and a maid, not in the least surprised by the habits of her mistress, entered the chamber bearing a card upon a silver tray. 'Oh! Lady Vane?' I started since I recognized the name that Mary had mentioned earlier. 'Show her to this chamber.'

'Tell me more,' I said.

'Oh, Frances was introduced to Society at the age of thirteen and fell in love with Lord William Hamilton a mere two years later. When both families opposed the match, they eloped. Unfortunately, her husband died after a year of marriage. Frances then married Viscount Vane, who seems to have been most disappointing sexually, for she kept running away from him. Lord Vane even offered a £100 reward in the newspapers for anyone who might discover the whereabouts of his lady. It was so ineptly worded, this wretched advertisement, that one would think he had lost some favourite spaniel bitch.' Lizzie and Jane could not restrain their giggles. 'Lady Vane eventually returned to our fair shores in the company of Lord Berkeley,' Mary continued. 'I am told that she does not pride herself on fidelity to any one man, which is but a narrow way of thinking, but she boasts that she has always been true to her nation and, notwithstanding foreign attacks, has always reserved her charms for the use of her own countrymen.' There was a tap upon the door. 'Talk of a she-devil! Come!'

'I'd love to, I'd love to,' said the lady who swept into the room and rarely have I seen one so beautiful. Her heaps of golden tresses cascaded down her shoulders, her face was slim and pale with high cheek-bones, she had startling eyes of azure blue, her bosom, puffed by a low-cut dress, was startling in its impact, and, judging from the way she swirled her skirts as she sat down, there was much to be said for her bottom. She sat there amidst the candles, shimmering in sparkling pink silk and smiling wickedly at the four of us in a bed. 'Typical, Mary,' she commented as a maid brought her a goblet of port. 'You haven't changed at all, have you? You always were,' she smiled, 'after the young ones. Now do introduce me.' Mary did so. Lady Vane smiled at Lizzie and Jane then added: 'Ah! And Lord Horby. Receiving a good education from Mary, I trust?' She drank her port lustily and giggled. 'I hear, Horby, that you are a good fuck. Is that the case?'

'Try me,' I replied, ' for despite delightful times, I have not actually had a fuck all evening.'

UNHOLY PASSIONS

'I shall,' Lady Vane replied with a very pointed look. 'No doubt Mary has been informing you that I am a very loose woman. On the contrary, I am much misunderstood. I know that it was some sort of scandal, heaven knows why, but when Lord Vane proceeded to persecute me with his wretched public advertisements, I made no hesitation in my choice, putting myself under the protection of a man of honour, Lord Berkeley, whom I esteemed, rather than suffer every sort of mortification from a husband such as Lord Vane who had become the object of my abhorrence and contempt.'

'Yes, dear,' Lady Mary smiled sweetly, 'and that is why you thence chose to abandon him and live with Lord Bolingbroke.'

'You bitch!' Lady Vane exclaimed, opening her fan and fluttering it irritably. 'From a mistaken pride, I chose to live in Lord Bolingbroke's house, rather than be maintained at his expense in any other place.'

'He did not last long, though, did he, Frances?' said Lady Mary.

'Oh, that's all over. Who cares about the past? I am only interested in the present and the future. I have come into an unexpected legacy, and so,' she fluttered her fan demurely, 'I can do precisely as I please. I am very happy at my house in Twickenham, recently purchased, so,' she smiled merrily, 'Mary, we shall be neighbours. And don't you think that Bubb-Dodington is an excellent neighbour, too? Why, we both adore Sir Francis Dashwood and his charming Steward, Paul Whitehead, has only just recently purchased a place just around the corner. We are, I think, in very good company.'

'And how is the love-life?' Mary asked.

'*Magnificent!*' Frances shrieked. 'You must know Sewallis Shirley...?'

'Not personally,' Mary responded, 'but I gather that he is a wickedly handsome man, a Dilettanti member and a friend of Sir Francis Dashwood.'

'Exactly!' Frances motioned to the emotionless maid for more port. 'And he can help us in our aim for Sir Francis' purported Club by introducing more ladies of quality so that we may exercise further feminine influence. We must have Lady Betty Germain. Why, she is in possession of the Aztec "scrying stone" of the great Elizabethan magus, Dr John Dee, which he used to "scry in the spirit vision". Would that not be perfect for the Magick which, one trusts, Sir Francis Dashwood intends?' (This device now reposes – until I can line up a wealthy customer for it – in the British Museum, having left Betty Germain's hands later for those of Horace Walpole: *Ed.*) 'Anyway, she is very beautiful and I simply cannot wait to tumble into bed with her. I am fascinated by her bottom and am sure that it is satin-smooth. Mmmm.' She licked her lips like a cat offered a vat of cream. 'I'm absolutely *dying* to meet Fanny Murray, y'know, the mistress of Sandwich. What *is* she like? I hear she is quite exquisitely luscious! How delightful!' Frances laughed throatily. 'Sir Francis tells me he desires "ladies of accomplishment". Well, the ladies I have mentioned are accomplished and one trusts that he will include the intriguing, vivacious and pretty, Mary Walcott, his half-sister.'

'Ah, yes,' said Lady Mary Wortley Montague, 'the "Sultana Walcotonia" as she was known in the Divan Club. Yes, she *would* be a valuable addition. Then there's the matter of the young "Sister Agnes", whom Paul Whitehead mentioned to me the other day. Her background is apparently in the shady side of bookselling but the Club may find that to be useful; and I gather that she is very pretty.'

'Bookselling, ah yes!' Lady Vane responded. 'The matter interests me since I have commenced a new career in literature.' Lady Mary raised her eyebrows. 'Are you at all acquainted with *Fanny Hill: Memoirs of a Woman of Pleasure* by John Cleland?' Jane and Lizzie giggled as Mary burst out laughing.

UNHOLY PASSIONS

'Of course,' I said. 'It has sold more copies than any other of our age, there was much talk of prosecuting the author for its allegedly scandalous obscenity and eventually the Government resolved to give John Cleland a handsome pension on condition that he did not write any more books again. He accepted the offer since he had nothing more to say.'

'Quite true, Horby,' Frances responded, 'but you see, *I* could not resist essaying a witty and partly autobiographical parody entitled *Memoirs of a Lady of Quality* and this will be published anonymously within the pages of his next novel, *Peregrine Pickle*, by one of the finest authors of our age, my dear friend, Tobias Smollett. *Such* a man of talent...' she sighed.

'I am delighted for you, my dear, and look forward to reading the work,' Lady Mary replied. 'Now do get those clothes off and come to bed with us.' Upon receiving the nodded assent of Frances, the maid proceeded to unloose the strings, stays, corset and hoops of the beautiful Lady Vane, taking a pleasure in the process until Mary saw that her friend was free and smilingly bade the maid her dismissal.

Frances leapt into bed with alacrity, squealing with joy as she first hugged Mary, and then proceeded to tickle the roseate young nipples of Lizzie and Jane, before sliding under the eiderdown and towards me. Her face was turned up towards me. I could not resist kissing her full upon the mouth. Her lips parted almost immediately to my rigid tongue that thrust inside her luscious mouth, slavering great loving caresses all over it. Her tongue in turn darted delicately in and out of my own mouth and her arms hugged my body to her. My own squeezed her body gently as my hands stroked her bare back.

Her skin was satin-soft to my touch. She lay back upon the bed, showing off her rounded apple-breasts with their proudly erect nipples; her nipped-in waist; rounded thighs and long, lissom, lovely legs. I drew my fingertips gently down her flat belly and her flesh fluttered beneath them. Naked I lay beside her, caressing her neck, arms, hips. My mouth showed my appreciation of her beauty, sucking on her breasts as if they held the milk of paradise, then giving her delicious cunt long, loving and lascivious licks. Her moans grew louder as her pretty bottom wriggled itself around upon Mary's silken sheets. Mary was meanwhile having both her cunny and her bottom licked and kissed by Lizzie and Jane.

I entered Frances Vane slowly and deliberately, then I rammed my sex inside her right up to the hilt and she gasped. She carried on gasping as I rode her in and out, going all the length, all the breadth, indeed, all the way, starting out slowly then working up to a quick-thrusting tempo of staccato jabs; she moaned with the rapture of its joyous succession. I moved my prick in strong, sweeping circles, rubbing every pore of that soft, wet cushion insider her as her hips gyrated with pleasure. Our loins fused together in a gallop so hard and fast, it was a blur of ecstasy that made my hips throw her cunny that extra inch which means another mile high: and then my arms held her closely and tenderly as she came.

The spasms that shook her body jolted me – and then I blasted away with my prick shooting for the stars, Frances sighing her delight at the sunbursts of my throbbing. For a few minutes, she lay quite still, eyes closed, as Jane and Lizzie sucked, licked and suckled Mary and I gazed down upon her face. Its contours had softened to a hint at a child-like vulnerability. I kissed her lips again. Abruptly, her eyes opened.

'Horby...' she sighed. 'Whore be!' she laughed.

CHAPTER ELEVEN

What a fine day it was, that first day of May 1751! A boat was ready at Twickenham at midday, to take all visitors to Medmenham Abbey, which Sir Francis Dashwood had prepared for our delectation. I had spent the previous six months taking Dashwood's advice to travel and had wisely appointed my dear old tutor, the Reverend Aloysius Herbert, so learned a man, to be my guide. His academic expertise had been flawlessly displayed as he lectured me well on the beauties of Paris, Berlin, Potsdam, Venice, Florence, Rome, Naples, Pompeii, Athens and Istanbul. Here it suffices to say that my education was excellent both in terms of culture and, to the horror on occasion of the affable Reverend Aloysius Herbert, in terms of sex. I had left England as a youth and returned as a man.

What an assemblage of persons of quality there was to behold in stepping aboard this boat! We were conducted on board by Paul Whitehead, the thin Steward, and welcomed thereon by Lord Sandwich, who had been appointed the Prior, the absent Dashwood, who was awaiting us, being the Abbot. Obviously, Bubb-Dodington, Thomas Potter and George Selwyn stepped on board. Frederick, Prince of Wales, entered the boat in uncharacteristically modest fashion. He was followed by Lord Bute, Sir Thomas Stapleton, Sir Henry Vansittart (on leave from his duties as an excellent Governor of Bengal); Dr Benjamin Bates, a nationally renowned physician; Sir John Dashwood-King, half-brother of the founder; the Earl of Orford, the Duke of Kingston, the Marquis of Granby; Lord March, later Duke of Queensberry; Joseph Banks, later President of the Royal Society; William Hogarth, the greatest artist of our age; and Guiseppe Borgnis, that charming Italian master of design. Finally for the men, making a party of twenty-two, there was a John Hall Stevenson Esq., who would, in the future and influenced by Dashwood, found 'Crazy Castle' in Yorkshire and assist that extraordinary and wonderful novelist, Laurence Sterne, the graces of whose *Tristram Shandy* are assuredly an adornment of our age.

The finest flower of English royalty, aristocracy, gentry and men of talent and intelligence stepped aboard the boat that day: and so did the finest flower of England's ladies. They were led by Lady Wortley Montague, followed by Lady Vane, the astonishingly beautiful and red-headed Lady Betty Germain and that delectable brunette and mistress of Sandwich, Fanny Murray; then Lady Mary Woolcott, half-sister of Dashwood, a slender, elfin wench; the rather shy and young Agnes, who was helped aboard by Whitehead (rumour had it that she might be an illegitimate daughter of Sir Francis); and then Mrs Charlotte Hayes accompanied by Sir Joshua Shawcross and followed by fifteen beautiful girls, including the willowy Millicent and Sarah, a splendid buxom blonde. Once on board, we were all served a choice of sparkling wine, claret, burgundy, port, brandywine and fruit punch in addition to smoked salmon, smoked eel, smoked trout, prawns, lobsters, crayfish and copious quantities of steak, kidney and oyster pudding, also pork-and-egg pie, pork sausages with sage and mustard, a side of ham and goose, pheasant and partridge.

'Just an appetizer, ladies and gentlemen,' Paul Whitehead murmured as the boat hauled anchor and commenced its sail along the River Thames. I noticed that Jane and Lizzie had

UNHOLY PASSIONS

been recruited under the wing of Mrs Charlotte Hayes.

'Splendid, isn't it, to go a-Maying, eh, Horby?' Bubb-Dodington exclaimed pleasantly. He tossed back his goblet of burgundy, wheezed cheerily, wolfed down two huge prawns and called for more wine, which was given to him instantly by the servants. 'Must say, I'm fascinated by the transport used by all who came to the Twickenham bower. Did not some of the girls come by waggon? Reminds me of a long, slow fuck. And some came by stage-coach: the best whores rode within, those on the way out rode in the basket behind it and those trying to get in clung onto the roof; ah, yes,' he drank deeply, 'it's a hard life for the whores, my friend. Of course, Mrs Charlotte Hayes arrived with her favourites in a brisk post-chaise. Now, a stage-coach reminds me of the sort of fuck whereby you go ahead steadily and stop after each orgasm. It is not acutely exciting but one eventually reaches one's journey's end with satisfaction. The post-chaise reminds me of those brisk, fast and rather ecstatic fucks.' He took a pinch of snuff and I joined him: this was the most satisfying, scented as it was with sandalwood. 'You, sir, of course, arrived in your phaeton. Why, that carriage can carry three ladies in addition to yourself. A series of fast galloping dashes yet done with elegance, isn't it, eh, sir? And yet did you see the arrival of Lady Betty Germain?'

'I have,' I replied, and I was mad keen to fuck her.

'She arrived in a gig, also called a "whisky" after that curious Scottish drink that is becoming quite fashionable these days. Fast and furious, wouldn't you say?' I nodded assent as we came up to Teddington Lock, where, and to my great delight, we were joined by a swift cabriolet which disgorged my dear friends, Lady Clarissa Hyde and the Hon. Arabella Marchmount for their joining of the boat. 'Fast and loose, containing two with space for a third,' Bubb-Dodington murmured as the ladies joined the boat and I greeted them with delight, which warmth they both eagerly returned. The river voyage was delightful and we eventually docked at the apple orchard of the Abbey.

'As Prior,' Sandwich stated, 'I say: "Ladies and Gentlemen, kindly step ashore." The Steward, the estimable Mr Whitehead here, now takes charge of a guided tour.' We stepped ashore indeed to be confronted after passing within some trees by a statue of Priapus, brandishing a huge and stiff flame-tipped phallus. A twist and a turn through the orchard showed us the statue of Venus stooping to pull out a thorn from her foot, with her beautifully sculptured buttocks blocking the entry to a small tavern.

'Instantly one recognizes a celebration of male and female energies,' Paul Whitehead pronounced. 'Sir Francis wishes to resurrect the vision of Rabelais. I am reminded of the noble words of that excellent poet, James Thomson, author of "Seasons" and "Rule Britannia", whom our noble Brother, George Bubb-Dodington, has assisted, when he stated:

'. . . There was but one great rule for all:
To wit, that each should work his own desire,
And eat, drink, study, sleep, as it may fall,
Or melt the time in love, or wake the lyre,
And carol what, unbid, the Muses might inspire.'

All of us were bombarded by a series of aesthetic sensations. We stared eagerly at the statue of Priapus. Beneath it was the inscription: PENI TENTO NON PENINTENTI – 'a penis tense, not penitence', venerating this flame-tipped expression of primordial male energy. The message was on further inspection reinforced by the pedestal upon which this statue stood. This consisted of a representation of Trophonius's cave, from which all creatures in mythology are said to come out melancholy. Trophonius was the builder of the Temple of Apollo at Delphi and myth has it that, after his death, his ghost haunted the Temple and inspired the priestesses of the Sun God to give enquirers truthful oracles. There were statues of a cock and a priest, both of whom get sex for nothing.

Closer inspection of the statue of Venus, with enchantingly proportioned buttocks, disclosed a Latin inscription:

' "Entry by the wrong route is deplored here," ' translated Paul Whitehead. 'Anyway, Sir Francis prefers to call her the *Bona Dea*, thus incorporating Aphrodite, Isis and Lakshmi of India into his worship. And just ahead, there is *The Temple of Cloacina*, also called *The Chapel of Ease*. Those with no imagination will simply call it the lavatory. Now let me take you to the Abbey itself.' We emerged to see a beautiful medieval Abbey that had been lovingly restored. Above its entrance had been lettered in gold: FAY CE QUE VOUDRAS, taken from Rabelais and his notion of the Abbey of Thelema and meaning: DO WHAT THOU WILT.

The interior vouchsafed the guests every possible comfort. We entered a large drawing room, furnished largely with damask sofas of green silk, amidst ornate Roman decorations conducive to conviviality.

'Outside on the landing, as you may observe,' Paul Whitehead informed us, 'you can see the male and the female once more affirmed in the shapes of two statues, both of them holding fingers to their mouths. The male is Harpocrates, the Ancient Egyptian God of Silence; the female is Angerona, the Ancient Roman Goddess of Silence. No doubt silence will be observed concerning these proceedings, ladies and gentlemen, or the appropriate curses from the God and the Goddess will follow. Now, here are glazed and framed prints of the kings and queens, hung all over the walls of the Abbey. You might notice that paper has been pasted over the face of King Henry VIII for closing down the monasteries. Ah, and if you look through here, that is the dining room – and, incidentally, the wine cellar is virtually inexhaustible. Sir Francis thought that you would all find something to please you among the following: anchovies, beefsteak pie, crabs, dove, eels, fried fish, grouse, haricot beans, idiotic dishes such as hot pickles and peppers, jam of cranberry and jelly of currant; lamb, delicately roasted; mint sauce, nuts of pine, cashew and almond; oranges; potatoes, soundly baked; quail's eggs; roasted haunch of venison, sirloin steaks of beef, tench from the lake, freshly fried, ultimate excellence of spinach soaked in raw egg, veal and ham pie, whole hock of bacon soundly boiled with root vegetables, excellent smoked salmon from Scotland, yams from the West Indies. And since Sir Francis, our Abbot, has recently met the King of Prussia, he offers the Prior,' Whitehead smiled at Sandwich, 'zandwiches!' Sandwich smiled as we all laughed.

'Now,' Whitehead continued, 'if you look there, you will see the Library. There are many rare works of ceremonial Magick there, which Sir Francis purchased in Paris and Venice, in addition to an abundance of literature containing occult, erotic and recondite wisdom, which you are all free to read. If you will come this way...'

I noticed quite a number of comfortable bed-chambers; and servants in attendance.

'There for your pleasure, ladies and gentlemen,' said Whitehead. 'And here is what Sir Francis and I call "the playroom".' We looked and saw a large room furnished with marble statues of Pan and Aphrodite. 'Here there is fruit and the juice of the vine. As my old friend Mr Johnson, presently compiling his Dictionary, said to me the other day: "Claret is for boys; port is for men; but he who aspires to be a hero, must drink brandy." There is plenty of that – and over there is a rocking-horse with a dildo, the *Idolum Tentiginis*, a phallic steed used in ancient fertility cults, which will give pleasure,' he grinned wickedly, 'to every lady who desires to take a ride upon it.' The laughter of the women was as wicked as the leer upon the faces of the men. 'There will be sherry for all now.'

Over our glasses of sherry, we all admired the Abbey. For my own part, I had one eye upon the delectable Lady Betty Germain and the other upon whatever was going on. The name of Dashwood kept coming up in all the conversations I overheard and all wondered why he was not present among us.

After a few more glasses of sherry, Sandwich whispered words to a certain number, including myself, and these left the room, leaving the remaining lords and ladies and gentlemen and commoners to disport themselves as they wished. This Prior then led the way to a room panelled in oak. Sandwich proceeded to discard his clothing, indicating twelve suits of white hats, jackets and trousers.

'More like a waterman's than a monk's,' Bubb-Dodington murmured.

'Hush, sir,' Sandwich returned, 'have you never heard of Charon, the waterman, who ferries the dead across the River Styx?'

'Are we all ready, gentlemen?' Whitehead enquired. When we had all given our assent, we had to sign pieces of parchment stating that upon our honour, we could never divulge anything that took place within the Chapter-Room nor the names of anyone involved. I give the names of Dashwood, Sandwich, Whitehead, Bubb-Dodington, Thomas Potter and myself for the Inner Circle, solely because they have, in later years, given me their permission. The second clause upon the parchment insisted that we would swear to be silent concerning the actual rites conducted within the Chapter-Room although we would be allowed to relate of anything that passed without it and also to describe a vision.

Very well, then: I break no oaths in stating that the most wonderful sight I ever saw, one which thrilled the head, heart and guts and which has been witnessed and captured by fine artists such as Carpentiers, Hogarth and Knapton, was the sight I beheld when entering this mysterious Chapter-Room. Dashwood was kneeling in prayer, wearing the plain robe of a Franciscan friar. As I looked out of the window behind him, I could vaguely discern a gloomy landscape, a stormy sky and some strange Gothic buildings. His left hand was placed devoutly upon his heart. His right hand was extended in the form of a thumb and first forefinger apart, that which I had learned in Venice, as he had, to be the sign of the Horned God. He appeared to embody masculine energy and to be directing it towards the ankle of a naked and voluptuous marble figurine, the Goddess, who reclined lasciviously upon the altar, apparently delighted by his devotions.

Upon this altar and to the left of Dashwood, death was symbolized by a Venetian carnival mask. In front of him, though behind the figurine of the Goddess, there was an open leather-bound grimoire, the pages of which revealed the pentagrams, hexagrams and other sigils of magick spells. To his right, there was a cross hanging upside-down from a string of pearls, in mockery of a rosary. This cross hung over a shining shield, which was slightly topsy-turvy and, to my way of thinking, symbolized the vagina as the cross did the penis. It crossed my mind that this shield of Sir Francis might possibly be the Holy Grail itself. So many delights had spilled out of this dish, including oysters, mussels, grapes, crayfish, oranges and other fruits that symbolize fecundity. One goblet had spilled flowers upon the floor. Another, exquisitely carved in gold, stood proudly upright and bore a coronet. I do not know whether it was a trick of the light or not, but I could almost *swear* I saw a halo above the head of Dashwood, just as the artists had done.

At this point I trust that the reader will pardon me, for I cannot break my oath of silence and secrecy concerning what went on in the Chapter-Room other than to state that here were prayers beautifully composed and exquisitely spoken, gestures

UNHOLY PASSIONS

of ancient ceremony, the heady scent of incense and the drinking of a deep communion, that sacred libation to She whom Dashwood called 'the Goddess without eyes'. I had never known such ecstasy in the course of a religious ceremony and tears streamed from *my* eyes. My fellow members were also shivering, shaking and quaking. Perhaps it was the beauty of the language, possibly the nobility of the actual gestures, or there was even the possibility that the Great Goddess herself was present with us upon that noble night.

We went from the Chapter-Room to the Retiring-Room, where thirteen lovely and lascivious ladies had been assembled by Lady Mary and Mrs Hayes to give us tidings of great comfort and joy. I certainly break no oaths of secrecy here by stating that we all took copious cups of wine and entered into a merry swiving. It was a great pleasure for me to fuck Mrs Charlotte Hayes herself, who was quite exquisite, what with the way in which she kept swishing her gorgeous, smooth bottom back and forth over the palms of my hands ... I thrust into her time and time again as her narrow channel repeatedly squeezed my rampant pego, making me all the more eager to ram her stiffly. My pubic bone slammed so hard against her that she sighed as she expired in orgasm.

'Well, I'm sure, gentlemen,' said the petite Lady Mary Woolcott, half-sister of Sir Francis Dashwood, 'that I did not fancy that your undergarments were so indecently short.' Francis, with a laugh, caught hold of his sister's chemise and with a great roar, tore a great piece off all around, so that she was now in quite a short frock, which only half-covered her fair bottom. Mary Woolcott was crimson with blushes and inclined to be angry but, recovering herself, she laughed:

'Ah! Francis, what a shame to serve me so. But I don't mind if you make us all alike.' The girls screamed and the gentlemen made a rush. It was a most exciting scene: the young ladies retaliated by tearing the shirts off their tormentors and this first skirmish only ended when the whole company was reduced to a complete nudity. All were in blushes as we gazed upon the variety of male and female charms exposed to view.

'We've all heard of *Nuda Veritas*,' Sir Francis declared as he popped open some magnums of champagne, 'so now let us drink to Her health and to the first time we have been in Her company. I am sure that, given this toast, She will be most charming and agreeable.' All joined in this toast, the sparkling wine inflamed our desire and there was not a male organ present but was in a glorious state of erection.

'Look, ladies, what a lot of impudent fellows they are!' Lady Vane declared amidst hoots of laughter.

'And they should not think that we are going to surrender anyhow and any way to their manly lust,' Lady Betty Germain, whom I fancied so madly, concurred. 'They should all be blindfolded and then, ladies, we will arm ourselves with good birch rods. Then let it be everyone for themselves and Cupid's dart for us all.'

'Hear, hear,' responded all sides, and handkerchiefs were soon enough tied over our eyes as good birch rods were handed around to the ladies by Mrs Charlotte Hayes.

'Now, gentlemen, catch us if you can,' Lady Betty Germain chortled, slashing right and left into our manly group, her example being followed by the other young ladies as one heard Lady Mary Wortley Montague and Mrs Charlotte Hayes laughing with glee. The room was quite large enough and a fine romp ensued. The ladies were as lithe and active as young fawns and for a while sorely tried the posteriors of their gentlemen friends, for we tumbled about in all directions, only to receive an extra dose of the birch upon our bottoms before we could regain our feet.

At last Lady Betty Germain stumbled over a prostrate gentleman, who happened to be me. I had surreptitiously loosened my blindfold so that I could spy out my prize. I grasped her firmly around her slender waist and clung to my struggling reward as a shower of birch-cuts greeted the writhing of our pairing.

'Hold, hold!' Frances, Lady Vane cried out. 'She's fairly caught and must submit to be offered as a victim on the Altar of Lust!'

Both Lady Mary Wortley Montague and Lady Mary Woolcott quickly wheeled a small couch into the centre of the room. The gentlemen pulled away their blindfolds and all laughingly assisted to place us in position, the lady underneath with a pillow under her dimpled buttocks and myself, on my knees, fairly planted between her thighs.

'Are they novices?' Lady Vane laughed cruelly.

'Nay, a more beautiful couple it would be impossible to imagine,' Lady Clarissa entered the conversation. 'He is a fine young fellow with dark hair and eyes and her complexion is almost a counterpart of his; their eyes are similar also.'

'Indeed, Madam,' I murmured, noticing that Betty's cunny and my instrument were both finely ornamented with soft, curly, black hair.

'Oooh!' Betty exclaimed as she publicly fingered my stiff prick. 'With the skin drawn back, the fine purple head of your cock looks just like a large ruby.' I presented it to her lusciouslooking vermilion gap, the lips of which were just slightly open as she lay with her legs apart. This touch seemed to jolt her; and her blushing face turned to a still deeper crimson as my dart of lust slowly entered the outer lips of her quim.

Feeling my steed to be fairly in contact with the throbbing joxy of the lovely woman beneath me, I at once plunged forward to the attack, pushing, shoving and clasping Betty around the body with all my strength and I stifled her wanton cries of rapture by gluing my lips to hers. It was a case of *Veni*, *Vidi*, *Vici* and, one might add, *vagina* and *veneris*. My onset was too impetuous to be withstood and she lay in such a passive, favourable position that I was soon, after my first charge, in full possession of my dame up to the roots of my pubic hair.

'Ah!' she exclaimed with a faint smile. 'That was indeed sharp but I can already begin to feel the pleasure of lust!' This came as no surprise to me since the juices of her love were pouring upon the palms of my hands, placed beneath her silken soft bottom. 'Go on now, dear boy, for our example will soon fire the others to imitate us.' She heaved up her gorgeous bottom as a challenge then pressed my face fondly to her bosom. We ran a delightful course, the sight of which filled the spectators with voluptuous excitement and as we died away in a mutual spend, someone snuffed out the lights. All was laughing confusion, gentlemen trying to catch a prize ... and there was much kissing and sighing.

'Oooh!' the Hon. Arabella Marchmount squealed, 'I feel myself seized by a strong arm ...'

'A strong hand,' Lady Clarissa sighed lazily, 'is groping for my cunny. How delightful!'

'I know it's you,' I heard Dashwood murmur, 'my dear young Millicent. I can't make a mistake even in the dark as yours is the only hairless quim in the company. Kiss me, my dear, I'm bursting to be into your tight little affair.' Lips met lips in luscious kisses.

Somehow, Betty and I found ourselves close to a divan. I lifted her up and put her back on it and, taking her legs under my arms, I was soon once more pushing my prick up her longing cunny. Her quim nipped my cock as tightly as possible. I was in ecstasy and spent directly but, by keeping my place, I put her, through my previous rigorous action, into a perfect frenzy of lust. Spend seemed to follow spend, till we had each of us done it six times. The last time, Betty so forgot herself as to bite my shoulder and draw blood in her delight.

The room was still in darkness and love engagements were

going on all round. I heard Lady Vane murmur that she had enjoyed two more partners, though lamenting that there was only one go with each. I shall never forget that night as long as a breath remains in my body.

Later I heard that Dashwood had had his sister in the mêlée, which she afterwards admitted to me was a fact, although she thought he did now know it and the temptation to enjoy her brother had proved too much for her.

This orgy confirmed the establishment of our secret society amongst a certain circle of Brothers and Sisters. Anyone who gives a pressure of the hand and asks: 'Do you remember the birthday of Sir Francis?' is free to indulge in love with those who understand it. I have since been present at so many repetitions of that birthday fun.

CHAPTER TWELVE

Upon returning to the main drawing room, we found that those of the Outer Order were engaging in scenes of the most scandalous and salacious nature, at least according to the prudish (had any such been present). Violinists played merry tunes by Handel as couples copulated quite recklessly, with wanton abandon, upon the Persian carpets. Whenever a man or woman had finished a fuck, their goblets were instantly replenished by servants and maids. The more introverted of our members were quietly perusing the erotic delights of the literature that Sir Francis had so thoughtfully assembled in his library and the more scholarly were even studying the *grimoires* of magick spells as the more lively of the ladies formed a queue for the enjoyment of the rocking-horse with its dildo. Sir Francis bade us join him in the dining room for the alphabetical feast he had designed and that proved to be as delicious as he had promised. Ah! It was among the finest feasts that I have ever enjoyed. There was as much burgundy and claret as any sane man could desire and afterwards huge quantities of port and brandy were served. 'Genial gentlemen all,' Dr Benjamin Bates had told investigators in later years and that is quite true, although he (wisely) omitted mention of the many ladies.

In fact, to be a member of the Outer Order, nothing was required of one other than to be a genial and convivial fucker prepared to work with us politically. As for the Inner Order . . .

I was writing these words with my finest quill pen when my butler informed me that a certain elderly gentleman had requested admission. Naturally I acceded to the request and was delighted to welcome a senior member of the Inner Circle, therein also known as 'John'. He informed me that he had heard that I was penning my Memoirs, that he had been in touch with both English and Continental Freemasons, also those of the Scottish persuasion in the Ancient and Accepted Rite, and that all the Elders were of the opinion that I could write of the secret rites of the Monks of Medmenham provided that I did so in Latin. Naturally I thanked this gentleman who came and left wearing a broad-brimmed hat and a long black cloak – those of my few readers familiar with the doings of the Illuminati will readily guess my meaning – and with gratitude, feasted him royally. It was with joy that we reminisced, over our port, about our memories of the first day of Dashwood's launching of the Medmenham Monks . . .

'A story, gentlemen, a story!' Sir Francis cried out on that occasion. 'Bubb! Do you have one for us or is your tongue tied?'

'Gladly,' Bubb-Dodington replied, 'and particularly in view of the excellence you have organized. I wish to praise women!' The ladies cheered him. 'However, I shall reverse the general practice and instead of beginning with the head, commence with the leg and hope to get credit for so doing. A pretty face, sparkling eyes, rosy cheeks, a delicate complexion, smiles, dimples, hair dark, auburn or blonde have all, it is acknowledged, great weight in the business of love; but . . .'

'Get on with it!' Thomas Potter shouted.

'Indeed, sir,' Bubb-Dodington answered him imperturbably, 'so still let me appeal to every impartial and unprejudiced observer, which is he most curious to behold: the legs or the face of his favourite Lady? Do the face or the legs of a pretty girl who is clambering over a stile or mounting a ladder... which, gentlemen, most attract our regard? What is it,' Bubb looked at Lord March, 'Old Q', that notorious rake, 'that causes my lord to smack his chops in a wanton lecherous manner as he is sauntering up and down some lounge in Bond Street, with his glass in hand – or should I say spy-glass? – to watch the ladies getting in and out of their carriages? And what is it that draws together such vast crowds of the holiday gentry,' he looked at George Selwyn, 'at Easter and Whitsuntide to see the merry, rose-faced lasses chortling over a hanging at Tyburn? What is it,' he looked at Sandwich and Fanny Murray 'that causes such a roar of laughter and applause when a merry girl happens to "somersault" in her career and kick her heels in the air?'

'What is it,' George Selwyn drawled, 'and as the parsons say, what is it that makes the theatrical ballets so popular?' The ladies squealed with mirth since Selwyn was notorious not only for his necrophilia but also for his passion for young girls.

'Quite so, sir,' Bubb returned. 'It has frequently been remarked by foreign travellers that in no nation of the world are the ladies more nice and curious about their legs than in England; and to do them justice, there is perhaps no nation in the world where the ladies have greater reason to show them. Think of dirty weather, whereby the fear of passing for dragtails causes the pretty girls to hold their petticoats up behind and to display their lovely calves and ankles well above par. Consequently, I am infinitely more delighted with my muddy walk than were I making an excursion in the finest sunshiny day imaginable. There is a kind of magic in the sight of a handsome female leg, which is not in the power of language to describe. To be conceived, it must be felt.'

'But too well am I acquainted,' Prince Frederick interposed in a high heat of excitement, 'and from experience, with the magic which centres in a pretty leg, a delicate ankle and a well-proportioned calf. The first time that I was in love, and I perfectly well remember the circumstances as if it occurred but yesterday, the first time I could ever be said to feel what love is, I had to thank a pretty leg for it. I was then in my early teens, as harmless and innocent a young fellow as needs be.

'It was a beautiful summer's day,' the heir to the throne continued. 'I had strolled into the woods, laying myself down in a copse of young hazel trees, and alternately musing and dozing away when my curiosity was excited by a rustling noise close to the spot where I lay concealed. I was all attention; and, directing my inquisitive eyes to the quarter from whence the noise proceeded, discovered a wonderfully pretty, rosy-cheeked girl, who lay basking in the sun and who, deeming herself to be sufficiently remote from observation, was under no restraint in her motions. Presently she whipped up her skirts and petticoats and ungartered her stockings, contemplated her legs, turning them this way and that way and in short practised a thousand manoeuvres ... ah, suffice it to say that not a single movement was lost upon me and from that hour to the present moment, I never see a pretty leg but I feel certain unutterable emotions within me. My misfortune was that she continued to tease me and I did not have the courage to approach her.'

'Would you know her if you saw her again, sire?' Dashwood asked.

'Certainly, Sir Francis. Millicent, who later attended to my education in divers ways, is sitting here at present.'

'Well!' Lord Sandwich gave her an evil smile, 'well, well well. A lady's legs are certainly beautiful, though myself I prefer the sight of a lady's bottom. Furthermore, Sister Millicent has informed me that she is desirous of joining the Inner Order. How fortuitous! Sister Millicent, we welcome you,' said the smiling Prior. 'Are you willing to take the oaths of secrecy and to be initiated into the mysteries of the rod?'

'Yes, my Lord Prior.'

'You must be submissive to all our rules and regulations,' said Sandwich. 'In order to prove your loyalty,' Dashwood nodded his approval, 'you must now strip.' Charlotte Hayes and Sarah assisted in disrobing the novice who blushed as they took away her dress and removed her petticoats.

'Oh! I never expected this!' Millicent exclaimed. 'It is so indecent.'

'Make haste,' Sandwich instructed the ladies of the stripping that was to facilitate a whipping. 'Your improper remarks must be checked. We have no patience with prick teasers here and your bottom will smart soundly for it.'

'Pray permit me to apologize, for I had no idea that the members were liable to chastisement . . .' Millicent responded in a faltering voice, since she was evidently in great confusion. 'I thought you amused yourselves by whipping charity children sent up by schools for punishment.'

'What impertinence!' Lady Vane exclaimed.

'You will have to do penance under the rod,' our Abbot, Sir Francis, told her severely. 'We are quite above tickling the bottoms of school children here; although it is indeed the duty of every member to exercise proper discipline in any house or place where he or she may have authority.' Millicent fell silent but her crimson face and the nervous twitching of the corners of her mouth attested to how she felt about the approaching taste of the rod and presently, with nothing but her drawers, chemise, boots and stockings on, she was led to a ladder as we all rose from the dining table to cluster around our victim.

'Have the ladder nearly upright,' Sandwich, our Prior, commanded, 'with her wrists secured high up, and let her toes only just touch the floor.'

'Woe to her bum,' George Selwyn murmured, 'if she dares to step upon the bottom rung of the ladder without orders.'

Millicent, with tears of shame and apprehension, protested against this disposition of her body as being too painful and cried out for mercy as she felt her chemise rolled up and fastened under her armpits and her unbuttoned drawers pulled down to her knees.

'Ah! Ah! Oh! Have mercy, dear Mrs Hayes.'

'Um ... no,' said Charlotte.

'Don't show the white feather, young lady,' said Dashwood.

'We are going to initiate you into a most delightful society,' said Sandwich, 'for you will soon be one of the most active of the sisterhood.' Charlotte offered Prince Frederick a most elegantly tied-up rod, ornamented with blue and gold ribbons. Prince Frederick used it to switch the victim's bare bottom lightly.

'Now ask me to birch you properly,' the Prince commanded, 'for teasing me in my youth and flaunting what I could not then enjoy. Beg pardon also for your frivolous objections.'

'Oh! Is there no getting off?' Millicent shrieked in a tremor of fear, adding with faltering voice: 'Why must I be cruelly whipped?'

'There, that's a slight taste, you stupid bitch,' snapped the Prince with a smart swish across her beautiful buttocks, which at once brought the roses to the surface. 'I can't waste more time. There ... *there*, THERE!' He issued three more sharp cuts in succession, each leaving their respective (and respected) long, red marks. 'Perhaps in a few minutes you will think it worth your while to obey orders and beg my pardon.'

'Ah!' Millicent screeched. 'Ah-r-r-re! It is cruel, oh! oh! I am sorry for saying so! The cuts smart so it is impossible to think what I am saying. Oh! pray forgive me and punish me properly ... but ... but oh! Be merciful!' She writhed and wriggled under the painful swishes which had already begun to weal her delicate, tender white skin.

'Very well,' said Sandwich, 'you have done it after a

UNHOLY PASSIONS

fashion; but now, as you are becoming one of our members, pray, have you got a sweetheart?'

'Aargh!' Millicent yelled upon receiving an extra sharp cut. 'Oh! oh! I can't bear it, it's like a hot knife cutting the skin! Indeed, I have not got a lover, if that is not allowed . . .' and she put her feet on the rungs of the ladder to ease the painful strain on her wrists.

'How *dare* you alter my disposition of your body by putting your feet upon the ladder!' His Royal Highness snarled and dealt her a tremendous whack across the calves of the legs, which made Millicent fairly spring with agony. He returned to swishing her roseate, twitching bottom until the poor girl capered like a cat upon hot bricks. 'Now, about lovers, you *have* had one, if not just at present?'

'Oh!' Millicent returned in smarting pain. 'My poor legs! My poor bottom!' At this we all burst into a loud laugh and thoroughly enjoyed poor Millicent's shame and confusion.

'Cheer up, Sister Millicent,' Mrs Charlotte Hayes urged her. 'You have only to do what we call *stepping the ladder* and some day, perhaps, you may have a chance of revenge. Meanwhile you will find Lady Mary Wortley Montague here to be quite as cruel as I am, when she uses the birch in her skilful style upon your half-cooked arse. Come, my dear,' Charlotte beckoned to Lady Mary as we watched eagerly, 'I think she is ready for the second edition of her punishment.'

'Oh! oh! how *horrible*!' Millicent squealed. 'My bottom is so sore that I really cannot bear it to be touched. Oh! No! Not again with that awful thing . . . !'

Lady Mary brought down her rod with a tremendous whack across the trembling girl's scarlet, glowing bottom.

'Confess!' she shrieked in between her strokes, looking with delight on the red marks her cut had left upon the white flesh of her victim, 'One!' She made her birch flourish through the air with a hissing noise. 'Pretty well, now, now, NOW!' she smiled. 'Two. Three!' And she issued a couple of strokes with a good interval between them, to make the victim feel the effect as much as possible. Millicent cried out fearfully upon receiving each swish.

'Ah!' she sobbed hysterically, 'how dreadful! The skin of my bottom will burst, it's getting so tight...'

'Glad you enjoy it so, dear,' Lady Mary answered airily. 'I'm sorry to hurt you,' she added as she looked delightedly around at the other members. 'Now... *now* ... NOW!' She declared with another flourish, 'four!...FIVE!' Millicent groaned as her bottom twitched and Lady Mary handed the rod to an eager Lady Vane.

'Steady, keep your bottom well out,' Frances commanded, switching her lightly underneath so as to tickle the exposed pussy. Then there was another grand flourish of the birch. 'Six! Seven!' These were awful crackers but the victim kept herself steady and her pluck was greeted by a clapping of hands all around as her punished bottom twitched and writhed in response. She was clearly fixed in a most inviting attitude for further flagellation. 'Thank you, Millicent,' Lady Vane cooed, 'very thoughtful of you. I hand over now to my Sister in the Order, Lady Betty Germain.' There was a round of applause: the lady accepted the rod gleefully.

'Now, Sister Millicent,' she declared in her high, cut-glass voice, 'before you are let off, you must tell us all about yourself and young Frederick, His Royal Highness.' She whisked the tightly bent bottom in a playful way with her rod but the victim was evidently so sore that even light strokes made expressions of pain pass across a fair face so reddened with shame.

'Oh! Oh! Pray don't begin again,' Millicent pleaded, her front teeth momentarily chewing her fleshy lower lip as her slim, glowing bottom twitched and her customarily prissy, snobbish manner was hereby humiliated. 'I tell you, he took

UNHOLY PASSIONS

liberties with me, what more can I say? Oh! Oh! Please don't touch me . . . the least whisk of that thing gives me awful pain.'

'Then, you silly girl,' Betty Germain addressed Millicent sternly, 'why do you persist in keeping back the truth? Did you not encourage him?' She made the victim writhe under her painful touches which, although not very heavy, seemed to have a great effect upon the burning female bottom, positioned so tightly by the ladder to which she was bound.

'Oh! Spare me!' Millicent cried out in great shame and confusion and appearing crimson all over at the realization of her degradation before us all. 'If you know all, have mercy!' she pleaded. 'Consider my feelings . . . oh, and how painful such a confession must be. Ah, you are shameful girls to be enjoying my pain and shame so.' And she sobbed as though her heart would break.

'Come, come, young Miss,' said Dashwood, upon receiving the sceptre of the rod from Lady Betty Germain. 'It is not as bad as that. Make a clean breast of it and be one of us in the future. You will enjoy such scenes yourself when the next novice is admitted: but I cannot play with you. There, *there*, THERE!' The Abbot cut three brisk strokes upon the proffered bottom and handed the rod to the Prior.

'Ah!' the penitent shouted out. 'Please! Oh! – or I shall faint again dead away. It is like burning with red-hot irons. Oh! You know he seduced me and . . . I must confess I did not resist as I ought. Something tempted me to taste the sweets of love and your Abbot's birching brought all the thrilling sensations back to me and when I fainted, my dream was all about the bliss enjoyed in the arms of this wonderful man.'

'A little better,' Sandwich murmured as he lightly whisked the rod across her blazing flesh, 'and getting nearer the truth: but you still prevaricate in trying to excuse your own fault. Now: did you not endeavour to seduce the youth prior to his alleged taking of advantage from you?'

'Oh! Pity me ... I saw him lying asleep on the grass in a secluded part of the garden. He was so sleepy that I failed to wake him but I since believe he was shamming.'

'And he was not the only one,' Prince Frederick muttered.

'Noting a lump of something in his breeches,' Millicent continued her confession, 'I gently pressed it with my fingers to see what it was, whereupon it gradually swelled under my pressure and became like a hard stick throbbing under the cloth. My blood was fired. I cannot tell you how I did it but presently, when he opened his eyes and laughed at me, I found myself with his exposed shaft in my hand. He jumped up, sprang upon me and, taking advantage of my confusion, I own he had an easy conquest. But something of the sort will happen to every loving girl at some time or other. Oh, now I have told you all, so have pity and let me go,' she sobbed, looking dreadfully confused and distressed.

'There is only one problem,' said Sandwich, flicking the birch twigs around Millicent's blazing bottom for the sheer pleasure of watching it twitch. 'The account of Brother Frederick is at variance with yours, albeit that there are some inconsistencies.'

'My account is true, Sir Prior!' Prince Frederick shouted indignantly. 'Consider please, ladies and gentlemen,' he addressed us stiffly. 'A man likes to tell stories of sexual success, not of frustrated and ignominious sexual failure. I swear to you that this Sister of ours taunted and teased me and that I never received the honest happiness of a good jolly rogering! Had I done so, all those years ago, I would never have permitted the present punishment.'

'Well, Sister Millicent,' Sandwich smiled gleefully, 'you can be released providing that you swear solemnly to spend a night in one of our cells with Prince Frederick, our dear brother Fritz.' Millicent gave her assent and we all applauded the justice of the Prior's decision.

UNHOLY PASSIONS

Millicent was let down from the ladder and we all crowded around her, giving affectionate kisses and welcoming her as a real Sister of the Medmenham Monks. The poor girl was very sore and sobbed over her smarting bottom.

'Oh!' she squealed sexily, 'oh! I can't sit down, it will be weeks before I can do anything with comfort. Ah! You pretend to be kind now after all that dreadful cruelty . . . one day, Fritz, I would love to give you a good thrashing. You impetuous boy,' she kissed him, 'it would do you good.'

Paul Whitehead guided us to our 'cells'. These were furnished with large beds and commodious coverings. There was not a man or a woman who did not get laid that glorious night. For my own part, I had an absolutely fabulous fuck with Dashwood's half-sister, Lady Mary Woolcott, who proved to be as libidinous as Sir Francis himself, to my great delight.

Awakening in the early hours, I contemplated with pleasure the remarkable paintings in tempura upon the ceiling which unashamedly showed the Gods, Goddesses, fairy folk, satyrs, nymphs and fauns in ecstatic acts of copulation. I reflected that no grouping hitherto had ever given me so much wisdom and delight in my life and I resolved again to be loyal to this wonderful Club, anticipating the time when Prince Frederick would become King and we would run the country.

CHAPTER THIRTEEN

'It is very unfortunate, Horby,' Bubb-Dodington informed me as we strolled through Vauxhall Pleasure Gardens. The music and the fireworks did little to clear his furrowed brow and the passing by of elegant ladies swishing their petticoats did little to lift the gloom of his countenance. 'Prince Frederick is dead.'

'Oh!' I gasped. 'I am sorry to hear of it.'

'It won't be pudding time yet,' said Bubb. 'Pity, because he was an affable, generous person. Still owes me £6,000 for the purchase of Carlton house in Pall Mall, but never mind. Let's face it, he was an honourable and decent fellow, ill-treated by his parents, who could have played his part in realizing a vision by becoming an excellent King. Our King George II apparently just grunted: "*Fritz ist tot*," and appeared to be relieved. Charming fellow! Ah! Let us take some port with friends and Brothers, my dear sir!' We approached a table where refreshments were being served among the trees and lawns and amidst fireworks and the music of Purcell and Handel. It was a pleasure to see Thomas Potter and Lord Bute. Potter raised his glass and directed his gaze towards the River Thames, the surface of which shimmered in the full moonlight, declaring:

'Here lies Fred
Who was alive and is dead.'

'Had it been his father,
I would much rather,' Bubb pronounced.

'Had it been his brother,
Still better than another,' I said, joining in the game.

'Had it been his sister,
No one would have missed her,' said Bute.

'Had it been the whole generation,
Still better for the nation!' Potter laughed cruelly.

'But since 'tis only Fred
Who was alive and is dead . . .' Bubb stated cautiously.

'There's no more to be said.' I capped it, winning the plaudits of the company as we quaffed our cups of wine and called for more.

I have never forgotten the conversation that we had that night. Essentially, Bute revealed that with the willing consent of the late Prince Frederick, always a keen womanizer himself, he had become the lover of his wife, Princess Augusta, on account of which he had been appointed Tutor to her son, George, heir to the throne now as the future George III.

'Patience, sirs,' said Bute. 'I shall endeavour to inculcate all our principles into the young and malleable mind of my charge.' He took a pinch of snuff. 'If Prince George can be made to realize his duty as a Patriot King and the power which the Crown still has, he might restore the true Constitution. He might break the Whig oligarchy, end corruption and placemanship, deliver Parliament from the grandees and manipulators and govern his people with an equal hand through ministers of different parties and no parties, restoring public liberty as we of Medmenham conceive it.'

UNHOLY PASSIONS

'Well spoken, sir!' I exclaimed warmly. 'But for how long must we wait?'

Writing in retrospect, it was a very slow process. The lowest point was when Bubb-Dodington was dismissed from office; yet, having charmed Princess Augusta, the future Queen Mother, he bounced back as Treasurer of the Navy. From there he intrigued to advance the position of Bute. I stared at this languid, handsome man and envied his good fortune in fucking Princess Augusta, an exquisitely pretty and gracious woman. Bute was now the salaried head of her official household.

Although John Stuart, third Earl of Bute, came from a relatively old Scottish family, his property consisted solely of the island of that name. This Eton-educated man, descended from a bastard son of Scotland's King Robert II, had parlayed his pedigree into a marriage with the daughter of Lady Mary Wortley Montague. I knew that money remained a problem, however, and for a while Bute was renting a small house in Twickenham. It was said that His Majesty the King detested Bute. Upon Bute's appointment as Groom of the Stole, the King declined to receive the Earl but reluctantly acceded to the appointment of a Stuart, instructing the vain and idle Duke of Grafton to slip the gold key, that badge of office, into Bute's pocket. He was holding a golden key indeed for, in addition to his happy and affectionate marriage to Mary Montagu, he was obviously making love to Princess Augusta and was also reputed to be enjoying an affair with the lascivious Lady Howe. In my opinion, Bute was intelligent, charming and socially accomplished, if somewhat vain and arrogant. I had not forgotten the words to me of his late patron, Prince Frederick.

'Bute is a fine, showy man,' His Royal Highness had said. 'He would make an excellent ambassador to a court where there was no business.'

This was the man for whom we all plotted to put him into power. We would no doubt have plotted for many more hours had we not suddenly been hailed by Lady Clarissa Hyde and the Hon. Arabella Marchmount, who were evidently enjoying the sights and sounds of Vauxhall Pleasure Gardens as much as we were. There were warm greetings exchanged and the ladies agreed to join us to share a bowl of strong, cold punch.

'How are matters with you, Arabella?' I enquired.

'Before I deliver the good news,' she responded, 'let us have what some may regard as the bad. I have been under the tutelage of a dancing master, and he has instructed me to abandon the regalia of baroque stage costume and to wear only a simple muslin robe, draping me as if I were a Greek statue, and to let my hair down so as to allow me greater freedom.'

At this instant, Arabella pulled pins out of her hair and let it flow down freely. This was quite in keeping with the atmosphere of Vauxhall Pleasure Gardens, where everyone, metaphorically speaking, let down their hair, for many had wigs. And it was such a joy to witness the fireworks, the fountains, the harlequinade, the puppet shows and also the open copulation of couples amidst the trees.

'Speaking of freedom,' Clarissa murmured, 'how large was the bulge within the dancing master's leotards?'

'Clarissa,' Arabella replied, 'his testicles were smaller than coconuts yet possessed a hardness of chestnuts. It was not possible for him to disguise what lay and throbbed underneath his tunic. Ah!' she rhapsodized as she allowed Bute to give her more cold punch, 'with one toe I would pirouette and then he would take me into his arms.'

'Was his name by any chance Laval?' Bubb queried.

'Yes,' she answered. 'I think he makes love to all his students: yet how can one deny a man so handsome? His buttocks are so firm and tight!'

'Did he jump into the air and perform a *cabriole*?' Bute

enquired. Discerning that Bubb and I were perplexed by this technical term, he added: 'It is a feat of matching the high leap of a trained horse.'

'Much better than the finest stallion,' Arabella answered. 'Thank heavens he was hardly a Rosinante, that worn-out hack of Don Quixote. Yes, he made a great impression upon me.'

'And what is your impression of Sir Francis Dashwood?' Bubb enquired.

'I remember the first time I was invited to Medmenham Abbey,' Arabella responded. 'He is a man of rank and fashion. He declined to wear a wig. His own hair reached to his collar in dark curls and I longed to run my fingers through his locks. Upon our first encounter, I wore a gown of purple silk with elbow-length sleeves and a tight bodice to push my breasts up in an enticing and inviting fashion. Beneath my ankle-length gown, belled out by small hoops, I wore an embroidered petticoat and under that a shift of linen with silk stockings gartered above the knees.

'I tantalized him with my cleavage,' Arabella continued easily, 'and then I looked into his eyes. His stare was bold and forthright.

' "I trust that you will be contented with a simple dinner," he said. "There is merely a leg of boiled mutton and capers, a broiled fowl and an ox-tongue, a batter pudding in the Yorkshire style, a fine turkey roasted, fried rabbits, tarts, custard and jellies, almonds, raisins, oranges and apples and plenty of port wine."

' "Sir Francis!" I exclaimed. "I applaud the excellence of your hospitality but this is surely overwhelming in volume!"

' "Have no fear, my dear," he responded genially. "No food in this house is ever wasted and my servants eat the finest foods in England." In fact, the dishes had been cooked so well that I had a rapacious appetite and an insatiable thirst, gladly gratified by the frequent signals of Sir Francis to his servants for more fine claret. Following our excellent repast, a maid escorted me into a drawing-room and I requested a cup of tea, which I enjoyed in temporary solitude as I admired his collection of paintings.

'Logs blazed upon the inglenook, yes, a fine fire burning upon the hearth. There was the sound of a dog snoring lightly, the crackle of the logs of an evergreen tree and in my nostrils the scent of burning cedar. In my dreamy state, I sensed the spectre of the Brocken wild man, a shadowy image upon the mountain top I used to see in my childhood... and he descended and as he did so, his visage became clearer, there was a light touch upon my noddle and then I realized that my snood had been removed.

' "How many hours have I slept?" I asked.

' "Is it really so essential that you worry about time?" Sir Francis answered. He held up a sand-glass and I watched the sand slowly descend from the upper to the lower bulb.

' "Sir Francis..." I could not even finish my sentence before he took me into his arms and kissed me and then I felt a throbbing within my pudendum, a whirling pulsation, a touch of a tickle in order to tingle, and I fell a prey to a passion.'

'Oh, I know the sensation, my dear,' said Lady Clarissa, 'and perhaps you know the song:

'Oh, Sir Francis do not touch me
'Oh, Sir Francis do not touch...
'Oh, Sir Francis do not...
'Oh, Sir Francis do!
'Oh, Sir Francis!
'Oh, Sir...
'OH!!!
'And she lay between the lily-white sheets with nothing on at all.'

UNHOLY PASSIONS

'She's a most immoral lady!' Potter sang, in tenor.

'She's a most immoral lady!' Bubb joined in, in baritone.

'She's a most immoral la-a-dy!' sang Bute, in alto.

'And she lay between the lily-white sheets with nothing on at all,' Arabella trilled.

'Oh, yes!' this delightful soprano shrieked out. 'Thank heavens for our times when women can fuck men and openly admit to our great joys in the pleasure! Men have always been permitted to discuss this but it is only now that women can do so publicly. And so I have not the slightest shame in admitting that Sir Francis lifted up my gown, my embroidered petticoat and my linen shift, removed my garters and slowly rolled down my stockings while kissing me salaciously upon my inner thighs, the backs of my knees and then my calves and he then nipped gently upon my Achilles tendon, the cord connecting the calf to the heelbone where there is a weakness. Reaching the lowest extremities of my anatomy, he proceeded to suck upon my big toe, which made the outer lips of my womb all aquiver.

' "It is essential that you find the Holy Grail," he said.

' "And how is this to be accomplished?" I enquired.

' "Through sex, the sacred act of coitus." '

At that instant, there was an astonishing explosion of fireworks in the sky accompanied by music which ravished the feelings.

'Madam,' Potter said to Arabella, 'all of us agree with Sir Francis and we see and hear it before our senses now. Look! The coming of colours in the air, just like a rainbow! And bangs! Ah! And the music of Handel with the female chorus going "HA! HA! HA! HALLEJUYAH!" Orgasms all round!'

'Quite agree,' Bute murmured quietly, 'but I hope that Arabella will continue with her tale.'

'Tail or tale or possibly some head,' Bubb muttered in an undertone.

'I responded by slipping off his jacket,' Arabella resumed her story excitedly, 'and began to unbutton his britches. Turning them down, my eager hands wandered under his shirt, feeling the firmness of the ivory-like flesh of his deliciously rounded buttocks whilst my eyes did not fail to detect how far his linen stood out in front. He seemed to understand me now and, in a trice, he was as naked as Adam in Paradise. My roving hands took possession of his beautiful cock-of-the-walk, quite six stiff inches long, broad and throbbing, and ornamented around the tight-looking balls by a mass of curly brown hair.

' "What's this, Francis, are you often wet like this?" I teased him as I called his attention to the glistening sperm that was moistening my fingers. "What a big fellow this is, quite enough for any man." I could not resist drawing his prick to my lips and sucking it deliciously for a moment or two until I felt he was getting near his spend, to judge by his sighs.

' "Oh, do kiss me!" I implored him, letting him go as I reclined upon the sofa and opened my legs whilst his hands opened the slit in my drawers and exposed the lips of my cunt to view. His mouth was glued to it in a moment and ah! *O!* How his lascivious tongue made me spend in a second or two whilst my unslippered foot was rolling his prick upon his thigh. But I was afraid of losing the next emission of his love juice so I gently drew him over my body and directed his dart of love into my quim. His unruly member entered me and I could not contain myself.

'The love-milk flowed from within my cunny, since I had secreted an opaque white fluid sweeter than ambrosia. In response to him, I was endeavouring to offer a greater sacrament, perhaps; a visible, not an invisible, sign of inward and spiritual grace.

'What ecstasy there was as I felt the slow insertion of his

thick prick! How it seemed to swell inside the luscious sheath which received it lovingly! Yet Sir Francis is skilled in matters of lust. At first we lay motionless, billing and cooing with our lips until I began a slight motion with my bottom, to which he was not slow to respond.

'How I enjoyed that man! The knowledge that I had a really experienced cock within me added such a piquancy to my enjoyment that I fairly screamed from excess of emotion as I spent and felt his balsam of life shoot into my longing cunny.

'He had to fuck with me three times before I would let him dress and go about his business,' Arabella went on naughtily. 'He had been with me for over four hours but the time had been well spent in making love, not to mention our eating and drinking and talking. You know how free men tend to be with words just five minutes after a satisfying fuck, surely . . . ? Why, he found some cause to delay business which he had previously told me was urgent and instead told me all about the secrets of the Medmenham Monks.'

'Surely not . . .' Bute murmured uneasily.

'Oh, but of course!' Arabella squealed. 'You men think that you have all the Secrets in the Inner Chapter and that women are excluded from them. That is ridiculous because it is from women, from the high priestesses of ancient times, that these secrets come, and, a lady might add, go.'

'Be careful of what you say, Madam,' Bubb cautioned her as a rocket sped skywards to explode in silver stars whilst upon the grass nearby us there was a fiery shower of golden rain. The heady smoke of gunpowder swirled in the air.

'Why *should* she be careful?' Clarissa suddenly snapped. 'We women know all the secrets of your Inner Chapter Room or Temple and are united in approving everything you do apart from this shrouding in preposterous secrecy. It is that which will lead you to being accused of Devil-worship and of being a Hell-Fire Club, fit only for infantile blasphemy. We *know* that all you genial gentlemen do not believe in that preposterous superstition called Christianity and since you do not believe in Jesus Christ, you are sufficiently intelligent not to believe in that childish bogey-man, Satan. Therefore we *know* that in your Inner Rites, to which we women are forbidden, you are worshipping the male and the female principles of Nature in the form of Graeco-Roman gods and goddesses. As for the forms of your rites and ceremonies, these have been selected from the books, largely purchased in Venice, and are freely available to all, including women, who are given access to the Library of Sir Francis.'

'Madam, I am amazed by your perspicacity,' said Bubb.

'Oh, one doesn't have to be intelligent to work it out, Bubb,' Clarissa drawled back with a drip of acid, 'merely a woman. You know, I've never forgotten one occasion when dear Sir Francis invited me up to Medmenham. Do not mistake me, sirs, I have the highest respect for my darling Dashwood and certainly I shall assist his vision in any way I can in the hope that it may come to pass.

'Dashwood is a very thoughtful man,' Clarissa continued. 'He is also a wonderful friend. On and off, we have been fucking one another for years, and he can be a wonderful lover. On this occasion, however, he told me that he was tired and so we simply enjoyed a fuck that was fast and friendly, like a quick kiss. He knew, of course, that I could do with more sexual satisfaction and to this end had hired two handsome young men, as he sometimes does to ensure that the ladies are properly pleasured. For his own part, he appeared to take his own pleasure in escorting me to my bedroom and then taking his leave with the utmost propriety, giving me a brotherly good-night kiss upon the cheek.

'I entered my candle-lit room to see two young, strong and very handsome men, one white, one black, reclining upon my bed, taking snuff, quaffing from huge goblets of port and

UNHOLY PASSIONS

grinning insolently as their eyes inspected the curves of my bosom and my bottom.'

'Shocking . . .' Bubb murmured.

'Delightfully so,' Clarissa responded sweetly. 'In a low, throaty voice, I invited them to strip me bare and then I insisted upon stripping them, a game I call "Strip Jack Naked". Naturally, since all was free between us now, my hands groped for their pricks. I found them both to be as long and thick and stiff as possible and could not resist pressing their naked bodies against my own belly, where the contact of the throbbing pricks upon me had so great an effect on me that . . .'

'Who *are* these men?!' Arabella cried out. 'And where are they? I demand to be introduced. What are their names?'

'Oh, I don't remember their names, dear,' Clarissa sighed languorously, 'I merely recall them as Biffo and Boffo. They had no brains at all, same as horses, and should have been born in the bodies of stallions and put out to stud. I am grateful, however, that they *were* born into manly bodies, for that is what I enjoyed.

'Selecting Biffo by the size of his affair,' Clarissa resumed her story, 'I backed towards the bed and drew him upon me. What a great dick it was! It was so large that my cunt was fairly gorged with this delicious meaty morsel, which on account of my vaginal squeezes spent before it was well and truly into me. My arms held him firmly around his waist, and I sighed for him, after a brief rest, to go on with his delicious fuck. Just to stimulate him, I wriggled a cool, long finger into his behind, to make him do his work well with me. The effect was to give my cavalier quite double energy.

'I then requested Boffo to push his prick into my bottom. The latter was nothing loath and, although the want of lubricant was rather an obstacle, my second young man soon succeeded in his aim. I am always telling young men to have an aim in life. My hand passed behind me and played with the lower shaft of his prick and appendages as he buggered my bottom delightedly.

'This made for another prick I was enjoying. Fancy taking an experienced man and two lusty youths in one day!' She laughed with glee. 'It fired me with the most lustful sensations. Looking at the handsome black face of Biffo, I became aroused almost beyond bearing by his negritude. How my quim throbbed on his glorious black prick! How we spent in torrents of that elixir of love which makes us die in ecstasy at each fresh emission. What heavenly joys to spend together, as we did, three times without withdrawing. I know such excesses are only tending to shorten my life,' Clarissa added with biting sarcasm, 'but reason is powerless to resist the attraction of such Cytherian joys.

'I arose and lit the candles,' she resumed, 'and the light of a dozen showed everything to the best advantage. The figures of two youths like fauns, reflected in the looking-glasses around the room, appeared to fill the apartment with lusty young gladiators, dark and fair, both with limp, glistening pricks, just as they had withdrawn from the combat of love.'

'An excellent tale, Madam,' Lord Bute remarked. 'Sir Francis certainly knows just how to be attentive to the needs of his guests.' He added a wry smile.

'You may well smile, sir,' Clarissa responded coolly, 'but within this apparent crudity lies in fact the quintessence of Wisdom. There is nothing in life to match the *ecstasy* of the sexual act undertaken with love, and in that instant of rapture, one can perceive truths about the Universe we inhabit way beyond our conscious thinking, which is merely a creature of custom and habit.'

'Phew! You sound like Lady Mary Wortley Montague!' Bubb wiped sweat from his brow with a white silken handkerchief. 'Didn't know you were such a blue-stocking,

UNHOLY PASSIONS

Clarissa. You know,' he wheezed and chortled jovially as he took a pinch of snuff, 'we really must discuss these matters further and in greater depth at some future date convenient for everyone, if we're all agreed? Yes? Good, I'll see to it that there's a date for that. Jolly interesting, I'll say! But it is getting on a bit, talking of the time, and so I wondered if...'

'Oh, *do* get on with it, Bubb,' Thomas Potter drawled. 'We want to bring a good evening to a good end, don't we? The question before us therefore is, who will be fucking with whom?'

'Quite so,' the ladies said in chorus.

'Clarissa...' I murmured softly, staring hard into her beautiful azure eyes.

'Yes, John Horby,' she replied in a voice like hard cut-glass yet with a gaze that was as soft and yielding as the pure water from a gentle spring.

'Arabella,' said Thomas Potter. 'You are a beautiful woman and I want to fuck you and fuck you well. Come with me, you gorgeous lady, to enjoy at my home excellent food, excellent drink and excellent lust!'

'There's no subtlety about you at all, is there, Thomas?' Arabella burst out laughing. 'Yes, of course I'll accept your invitation, you lascivious rogue. And your fucking had better be as good as your meat and drink: or is it the other way around?' I think that Potter was vexed to smack her bottom for her cheek but could not do so owing to her hoops.

'Well, a delightful and instructive evening. I warmly relish the company of you ladies and gentlemen.' Bute bowed courteously and, twirling his cane, took his leave with the utmost style. Men and women regarded him as he strolled away and upon the faces of some women, there was open sexual admiration. He appeared to be so handsome, proud, aristocratic and lofty, almost destined for high office. The men envied his figure, which made them finger their own paunches, and pondered the fact that he was educating the heir to the throne and going home to a palace to fuck the future Queen Mother.

CHAPTER FOURTEEN

'Would you like,' Thomas Potter had asked me, 'to come and meet an interesting man?' This was in the early 1750s when the Club was going well and I had no idea about the havoc this man would eventually cause. Initially, indeed, John Wilkes appeared to be a charming and ingratiating fellow when Potter introduced me to him at Garner's Coffee House. There the coffee was as good as ever and I always enjoy meeting an interesting individual. As it was, I had already learned something about the man whom his future Majesty King George III would come to call 'that Devil Wilkes'.

In appearance, he was a goggle-eyed son of a bitch. Potter had told me that John Wilkes was the son of a London merchant who disapproved of his son's wasteful and extravagant life-style. This had caused him to marry a sleepy and physically attractive but pleasant woman who had some money. He remained a rake but he was unfailingly kind and considerate to her: and the daughter his wife bore him absolutely adored her father.

'Sir, you have probably heard terrible stories about me,' Wilkes declared.

'Indeed, sir,' I replied. 'I have only this day heard William Pitt state that you are "a blasphemer who does not deserve to be ranked among the human species". What do you have to say to that, sir?'

Wilkes burst out laughing.

'He would say that, sir, would he not?' Wilkes replied. 'My impassioned advocacy of Democracy and crusade against corruption have indeed made me many enemies.' His well-adorned slim body appeared to quiver with righteous indignation. 'Why, sir, only the other day, a newspaper owned by this wretched Government stated: "There was no corruption that he had learned anywhere but he was able to duplicate it." Can scurvy untruths go further? Yes, they can, sir, and do so every day in papers owned or subsidized by our appalling Government.'

'There's more, Horby.' Thomas Potter smirked, holding up a journal which at first glance seemed to be hot off the press and badly printed on cheap paper. 'Here it is said of Jack: "There is not a friend Wilkes would not sacrifice for a scurvy jest." That's an odd saying, y'know, since the same article accuses me of being "Wilkes's Evil Genius!" Ho! ho! Hup-two, hup-two, hup-two, POTTER!'

'I have every vice but one, sir,' Wilkes responded coolly, 'I am not an hypocrite.' I found this to be the case during the course of our afternoon's conversation. The wit of Wilkes gave charm to every subject he spoke upon. I had to laugh when Potter taunted him about his squint. 'Give me half an hour to make up my face,' Wilkes answered, 'and I'll seduce a woman ahead of the handsomest man in Europe.' Wilkes later made good his boast in Paris, where he tumbled a dame Casanova had unsuccessfully laid siege to for many moons. 'My secret is that I genuinely *like* women. Potter, my dear sir, you do not *like* women, you merely want to fuck them.'

I rather liked the robust agnosticism of Wilkes whom I found to be conspicuous for wit, political flair, journalistic verve, disreputability and scorn for religion.

'I,' he declared with passion, 'can bring Libertinism and Liberty together if anyone can. What you gentlemen are doing is all very well but you have no sympathy with the people. *I* am the one to reach them.'

UNHOLY PASSIONS

Well, I seconded Potter's proposal to elect John Wilkes to our Club though, for the present, only to our Outer Order. Thereafter, Wilkes was made High Sheriff of Buckingham and used his wife's money to buy a house in Aylesbury. Dashwood liked Wilkes sufficiently to make of him his Lieutenant-Colonel in the Bucks Militia he had founded. In 1757, Wilkes would become the Member of Parliament for Aylesbury. Until the crisis came, Wilkes was frequently to be seen and heard enjoying himself at Medmenham Abbey, calling his copious quaffing of wine and fucking of tarts his 'Private devotions'. Although he recognized Dashwood as a man of 'very, *virry* real mental abilities, sir!' Dashwood never saw fit, wisely as it turned out, to invite Wilkes into the Inner Order and the Chapter-Room, which Wilkes late opined to be the place for the celebration of 'the English Eleusinian Mysteries'. Nobody who was not there has come so close to the truth.

'And how do you propose to reach the people, Jack?' Potter was asking slyly as the most famous poet in all of England entered the coffee-house and greeted John Wilkes with a joy that was visibly reciprocated. This was Charles Churchill and it would be hard to imagine anyone looking less like the common idea of a poet. He was as huge and clumsy as a bear with astonishingly thick arms and legs. I knew him slightly since he had visited Medmenham Abbey in the Outer Order a couple of times. Despite the atmosphere of scandal and violence which surrounded his private life, he was unquestionably generous to his friends and charitable to the poor. His latest volume of poetry must have sold exceptionally well, since his talent was blessed by personal animosity, causing him to pen wicked and even vicious social and political satire, and now he swaggered towards us wearing a gold-laced tricorn hat, a royal blue coat, white silk stockings and silver-buckled shoes of gleaming Spanish leather. However, as he approached us, one Sir Archibald Mortimer, a notorious bore who was sitting alone at an adjacent table, jumped to his feet, waved his arms in the air like a monkey and yelled obscenities at Charles Churchill, obviously on account of the fact that the poet had made of him the victim of his satire.

Churchill responded to the stream of voluble insults by walking towards Sir Archibald Mortimer, picking him up as one would a rag doll, slinging him over his burly right shoulder and carrying him outside, whereupon he dumped him in a deep and muddy puddle. We all pointed and laughed at the sight of the wet and wretched Sir Archibald Mortimer and applauded Charles Churchill as he re-entered to declaim some verses:

'From Hell Itself his characters he drew,
And christened them by every name he knew.'

'Sit with us, sir!' Wilkes cried out, 'and you may yet satirize characters from Heaven!'

'Humph!' Churchill grunted, not very poetically, though he took his seat with us.

'Enjoying the delights of Medmenham Abbey, are you, Mr Churchill?' Thomas Potter enquired. Churchill replied in verse:

'Whilst womanhood, in the habit of a nun
At Med'n'am lies, by backward monks undone:
A nation's reckoning, like an ale-house score
Which Paul the aged chalks behind the door.'

'Well, I think that's a bit hard on Paul Whitehead,' Potter commented, but not before he had ensured that Churchill had been brought a cup of the strongest available unsweetened black coffee. 'Let's face it, your enemies state that you exaggerate the offences of your subjects beyond all bounds of

UNHOLY PASSIONS

truth and decency. Why, here you even satirize our sacred Club and our ambitions. Allow me to give you my own answer in verse, sir, and one trusts that you will enjoy in words what you have previously relished in action:

> 'The grasp divine, th'emphatic, thrilling squeeze,
> The throbbing, panting breasts and trembling knees,
> The tickling motion, the enlivening flow,
> The rapturous shiver and dissolving, oh!'

'Why, that is decent enough poetry, sir,' Churchill growled, 'but it all depends upon what will come of it.' He leaned back in his chair, took a gigantic pinch of snuff and sneezed violently, wiping his bulbous nose with a richly embroidered navy blue silk handkerchief.

'I answer your question, sir,' Potter instantly responded. 'Out of our Club will come the greatest government that the World has ever seen or that England has ever enjoyed. Poets of your calibre and artists such as our friend and Brother William Hogarth will be assisted and appreciated as never before. In the reign of a wise, well-educated and patriotic king of One Nation, the people will enjoy peace and prosperity as never before, as the wise few guide the ignorant many.'

'That is my problem, Mr Potter,' Churchill rumbled, 'since in common with my friend Jack Wilkes here,' he glanced at him, 'I think that our élite is no longer fit to rule and that what we require is an educated democracy.'

'Hear! hear!' Wilkes cried out. 'And what's your opinion, Lord Horby?'

'Democracy is certainly a very interesting development, Mr Wilkes,' I replied, 'though I recall that when it functioned in ancient Athens, the vote was limited to all *educated* citizens. You and Mr Churchill appear to advocate the doctrine of: "One man, one vote." In my view, this will lead to mere Mob rule and electoral victory will go to whichever party best pleases, deludes or bribes this MOB.'

'Have faith in the People, sir,' Wilkes answered with the spring of a snapping bowstring, 'for the Voice of the People is the Voice of God.'

'How nice that we all have our differences...' Thomas Potter chortled genially. 'Since the aim of Sir Francis is Liberty, there can be so many divers ways of compassing the matter. I don't think we need to quarrel over Politics, do you, gentlemen? Let us instead discourse regarding matters concerning which we are all agreed. Let me tell you about an absolutely fabulous fuck I had the other day:

'There are undeniable advantages,' said Thomas Potter, 'to being the son of the Archbishop of Canterbury, though my enemies call me the Archbishop of Cunterbury. One advantage is that it makes me Chairman of the Governors at a Church of England school for orphans, both male and female. A most enjoyable day out consists of the Governors' Inspection, when the pupils guilty of indiscipline are duly punished upon their naked fesses. I must admit that these boys and girls over the age of sixteen and begging for employment were most attractive physically. However, some of them had misbehaved themselves; therefore I had along with me a nice little dog-whip with a long lash on it.

'Arriving early after a night's drinking so as to invade the dormitory of the girls, I whipped at the surprised and timid young female beauties so ineffectually that I had only time to give about a half dozen cuts before they sprang from their beds and ran screaming around the room as I followed through fast from my initial clumsy move and plied my whip smartly over their tender bottoms. The sight of the thin weals which every cut drew on their tender skin, the shrieks of pain and the blushing effects on both faces and bums immediately so excited me that I longed to ravish the girls as roughly as possible. Yes,' Potter looked gleeful, 'I confess that at that moment, I felt extremely cruel and should have liked to see these girls suffer the most dreadful agonies under their defloration.

'I know,' he panted, 'that the delight of many men is intensified if they can only inflict pain on the victims they ravish . . . it is so. I gloated over knowledge concerning the sight to come, being literally mad with lust of blood and torture. Having marched in some of the boys, I lined up the girls and made them curtsey, kneel down, unbutton the boys' britches and kiss their pricks as they begged them to take their maidenheads.

'You ask any boy who went to this orphanage of the Church of England,' Potter roared, 'and I bet you, sirs, that he will tell you that his schooldays were the best days of his life. For instance, at this moment, I ordered Dave and Tom to lay Barbara and Ursula upon the soft Turkey carpet in the middle of the room with pillows under their buttocks. Then my two young champions, kneeling between their legs, opened the lips of the girls' wet cunts and proceeded to insert the heads of their pegos within the vermilion clefts of the victims. This was a most delightful sight for me as I witnessed the blushes and enjoyed every painful contortion of their faces as the boys' pricks were ruthlessly shoved into them under the influence of my whip, which I used without pity to push the boys on to victory. At last it was done and I could see that the boys had spent into them and I was sorry it was so soon over.

'The tears of the girls were changed to loving smiles as, by my directions, they all had another kind of hot and foaming wash. Then we sat down to jellies and wine, indulging in all manner of freedoms and jokes, until my boys began to feel their feet again and I dismissed them. My blood was up and I could discern that both the buxom Barbara and the slender Ursula were eyeing me most amorously. Power, gentlemen, is an aphrodisiac to a female. Nothing would do but that I must enjoy them both at once.

'Barbara and Ursula sat on either side of me and my flickering fingers soon informed me that both quims were ready for action. So I made Barbara to be properly sitted upon the fine, stiff prick I proffered and gently requested Ursula to slip a finger into me from behind. I was determined to have it so and the girls succeeded in accomplishing my erotic fancy. Then I wanted to be queened since both girls had such beautiful bums and they took it in turns to sit upon my face as I sighed with the joy of it and licked and kissed their gorgeous buns. All the while they tickled my throbbing prick and my testicles. I tell you, sirs, it is a great joy to be within a hooped petticoat, kissing the arse that you have previously whipped.

'"Enough!" I cried out, discerning that the cunts of both of these lascivious girls were distended by their lusts. I now demanded that I fuck them both, promising them jobs of Parliamentary assistance if only they could please me further. Where do you think most Parliamentary assistants come from these days? Anyway, their job is to ease the cares of State. Naturally, I kept my promise and these former orphans are presently doing well in assisting my Lords Grenville and Temple. But what I wanted to do at that moment was to fuck both their lovely young juicy cunts, plunging in and out of one and into the other, then back again.

'Description fails me in endeavouring to picture the excessive voluptuousness of this conjunction, *trio in uno!* My profuse thrustings so lubricated their cunts that they were soon quite comfortably rubbing up and down my delighted prick.

'"Ah!" Barbara screamed, "Oh! I spend! I die in ecstasy!"

'"Where am I . . . ?" Ursula sighed. "Ah!" she exclaimed as I pronged my rod from one quim into the other, "Heavens! Oh! God! Goddess!! What bliss!" That was when I screamed out and then almost fainted from excess of emotion, only to awaken directly to find the girls also in the frenzy of their emission. The excitement was so great that my champion retained its stiffness whilst the girls, not to be outdone, jumped up and down upon the bed and the voluptuous Barbara, turning again her bottom to my face, in turn buried Ursula's face between her thighs as she pressed her quim to her mouth for a gamahauch.

'My tongue, I assure you, proceeded to enjoy its revels both in Barbara's cunny and within her little pink wrinkled bumhole. Meanwhile, Ursula tickled my prick so exquisitely that I swear that my next shot of spunk hit the curtains of the four-poster bed. They would be excellent ladies for the Club, gentlemen. This went on until sheer exhaustion compelled us to separate: and how I hugged and kissed the pair of them until at last I allowed them to retire to their dormitories. These days they have good jobs and the orphanage boys earn well as runners on the Stock Exchange. We may well mock the Church of England, gentlemen, but it cannot be denied that it gives boys and girls at well-governed schools a decent start in life, especially if they are from impoverished families. More coffee!' Potter bellowed. 'And put more brandywine into it!'

'I was fascinated, Thomas,' Wilkes said to Potter, 'generally by your story and particularly by your delight in being beneath and within the hooped petticoat of a young female. Many events occur, let us face it, sir, in our hunt for the cunt. I am also fascinated by your description of the practice of *queening*, by which a woman places her bottom upon the face of a man and between us all I am reliably informed that this is the favourite practice of Princess Augusta in her conjunctions with our dear Brother, Lord Bute. Then there is the Society for the Promulgation of Petticoat Government . . .'

'Nay, sir,' Potter replied, 'I am not a Mollie.'

'I am sure not, sir,' Wilkes replied, 'since the Mollies are for men who *choose* to wear the clothing of ladies. I am speaking of a regime in which men are *forced* to wear the delicate garb of ladies. I am not a member, as it happens, but I know of some who are, of which possibly more anon. My own experience of petticoats consists of hiding beneath them.'

'What?' said Potter. 'Are you telling me, Jack, that you donned petticoats in order to avoid being stabbed or shot?!'

'Not quite,' Wilkes returned. 'Allow me to explain. This was hardly an occasion at which, like some lordly gentlemen, I was corseted, petticoated, hooped and skirted ... except in a curious way. I was fucking Lady Hester Temple, a most beautiful woman with gorgeous white bubbies, roseate titties and a satin bottom, one twitch of which could bring an erection to any man. Unfortunately, she was also the lover of Colonel Laidlaw, a fierce fan of the duel and accounted amongst the finest fencers and most accurate pistol shots in England. Now, regard my squint, gentlemen. I am an incompetent swordsman and my sight is so poor that I could not hit a barnyard door at ten yards with a blunderbuss. Unfortunately, Colonel Laidlaw returned to Lady Hester Temple somewhat earlier than expected, roaring: "That was a good kill! And I want a good fuck now!" as he stormed up the stairs.

'I am not a coward,' Wilkes stated, 'but any sane man could discern that I did not have a dog's chance in hell, being unarmed and in this particular, unfortunate situation. Consequently I responded eagerly to Milady's bidding, which was to hide beneath the hoops of her petticoats.'

'"Any visitors?" Colonel Laidlaw demanded gruffly as he strode forward to kiss his mistress peremptorily, then strode backward to help himself to a tankard of port. "How're things, m'dear?"

'Lady Hester said very little but obviously pleased him by her gestures, all of which made her petticoats shimmy and rustle as I hid beneath them. For me, there was a further problem since she was not wearing any drawers. Her quim was naked and before me, its intoxicating scent was within my nostrils and I was bewitched by her smooth and silken thighs. As her petticoats rustled, I pressed my lips to her soft thighs and then, brushing her soft down at her pubic mound, I kissed the welcoming lips of her quim and inserted my eager tongue within her gentle cunny.

"'Clever fox,' said Colonel Laidlaw, 'but we got him in the end, m'dear, I can tell you.'"

"'Uhhh . . . ' Lady Hester sighed as I licked her quim slowly. "That is wonderful, darling.""

"'Always been a good hunter,' the Colonel declared."

"'Oh, yes!' Lady Hester gasped as I licked her quim swiftly."

"'I made that kill so swiftly,' the Colonel proclaimed, 'that I still had time to engage in a spot of fishing. Caught a fine trout.'"

"'Wonderful, my dear,' Hester breathed as I started to suck her delectable vagina."

"'And then guess what happened?' the Colonel demanded."

"'I have no idea,' Lady Hester replied as her love juices oozed onto my face. 'But do – uh – please . . . tell me . . .'"

"'With pleasure, my dear!' the Colonel boomed as Hester's petticoats rustled, her hoops shifted and I continued to lick and suck away. 'As I was departing from the river with my catch, I espied a hare lurking in the shadows. Now I am a dab hand with a good fowling piece and so I potted him! Ah! Nothing like jugged hare!' I could hear him taking a deep draught of port and then taking more. 'What do you say to that, my beauty?'"

"'Absolutely fabulous . . .' Hester groaned pleasurably as my tongue flicked fast over her love buttom. 'But did you not tell me that you have an appointment at White's for a game of cards? Surely Lady Luck is smiling upon you this evening?'"

"'She is, Madam, she is!' the Colonel roared with approval. 'I shall therefore proceed to win at cards, return and fuck you," he announced with an air of decisive finality.

"'Oh! . . . how beautiful!" Hester gasped as my tongue probed every inmost recess of her soft and welcoming vagina. She came again as the worthy Colonel Laidlaw left. Well, gentlemen,' Wilkes concluded his tale, 'naturally I had a jolly rogering with the lady, who no doubt enjoyed yet another one when the goodly Colonel eventually came home, but I had somehow found the experience underneath Hester's petticoats to be among the most erotic of my short and wild life.'

'There are not many people I genuinely like,' said Thomas Potter, 'but you, Jack Wilkes, are one of them. Stick with me and I shall get you a safe seat in Parliament. Put a few wise heads together and we can overturn the Government of a nation!'

Unfortunately, although Potter kept his promise in ensuring that Wilkes was returned as Member of Parliament in the safe seat of Aylesbury in 1757, he did not live to see the fruits of his labour. His habits led him to fall ill from a combination of gout, scurvy and palsy. By 1758, he was on a milk diet. According to his friend and fellow necrophiliac, George Selwyn MP, this did not prevent Thomas Potter from spending all night upon a gravestone whereby he caught a fatal chill from which he died in the ensuing year.

His death was a grave loss to the Monks although his legacy would remain with us in divers unexpected ways for many a year. He was both a classic rake and a genuine wit. It is hard to discern any harm he did to anyone in his private life, unless one counts his behaviour in those Church of England schools which are still flourishing. Even here one would argue that orphans were assisted into flourishing livelihoods. Even so, there remains the irony that it was Potter who brought Wilkes into our Circles, who died before he could see us achieve our goal and who, by giving us Wilkes, made our position increasingly impossible to maintain.

UNHOLY PASSIONS

At the time, though, I was obsessed by the notions of Magick and Sex as reputedly possessed by Sir Francis Dashwood and was greatly looking forward to hearing his views this forthcoming Saturday, a day of the week which, I always maintain, should be one for the taking of risks.

CHAPTER FIFTEEN

'I do hope that you are not too hungry, Horby,' Sir Francis Dashwood remarked as the two of us dined together at Medmenham Abbey. 'I was thinking of starting with a potato.' I nodded a slightly puzzled assent and then these potatoes arrived. Bartholemew the butler served them in their rough but honest jackets, having sliced them open and squeezed them in a napkin until the delicious, floury whiteness within each potato gushed out to gladden stout British hearts. Lashings of deep yellow butter and copious quantities of chopped spring onions were packed into each tuber.

'This potato is as the fruits of the Hesperides,' I told Dashwood, since it was indeed so delicious. 'It is not for mortal lips, hardly.'

'Everything is for mortal lips,' Dashwood replied as our glasses were replenished with the finest of wines and the succeeding courses were served. I was amazed by the profusion of my host's hospitality. There was a dish of rabbits, all smothered with onions; a leg of mutton boiled with capers; a side of beef with peas; a roasted goose with some chickens and other game, roasted lobster, a dish of fish with their bellies stuffed with pudding, a currant pudding and a vast apple pie accompanied by thick whipped cream. 'Ale if you prefer it to wine,' Dashwood added. 'And do not worry about waste. I serve an excellent cold table at midday and if anything is not eaten then, why, my servants enjoy the finest pickings in the

World!' He leaned back in his chair and chortled genially. 'But Horby,' he continued with animation, 'you want to know the facts about life, don't you? You want to understand what we are *really* doing within the Inner Chapter? I can tell you. When you have eaten and drunk your fill, come with me, Horby, and I shall show you.'

'Gladly,' I replied, 'though one trusts that there is more port . . .'

'Surely, my dear Brother.' Dashwood passed the decanter and his port was quite exquisite. 'Meanwhile, allow me to tell you an interesting erotic tale. You have of course seen the books in my library, my magical *grimoires* which are simply *grammars*, enabling us to contact *praeter*-human intelligence. There is much scepticism about this matter, of course. These books give one precise technical instructions concerning how one can enter into communication with different orders of being alien to our own customary experience upon this planet. *The Greater Key of Solomon*, for example, invokes the Angels of God. *The Lesser Key of Solomon* evokes the spirits. *The Grimoire of Pope Honorius* and *The Grimorium Verum* and *The Red Dragon* evoke the demons.'

'Excuse me, Sir Francis,' I responded. 'What are angels, what are spirits, what are demons . . . could you kindly explain these matters to me?'

'I shall try to answer your questions as best as I can, my dear Horby,' Sir Francis responded evenly. 'Once upon a time I was asking precisely the same questions myself. I had been told that there was a secret sect in Venice to which I had an introduction and from whom I bought these books, which could give me answers. My connection was via the Borghese family; and it was within a *palazzo* of Venice that I witnessed and learned many extraordinary things. I was invited to attend a Black Mass.

'It was an altogether extraordinary occasion,' Sir Francis

continued, 'and it was all to do with blaspheming the Christian Church. The family in question had in fact purchased a church and therein they gave a good living to Father Giovanni who also was in charge of the neighbouring orphanage. It is said, I believe, that the Black Mass can only be celebrated by an unfrocked Roman Catholic priest. I suppose, therefore, that the Borghese family was blaspheming the tenets of satanism since, to my knowledge, Father Giovanni has not yet been unfrocked. The Church itself was beautiful and I especially enjoyed the sight of the statues, the paintings, the stained glass and especially that of a beautiful girl lying naked upon the altar. The congregation, largely dominated by women, appeared to hate the Roman Catholic faith as much as I do.

'The girls of the choir, whom I was required to inspect, were all dressed in the same costumes; blue silk corsets with scarlet silk laces and short skirts of white tulle, coming a little below the knee, so as to show all the beautiful legs sheathed within black silk stockings and high-heeled boots of glossy black Venetian leather. The outer dresses had been discarded to allow a greater freedom of movement and also a display of the glorious necks and bosoms of the girls, who were young and beautiful without exception, and flushed with excitement and anticipation. Their snow-white globes were heaving at each breath and were set off to the greatest advantage by bouquets of red roses placed between these lovely hillocks of lust.

'Now, there are connections, Horby, between London and Venice, conduits or even canals, one might almost say. As the honorary president of the occasion, it came as no surprise to me that the "virgin" lying upon the altar was none other than our dear friend, Lady Vane, who was looking more delectable than ever. Tall black candles burned as Father Giovanni approached the altar and commenced his hocus-pocus or *Hic est corpus* or whatever. He thrust a communion wafer into

Lady Vane's quim and then proceeded to murmur the Latin Mass backwards and the women moaned as Lady Vane writhed upon the altar. Every time that God or Jesus was mentioned in the ritual, the words "Satan" and "Lucifer" were substituted. Eventually Lady Vane was commanded to pee through the communion wafer as Father Giovanni caught her dripping squirts in the cup of consecrated communion wine.

'"Hail Satan!" the priest cried out.

'"Hail Satan . . ." we all intoned. The chalice was passed between us and so was the defiled bread of allegedly holy communion.

'"Well, my dear Sister," Father Giovanni informed her, "every venal sin you may have committed is hereby forgiven. You are now within one of the most powerful political institutions in the world, powerful because unsuspected, and its members have all sworn allegiance to the Devil." This thin man smiled at her sweetly. "You have sworn to obey us with both body and soul. In fact, my dear Sister, this holy sisterhood into which we have just admitted you will permit you to enjoy every possible sensual pleasure here upon earth and will ensure your heavenly reward as well . . ." The bright light of the candles showed us plainly the blushing face of Lady Vane, which was turning almost crimson as the confessor whispered something to her.

' "Ah! No! No! No . . ." she sighed.

'"The first act of sisterhood is always to do penance directly after admission, and you have taken the oaths to obey both in body and mind. Now you will submit your body to mortification of the flesh."

'It was Lady Betty Germain who stepped forward to make Lady Vane kneel upon a cushion and rest her arms and face on the rails of the altar. Lady Vane – such a fair girl – had nothing with which to cover her beautiful figure and Lady Betty Germain speedily adjusted a bandage over the former's beautiful eyes. Father Giovanni armed himself with a light martinet of small cords, fixed in a handle, whilst Lady Betty Germain eagerly bound her victim, Lady Vane, so as to expose fully her bottom, thighs, legs and back to castigation. Having performed her duties, Lady Betty seated herself upon my own knee, for I had made myself comfortable in a large chair close to the victim. I clasped Betty around the waist and pressed my lips to hers, whilst our hands indulged in a mutual groping about one another's private parts . . .

'The scourge of Don Giovanni before the altar of Satan fell upon the lovely bottom of Lady Vane, each stroke drawing a tender and painful sigh from the victim and leaving long red weals upon her soft and quivering flesh. The "confessor" continuedly lectured her on her future duties and made her promise to perform all his commands. The poor girl's bottom was soon scored all over, the sight of which seemed to enflame us, so that the confessor's affair stood out between the opening of his cassock whilst Lady Betty Germain spitted herself upon my own pego and rode it for a most gallant St George.

'"Now, Sister," Father Giovanni addressed the devout Lady Vane, "for the last mortification of your flesh, you must surrender your all to the Church of Satan." Saying that, he whipped the blindfold away from her eyes and laid her comfortably upon her back for his attack, with an extra cushion beneath her buttocks and in the most approved fashion. Then, kneeling down between her thighs, he opened up his cassock and we could see that he was naked underneath. He laid himself forward upon her gorgeous body, and whispered something in her ear, which was apparently a command to her to take hold of his lustful weapon; for she immediately put down her hand and directed his prick into her crack herself.

'Lady Vane was evidently fired with lust and longing to allay the raging heat of the part which had been so cruelly whipped, for she heaved up her bottom to meet his attack and so seconded his efforts that he speedily forced his way in, and the only evidence of pain on her part was a rather sharp little cry. They lay for a moment in the enjoyment of the loving conjunction of their parts but she was impatient, putting her hands on the cheeks of his bottom and pressing him to herself in a most lascivious manner.

'Just then, Betty and I, who had finished our course, arose. I had seized the scourge dropped by Father Giovanni and Betty had taken a thin cane lying in the corner of the desecrated chapel. She lifted up the cassock of Father Giovanni to expose a brown, hairy-looking bottom and then we both began to lay on to the priest in good earnest.

'Thus stimulated, and begging and crying for us to let him alone, he rammed furiously into Lady Vane, to her evident delight. She wriggled, writhed and screamed out in ecstasy, giving us such a sight of sensual delirium as I have never seen before or since. At last he spent into her and then withdrew herself from her clinging embrace, as she seemed to be trying hard to get him to go on again.

"'Hail Satan!" Lady Vane shrieked.

"'Hail Satan!" we all answered.

"'Fuck the Pope!" said Lady Betty Germain, "though he is probably incapable of fucking anybody anyway." The incense of sulphur and brimstone invaded our nostrils. As Father Giuseppe fainted by the altar, Lady Betty arose from my prick to approach Prince Borghese with her amorous advances. For my own part, I approached the altar upon which Lady Vane was lying lasciviously once again.

"'Now, Sir Francis," she shot me a sharp glance from her dazzling eyes, "no more of your impudent pranks. Pray let me recover my serenity." I responded by kneeling down and taking her hand, which she affectedly tried to withdraw. But I retained it, saying:

UNHOLY PASSIONS

'"Dearest Frances, Lady Vane . . . pity my passion. How can I help loving those killing eyes and luscious, pouting lips? That very fact that we are celebrating the Black Mass makes my determination to enjoy you the greater, Madam, at the first opportunity. It is useless to resist our fate. Why has the Goddess of Love given me such a chance as this?" She turned away her head with affected prudery but not a blush arose to attest to her horror at my speech. One hand of mine pressed her fingers to my lips but where was the other? Under her clothes? No, sir, for she was not wearing any.

'I first touched her ankle and then slowly moved it up her leg. She fidgeted upon the altar but, as always, I was impetuous and soon had possession of her most secret charms. Her suddenly languishing eyes were turned upon me as my own eyes gazed upon her lovely legs and, at the same instant, my lips became glued to hers. My hands gently parted her yielding thighs as I placed myself well between them, which was but the work of an instant. I put her hand on the shaft of lust and she guided it into the haven of love. In fact, we were both so evidently hot and impetuous that it was all over within a minute as the spectators cried out: "Hail Satan!"

'"Hail Satan!" Lady Vane declared. "It has been quite a rape, sir," she added heartily with a throaty chuckle. "But are you capable of doing the dirty deed again? Your first fuck has gone, fled like a shadow, but, sir, you must be mine. I cannot restrain the fires of lust which are consuming me and the very *notion* of sin makes the idea more delicious. Come, sir, if you can!" I always rise to a challenge and her first faint efforts to resist me were useless. "Oh, you're a fine, strong fellow," she sighed. In an instant I threw her back upon the altar and my hands took possession of her longing cunny. The furore of lust was upon me though she made a fair show of resistance and seemed only to yield to force, shutting her eyes as if afraid to see how I was exposing myself.

'I roughly forced her thighs apart and throwing myself upon her, she could feel the hot head of my cock thrusting its way between the lips of her vagina. The bitch deliberately struggled and contracted herself as much as possible but despite her faked and subdued cries of pain, I gradually won my way, which was at the last moment facilitated by her copious spend.

"Ah! Darling . . . how delightful!" I cried out as I lay with my weapon in her up to the hilt, throbbing and enjoying the lascivious contractions to which she now treated me. My lips were fixed to hers.

"Ah!" Lady Vane exclaimed as she broke away, "the soft, velvety tip of your tongue is a tit-bit I cannot refuse." She thence proceeded to suck it until I almost choked for want of breath. I spent again under the stimulating emotions with which she inspired me. Then I lay still for a few moments as we recovered our breath and then, with an upward motion of her beautiful buttocks, she challenged me to go on.

'This was a most erotically voluptuous love engagement. She could not exhaust me. I was continually shooting my love juices into her most insatiable womb and it was more than an hour before either of us would consent to a cessation of the game.

'"HAIL SATAN!" the congregation chanted as we came simultaneously.'

'Sir Francis,' I demanded, 'is it true, therefore, what your enemies say, that you can never lose the smell of brimstone and that you do indeed worship the Devil?'

'Oh, fuck off, Horby,' he drawled lazily as he refilled his glass of port and passed the decanter to me. 'If you believe that, why, then you will believe anything. The Devil does not exist. He is simply the God of any religion one happens to dislike. I don't believe in the Christian God so how can I possibly believe in the Christian Devil? Frankly, I found my

UNHOLY PASSIONS

experience of the Black Mass in Venice to be erotically enchanting yet utterly meaningless in terms of religion.'

'Dashwood,' I said, 'I concur with your view that merely to blaspheme the Christian faith is infantile. However, as I recall, you were to tell me about gods, goddesses, angels, spirits and demons.'

'Quite right, Horby,' Dashwood replied. 'Let us take our glasses and proceed to the Chapter-Room, where you have been on many occasions before.' I nodded and allowed him to lead the way. 'Isn't this Chapter-Room beautiful?' he breathed reverentially as we entered. This was undeniably true. The two of us stood in silence within this sacred space as I admired the stained glass and then the exquisite marble figurine of a naked Goddess, flaunting her charms as she bestrode the altar. Dashwood instantly saluted Her, holding up his right hand with his thumb and first forefinger apart and extended.

'This is the Sign of the Horned God, Horby,' he told me, 'and it is the sign, other than that of the erect prick, most pleasing to the Goddess.' Certainly the statuette reclined lasciviously upon the altar, apparently delighted by Dashwood's devotions. 'Do you see that which is to the left? Death: symbolized by a Venetian carnival mask. Do you see what is to our right? A cross hanging upside down from a string of pearls in mockery of a rosary and a misery. Do you see what is behind the Goddess? There is an open book of Magick though, from this vantage point, one cannot make out its nature. This book contains superb spells and I purchased it in Venice. Returning your attention to the cross, which is of course a phallic symbol perverted by the Christian Church, notice that it is hanging over a shining shield which symbolizes both the Holy Grail and the vagina, which may amount to the same thing. Many delights are spilling out of this shield or cup or disc, including grapes, pears, pomegranates, oysters, sea-shells and other totems of fecundity. Ah, that golden goblet there is spilling roses upon the floor. Oh, and this other one here, the silver one, stands boldly upright and bears a coronet.

'That is the whole point of Ceremonial Magick, sir, you see?' Dashwood rounded upon me, his eyes ablaze. 'Every word, gesture, light, sound, scent, touch and taste is herein dedicated to the Goddess so as to focus the will, imagination, intellect and sense into a blazing stream of pure energy!'

'Admirable, Sir Francis,' I replied, 'and I find myself greatly inspired by your meetings here. But could you please define the beings to which your books of Magick refer?'

'Certainly, sir!' Dashwood responded warmly. 'The Goddess we see before us now symbolizes the all and everything, the plenitude within the Universe. Now, do you believe in God, sir? He is within you, within me, within everything, and it is through the conjunction of God within us and Goddess without us that we attain ecstatic states of consciousness, allowing us great insights into the ways in which we move and live and go and have our being.

'Angels?' Dashwood continued very quietly. 'You do not have to agree with me, but I hold that there *are* extraordinary intelligences way beyond our ken who inspire humanity. Spirits? Yes, I think that there are non-physical orders of being who can help us or hinder us and that books of Magick, if scholarly, give us our best means of essaying communication with them. I think that they are of a somewhat lower order than angels: one might compare them to animals or even plants and stones. Demons? Yes, I think that there are ugly beings eager to suck your very life's blood from you and it is very easy to call up demons since they are always calling *you*. Perhaps they are just things within ourselves to which Science will one day give a name. Meanwhile, Magick has already done so. For my own part, I think demons to be irrelevant as long as one follows the one and only Law which I have found to be true: Do What Thou Wilt. But under that Law, sir, I discern the Law of Nature, the male and the female, energy, *energy*, ENERGY!!!' he roared like a lion. 'That's IT!'

CHAPTER SIXTEEN

'Oh... Horby,' George Selwyn drawled as we took tawny port at Mrs Theresa Berkeley's flagellation brothel in Mayfair, 'I have just witnessed an absolutely fabulous execution. Never seen the like. It was the execution of Damiens who endeavoured to assassinate the French King Louis XV. Unfortunately for himself, he failed and was captured.'

'I do not approve of assassination,' I replied, 'since I think that you are indeed a double ass if you try to murder anybody. But I trust that the execution was swift...?'

'No, no, sir,' Selwyn replied, smacking his thin lips with relish. 'The English have been condemned for hanging a man slowly, leaving him to strangle to death for especially revolting crimes, though in most cases halfway through this matter, whilst the victim is still alive, his innards are publicly drawn from him and burned after which his body is quartered. Our Continental neighbours, however, add subtlety and refinement to the matter. Damiens was given the thumbscrews and the rack prior to the occasion, incisions were made in his arm-pits and thighs and hot lead was poured into these.

'A vast crowd of roughly 20,000 people came to see the public execution of Damiens. Rooms overlooking the square had been booked, for many weeks beforehand and many ladies had arranged for their carriages to be at the forefront of the matter. It was the greatest public spectacle that Paris has enjoyed in quite a while. Myself, I purchased a front row seat yet chose to go there disguised as a woman.'

'Why so, Selwyn?' I enquired. 'I had no idea that you were a Mollie.'

'Oh, on occasion I enjoy wearing the garb of ladies,' Selwyn replied lazily, 'and why not, if it gives one pleasure? A second reason was that I did not want the journals to report that an English Member of Parliament was enthusiastically attending this particular execution. Unfortunately, I had already attended so many in France that the Chief Executioner recognized my face as I was trying to make my way through the pressing crowd to the front. "Mesdames, Messieurs!" he shouted, "let this gentleman through! He is a famous English amateur!" The crowd let me pass by. I was therefore in a good position to view the execution of Damiens. Four wild horses were tied to each limb and then whipped to make them pull his arms and legs apart.'

'How long did it take?' I asked.

'Oh, an hour or so before the first limb – and I forget whether it was an arm or a leg – was torn away,' Selwyn responded. 'The crowd cheered lustily and in due course the other limbs too were torn away. There was much shrieking and some streams of blood. The incredible matter, sir, is that after all this torture, which I greatly relished, the head and the torso were still twitching and living . . .'

'I know, Monsieur, for I was there also,' said an exquisitely pretty woman who had just entered the drawing room of Mrs Theresa Berkeley. She was welcomed warmly by George Selwyn and proceeded to enjoy port with us. 'Poor Damiens was then slit open to the gizzard, his entrails were drawn from him and he died watching them being burned upon a slow coal brazier. We are even more cruel in France than you gentlemen are in England. Cruelty would be so nice – if only it did not hurt so much.' She had a very soft French accent.

Selwyn smiled.

'Madam,' he enquired, 'you are not by any chance the gracious lady who declared her sorrow for the sad toil of the horses . . . ?' Now it was the turn of the lady to smile sardonically.

'Possibly so, sir,' she replied crisply.

'Horby,' said Selwyn, 'allow me to introduce you to a new member of our Club, Charlotte Genevieve D'Eon Beaumont.'

'A pleasure to make your acquaintance, Madam,' I replied as I kissed her right hand, adorned by a kid glove, as she fluttered her fan with her left.

In fact, I was in a high state of perplexity. George Selwyn, though always welcome at Medmenham Abbey despite his peculiar predilections, was not in fact a member of the Inner Chapter. However, on a previous Inner Chapter occasion and owing to the untimely death of Thomas Potter, Sir Francis had initiated and urged us to give warm welcome to the Chevalier D'Eon of France, a startlingly handsome young man. I cannot forget startling azure eyes and I was now virtually prepared to swear that before me sat the Chevalier D'Eon, disguised in women's clothing. Was this personage a 'he' or a 'she'?

'Take your places, lady and gentlemen,' Mrs Theresa Berkeley, the buxom brothel-keeper announced as she swept into the room with a swishing, rustling and crackling of petticoats. 'The port-holes are there.' She indicated round windows whereby we might view the ensuing scene. Selwyn made it clear that he was the host. 'We have a most interesting programme tonight,' our hostess continued. 'It consists of two items. First, a young lady of aristocratic birth has been brought here by her mother for making too free with young lads.'

'The sooner the better, Madam,' Selwyn responded.

'Very well, sir.' Mrs Berkeley left the room, plates of rare roast beef sandwiches with mustard and horseradish sauce were brought, our glasses of port were replenished and, taking our most comfortable chairs, the three of us drew them up to peer with glee through the port-holes and down upon the sight in another drawing-room which greeted our eager eyes.

We saw an elegantly furnished room, the centrepiece of which was a rocking-horse. I recognized two of the women who were sharing a settee and sipping sherry as being the voluptuous blonde, Sarah, and the slender red-headed Mrs Charlotte Hayes, both of whom appeared to be in greedy anticipation of the forthcoming proceedings. A bell rang and the willowy brunette Millicent, wiggling her bottom in an all too enticing fashion, entered the room.

Millicent held a red ribbon in her hand and the other end of this had been tied around the white, swan-like neck of the young lady she led into the room.

'This is Lady Olivia,' she announced to Sarah and Charlotte, 'and for her sexual misdemeanours, she is to be birched. Kindly assist me.' The ladies rushed forward eagerly so to do. I watched the process with not inconsiderable fascination. Lady Olivia had dark hair, and being about eighteen, enjoyed a well-proportioned figure. She was rather above the medium height and had a languid expression and large, pensive hazel eyes. She held a beautiful bouquet of red roses in her right hand and was adorned in a tight-fitting dress of simple white.

Mrs Theresa Berkeley now swept into the room, her arrogant face flushed with excitement. Lady Olivia curtsied to her and proffered her bouquet. Mrs Berkeley accepted this gesture of submission, then motioned to her assistants. Lady Olivia was promptly seized with almost indecent haste and placed upon the rocking-horse where she was bound with thongs of leather.

'No!' Lady Olivia cried as the skirts of her blue satin dress were pulled up to reveal numerous white petticoats of silk and tulle and a hoop, which was swiftly removed. Selwyn, Madame D'Eon and I all praised her white silk stockings, her beautiful blue garters with golden buckles, her smooth thighs encased in rather tight-fitting drawers, prettily trimmed with Valensciennes lace . . . and when these were abruptly whipped away by the ladies assisting at the chastisement, we all praised the beauties of the white, rounded bottom which the rocking-horse of Mrs Berkeley had thrust upwards for our delectation.

'Yes!' Mrs Berkeley snapped sharply. 'Millicent, bring me the birch!' Millicent did so and, with a sly smile, laid it at the shining black leather boots of Mrs Berkeley.

Mrs Berkeley motioned to Sarah, who picked up the rod, prettily tied with a red silk ribbon done up in a bow, and placed it within the right hand of Mrs Berkeley, which hand was swathed by a satin glove of shining silver, causing the candle-light to flicker upon it, thus shooting specks of starlight into the centre of the room. Mrs Theresa Berkeley poised and swished the rod in the air as her mouth smirked spitefully.

'Lady Olivia,' she spoke sternly in a high, clear, cut-glass voice, 'you have been found Guilty of Sexual Misbehaviour, Insolence and Insubordination. You therefore deserve to be punished, and punished by the birch at that. You have been forced to spend all day selecting twigs and then binding them to make a rod for your own bottom, haven't you? You have even obeyed my instructions in wrapping it with a ribbon for you know you must be chastised, don't you, you naughty girl, and upon your bare bottom.' Olivia's exquisite rear writhed at these remarks.

'I hold in my hand,' Mrs Berkeley continued evenly, 'the Wand of Venus.' With her right hand, she whisked it through the air and with her left hand, she whisked her skirts and petticoats in a delicious rustle and crackling. 'The birch is the most ancient, renowned, elegant, poignant, romantic and beautiful of all instruments of physical correction. It is the very symbol of corporal punishment in its most classic form. My dear Olivia, I do not intend to trouble you with too long a lecture, though your castigation will be of a most piquant description.' The nubile young buttocks of Lady Olivia quivered in dreaded anticipation. 'Matters of domestic discipline, which my strict regulations so often bring under notice, require the exercise of my beloved rod. Ladies,' she smiled at her guests, 'I trust that you concur that my cure of recalcitrant girls has brought me very considerable fame amongst a large circle of acquaintances and friends since I have devoted myself to promoting a Ladies' Club exclusively for the admirers of Birch Discipline.

'I hope,' she trilled, 'that for your amusement, I have the means of affording us the most exquisite enjoyment, by bringing out a young lady's modest shyness so we may study her distress and horror at finding herself stripped and exposed for flagellation before the Sisters of the Rod!' With that, the birching began.

'One! – two – three – four!' Mrs Berkeley shrieked as her birch whistled through the air. 'Ha! ha!' she laughed cruelly. 'You will be marked for many a day. I'll wager you will not misbehave as long as these marks remain.' She increased the force of her blows scientifically with each cut and soon enough made her victim's bottom squirm.

'Ah!' Lady Olivia squealed. 'Ah-r-r-re! Have mercy, Madam!' She writhed in such agony, or pretended such, that her bottom jutted higher in the air than I had believed anatomically possible, though perhaps the quivering, straining action of her bottom testified to the intensity of her pain. 'Oh! Mother!'

'That's right, call your mother, she'll soon help you . . . ha! ha!' Mrs Berkeley was becoming visibly more excited. 'She gave her consent for me to punish you as I like. Five! Six! Seven!' She went on counting as she thrashed the girl. All the spectators were greatly moved and enjoyed the sight of Olivia's writhing, scarlet, glowing bottom. The victim's head drooped forward and her moaning and sighing became fainter and fainter and the rod was stopped at the twelfth stroke.

Mrs Berkeley was quite exhausted by her exertions and, with flushed face and heaving bosom, she sank back upon a sofa, fondly to embrace her friend Charlotte, describing to her all the thrilling sensations she had enjoyed during this operation. The glowing face and sparkling soft large blue eyes of Charlotte proclaimed her own appreciation of this spectacle. Meanwhile, Sarah and Millicent untied Olivia and laid her on the floor. Sarah sprinkled her face with water whilst Millicent used a very large fan most effectively. Olivia's lacerated bottom was sponged with salt and water and she soon showed signs of regaining animation.

'Where . . . where am I?' Olivia sighed and sobbed. '*Oh*! I remember. Mrs Berkeley has cut my bottom to pieces. Oh! Ah! How it smarts and burns!'

'Now for the finishing touch.' Mrs Berkeley disengaged herself from her amorous embraces with Charlotte Hayes. 'Sarah, I trust that you have the feathers? And Millicent, have you brought the tar from the kitchen?'

'Oh, haven't you done yet?' Olivia wept piteously. 'What more have I to suffer?'

'Ah. Here!' Theresa Berkeley exclaimed with satisfaction. 'We won't keep you in suspense, you naughty young Miss.' She seized a brush from a pot of warm tar, brought by Millicent. 'This will heal your weals.' Sarah and Millicent brought Olivia to her feet and Mrs Berkeley painted all over Olivia's glowing posteriors and the lower part of her belly inside her thighs and even within the crack of her bottom. Lady Olivia shrieked out in fearful distress and shame at this degradation. 'My dear,' Mrs Berkeley chortled, 'this is to heal you. We're going to cover your bottom with nice warm feathers. You have never felt so comfortable in your life as you will presently.'

This ceremony was both amusing and exciting but it would

be hard to describe the young girl's dreadful shame. Her shrieks and appeals were ignored as the Ladies of the Rod lifted up Olivia and rolled her bottom and vulva in a great heap of feathers, taking care to shove them in everywhere so as thoroughly to cover all the tar. She was thence led from this particular scene of punishment and degradation to another, a white corner. She had to press her nose to the walls, hold the birch, the instrument of her chastisement, with her right hand and with her left hold up her dress and petticoats to display her punished, birched, tarred and feathered bottom.

'Most enjoyable, eh?' George Selwyn's tongue flickered upon his thin, serpentine lips. Madame D'Eon and I nodded our assent. 'What's next on the programme? I believe there is a second item.'

There was indeed, and as we peered through our port holes, we saw that Lady Clarissa Hyde, the Hon. Arabella Marchmount, Lady Mary Wortley Montague, Lady Mary Woolcott, Lady Vane and Lady Betty Germain, all evidently Sisters of the Rod, had arrived to be warmly welcomed with great goblets of sherry. They inspected the punished bottom of Olivia, plucked some feathers and made laughing remarks concerning its changes of colour. Mrs Berkeley swanned around her drawing-room, so inwardly excited, I fear, that her heaving bosom and thrusting buttocks threatened to split her newly fashionable hoopless gown. Further refreshments were served by maids both in our chamber and downstairs, though I could not help wondering why Madam D'Eon was not sitting with the ladies, charming though she was.

There is nothing like a good, chilled German hock to refresh the palate, I find, and this was now served in copious quantities for us to enjoy as the gorgeous buttocks of the feathered Lady Olivia continued to quiver. Both upstairs and downstairs, we were served a banquet of smoked fish: hot, buttered kippers with toast; and salmon, eels and trout with fresh lemons and horseradish sauce. After a while, a very attractive and voluptuous woman entered the room, gazed with approval at Olivia, took some refreshments and then, since she was obviously the mother of Olivia, accepted her daughter's curtsey as the latter was released from her corner, and departed with the young lady swearing her resolve to lead a more sober life in the future.

As we waited for the next show created by Mrs Berkeley, Madame D'Eon produced a golden thumb-screw from her hang-bag.

'You like pain, don't you, Mr Selwyn?' she declared. 'Here, *mon cher monsieur*, let us see how much pain you can yourself endure, for this is graded on a scale from one to ten.' Selwyn accepted the challenge and promptly screwed this fiendish instrument of torture onto his thumb. At 'four' he began to squeal and at 'five' he gave up. I accepted the challenge and at 'five' I began to squeal and at 'six' I gave up. To our absolute stupefaction, Madame D'Eon screwed this dreaded instrument of torture onto her own thumb all the way up to 'ten' without the slightest perceptible sign of pain and both Selwyn and I gasped audibly.

'Gentlemen,' she declared, 'I could say that I succeeded in this matter because I am a woman and women possess a greater capacity for the endurance of pain. I could state that my acquaintanceship with those remarkable men and magicians, Casanova, Cagliostro and the Count of St Germain, not to mention Mesmer, have given me great esoteric techniques. But here is my esoteric technique, which I have in fact learned from the aforementioned.' Her forefinger flicked to indicate a concealed knob within the thumbscrew that rendered it quite useless. 'The moral of this story is never to allow your toughness to get ahead of your intelligence. Ah! I see that there is a Second Act.'

We looked and saw that a dazzlingly beautiful young lady,

who on closer inspection turned out to be the Hon. Emma Featherstonehaugh, was beckoning a somewhat shame-faced but exceedingly handsome young man into the room.

'Behold!' she cried out. 'This is my fiancé, Mr Robert Scrimshaw, arguably amongst the finest of merchant bankers in the City. I am honoured by his courtship and attentions . . . or at least I was until it came to my notice that he was consorting with another woman.'

'Shocking . . .' the Ladies of the Rod murmured.

'Oh, it's obvious, Horby,' Selwyn muttered in my ear, 'the poor chap has gone into debt and needs her in marriage: he must have her title and money in order to restore his fallen fortunes.'

'For his insults to Womanhood,' Emma demanded shrilly, 'I want a Hoop-La! Yes, I want this young man punished, hooped and *petticoated!*' She sipped some hock. 'I want him to understand that he will be hoop-la'd and under petticoat rule from now on and throughout our marriage.'

'Well spoken, Emma,' Mrs Berkeley glanced at Robert and appeared to be erupting in glee, to judge by the heaving of her bosom. She looked at the other ladies. 'Strip him!' she commanded. 'Deprive him of his britches!' With a great cry, the ladies fell upon the male and denuded him. He stood helplessly before them in more ways than one since his prick was stiff, thick and throbbing.

'Hoop-la!' Sarah shrieked and, having seized the young man, the ladies laced him into a tight corset, put stockings and suspenders upon his legs, made him step into hoops, and over these hoops tied on a variety of petticoats variously consisting of silk, satin, linen, tulle and calico, before crowning their endeavours with a silken dress of the brightest pink, tied behind by a big satin scarlet ribbon. I fair thought that Robert would die for shame since his face was virtually as crimson as his dress.

To add to the humiliation, Emma placed Robert over her knee and, whipping up his dress, petticoats and hoops (which were collapsible, as all ladies know to their convenience), proceeded to administer a sound spanking, the strokes of which were echoed by the ladies as their gloved hands came together in delicate applause. After the buttocks of Robert had been turned as crimson as his silken dress, he was made to stand in the corner as the ladies took tea and exchanged gossip. Eventually he was released, he had to apologize to his fiancée and promise to be a good boy in the future and, amidst the laughter and applause of the ladies, the Honourable Emma Featherstonehaugh led him away.

'I do not know,' Madame D'Eon murmured, 'whether the custom of *hoop-la!* and petticoating is more general among the upper classes in England or in France, but certainly what we have witnessed, Mr Selwyn, gives more pleasure, surely, than the barbaric execution of Damiens . . . ?'

'Madam,' Selwyn replied, 'we are all entitled to our various pleasures. I must admit that only two years ago, I was invited to a petticoating in Paris of a very vain and aristocratic young man with royal connections. It was certainly a *hoop-la!* He had a title but no money and she had money but no title. Only women were allowed to witness this auspicious occasion. I was there solely because I can be quite effective in disguising myself as a woman. The young man was duly flogged and stood in a corner as the ladies took tea. However, after half an hour, his affianced beauty approached this young man, standing obediently in the corner and, to the great delight of the ladies present, proceeded to caress him with her cool, long fingers.

'Eventually,' Selwyn continued, 'he began to shiver and shudder at her touch. His entire handsome body quivered when she inserted her hands beneath his skirt and petticoats to finger and tease his rampant penis. His petticoats fluttered delicately as he sighed and came. How the ladies loved it as they exchanged gossip and the young man remained cornered. The Parisians add an undeniable sense of style.'

'Ah!' Madame D'Eon cried out, 'how cruel we ladies can be when we have a man cornered! But Monsieur Selwyn, do you regularly dress as a lady?'

'Now and again,' Selwyn answered. 'Do you?' Madame D'Eon flushed deeply and fluttered her fan furiously.

'What do you mean by that, sir?' she replied stiffly.

'Conceivably it takes one to know one,' Selwyn responded lazily. 'All I am asking is whether in fact you are a man or a woman.'

'That,' D'Eon replied with a rustling of petticoats, 'remains to be seen.'

The results of this meeting were really quite extraordinary. Bets began to pile up as to whether D'Eon was a man or a woman. Selwyn bet heavily that 'she' was a man. Dashwood, Sandwich and I employed agents to investigate the matter. They discovered that this strange personage was born in 1728 and although 'his' baptismal name was Charles, 'he' was also called Genevieve and was dressed in girls' clothing from the age of three to seven. After that, 'he' received a male education. This led to 'his' joining of the French secret service under King Louis XV. D'Eon had thence gone on a mission to St Petersberg, disguised as a woman, and there he persuaded the Empress of Russia that 'she' was a lady. Returning to France in 1758, 'he' became a Captain in the Dragoons but had donned petticoats for a mission to London where nevertheless 'he' had assumed another name and proceeded to give expert lessons in fencing.

No one who dealt with this intriguing individual could doubt that he/she was an able diplomat who would greatly assist us in later years by a substantial contribution to the making of peace with France so as to end the Seven Years War in 1762. Sandwich particularly took a liking to 'her' and, when threats of murder were made, he sent agents to ensure that there was protection. As for the sex, D'Eon kept us guessing since there were no reports of any interest in either heterosexual or homosexual activities. The total sum of bets laid on the matter came to £120,000. (*Editor's note*: This is approximately £6,000,000 in today's terms.)

There was an endeavour finally to settle this matter at Medmenham Abbey, on 24 May 1771. It was agreed by the men that the matter should be decided by a committee of aristocratic ladies. One of our artists subsequently drew a picture of D'Eon sitting on a table wearing a towel, a cocked hat and a French governmental decoration for meritorious service. The ladies are inspecting this person with lorgnettes, magnifying glasses and even telescopes. They declared that they had made 'a most thorough investigation', yet they returned a verdict of 'doubtful . . . ?' All bets were off.

Six years later, a French jury ruled that D'Eon was a woman and she was commanded to wear the clothes of 'her' gender for the rest of 'her' life. 'She' returned to England to spend her old age, one gathered, in the company of a certain Mrs Cole. I always liked her as she helped us in ways to be described and I wish her well.

(*Editor's note:* The 1810 post-mortem made it clear that D'Eon was in fact a man.)

CHAPTER SEVENTEEN

'I have terrible news for you, gentlemen,' a buxom serving wench declared to Bubb-Dodington and myself as she served us with our foaming tankards at The George & Vulture. 'Our dearly beloved King George II is dead.' To her absolute stupefaction, Bubb and I whooped with glee and threw our hats into the air, causing her to spill our brews upon the flagstones.

'Never mind, miss, never mind!' I shouted. 'Bring us more and have one for yourself. We want to toast the health of King George III!'

'It couldn't be better, Horby,' Bubb murmured. 'Why, I have been working towards this moment for years. Ah! *Now* we shall be seeing some good, sensible government!'

Bubb and I became thoroughly drunk that night, fucked a couple of whores and by the following afternoon were fit enough to analyze all the reports. King George II had indeed died as vilely as he had lived: upon a lavatory seat.

There is no point in wearying the reader with the minutiae of the various intrigues which followed and in which, needless to state, Bubb-Dodington played a leading part. The fact is that in 1761, King George III, crowned in the previous year, was able finally to dismiss the Whig government which had governed Great Britain so badly for so long, and as his chief Minister, he appointed his Tutor and the lover of his mother, the Earl of Bute.

Naturally the paid Whig pamphleteers savaged his appointment in the press, calling it the regime of 'The Boot and the Petticoat'. For my own part, since I was privy to certain secrets, I wish to state that however vain 'the Boot and the Petticoat' may have appeared (and certainly the Queen Mother, so to speak, Princess Augusta, was on occasion guilty of arrogance) nevertheless the intentions were honourable. I have never forgotten the meeting that took place at Medmenham Abbey immediately following the appointment of Bute to the highest office in the land.

'Sir Francis,' said Bute, 'I thank you warmly for your hospitality and forthcoming celebration and would wish to appoint you Chancellor of the Exchequer.'

'I am honoured, my Lord,' Dashwood replied graciously, 'though as my friend and our fellow member John Wilkes has said of me: "Dashwood can't even add up a tavern bill." Why, the boys will point at me in the street and jeer: "There goes the worst Chancellor that England ever had!"'

'Sir Francis, you are too modest,' Bute responded. 'There are civil servants to deal with all the details you may find to be tedious. As for John Wilkes, although he may well be a friend to you, I do not share your high opinion of him since I think he is a man of ambition devoted solely to the advancement of his own self: and I thank you for obliging my request *not* to have him among our company tonight. I do not find,' he sniffed, 'his opinions to be relevant to the issues before us. A plague upon his notions of Democracy, gentlemen! I am committed to Aristocracy, rule by the best, government by the wise few for the benefit of the ignorant many. And that is why, Sir Francis, I would be honoured and gratified if you were to assist me by taking the second position in steering this ship of State. There is vital work to be done, gentlemen. The seven years of war with France have cost us dearly although we have emerged victorious. Now peace must

UNHOLY PASSIONS

be made and the war must be paid for. I rely upon the advice of my learned friend Sandwich here so that we can undertake a peace treaty which is to the lasting advantage of British interests. As for party politics, I am frankly not especially interested. Young King George III concurs with my tuition in wishing to be a Patriot King, just as his father Frederick orginally hoped to be. Whig or Tory? A plague on both your houses! I want men around me who put the national interest first.'

'Well spoken, sir,' Dashwood replied. 'Given your attitude, I will gladly accept the position that you have most graciously offered to me.' Bute inclined his head. 'You remind me a little of my dear acquaintance, Lord Chesterfield, who declared: "Talk often but never long for then, if you do not please the company, you are sure not to weary them." Now, sirs, we must feast! We shall have a feast of shell-fish, sacred unto Venus who, as the wonderful painting of Botticelli informs us, emerged out of the seas and upon the sands of Cyprus from an oyster shell. We shall therefore commence by eating oysters!'

'Oysters, Francis?' Sandwich queried. 'Oysters and poverty customarily go together and I usually feed them to my cats.'

'That may be so, John,' Dashwood responded, 'but the taste is absolutely delicious and reminds me so much of cunts. Paul!' he cried out to our excellent Steward, 'ensure that these are served.' Whitehead commanded the servants to do so and we ate them with brown bread and butter, fresh lemon and hot pepper sauce from the Caribbean Islands. 'I'm told that the great lover, Casanova, eats forty oysters a day,' Sir Francis commented. We then enjoyed buttered shrimps, prawns with a mayonnaise sauce, mussels cooked with onions and tomato, cracked and dressed crabs, scampi from the Mediterranean Sea, brought packed in ice; crawfish from the river; and lobster from the sea, all accompanied by portions of buttered spinach and thinly sliced fried potatoes. There were jellies, custard tarts and sherry trifle to follow, all of which were accompanied by white wines sent by King Frederick the Great of Prussia, presently our ally in the war against France, fine claret from Bordeaux, exquisite port from our oldest ally, Portugal; and good brandywine from Spain. 'And now I have another surprise for you gentlemen,' Sir Francis announced gleefully. 'As we have been discussing Politics, ladies have been dining in the room next door to us. Shall they join us?' All the men murmured their assent.

The red-headed Mrs Charlotte Hayes promptly entered the room, leading a team of ladies, at the instant that Sir Francis rang a bell. I noticed that her wealthy husband Joshua was not with her.

'Joshua, Joshua, what a lemon squash you are,' I heard Sandwich murmur.

The women led into the room as we celebrated our seizure of Government were certainly most attractive. All of them were offered further refreshments and all of them gladly accepted this offer. Sarah was a really splendid woman, a blonde with a fully developed figure, prominent blue flashing eyes and possessed of a most sensual chin. The willowy Millicent was also a fine woman with a very pretty, classic cast of countenance whilst the darling Charlotte seemed to be more beautiful than ever. Sarah and Millicent both kissed her with rapture, a gesture to which she lovingly responded. More fine and willing ladies stood behind them.

'Now what is the programme?' Sarah demanded of Charlotte.

'The Abbot and the Prior,' she glanced at Dashwood and Sandwich, 'tell me they are both keeping themselves in reserve for some grand ceremony. What weak things these men are! As if *we* wanted to be kept in reserve! Why, we ladies never get enough: the more we have, the more we seem to require and the less able they become to satisfy us. Talk about women's rights! They ought to compel men to find substitutes which can be used when they can't do it for us.' That said, Charlotte produced from her bag dildoes of monstrous size, made of the finest African ivory, beautifully moulded and finished, with all appendages complete. The ladies eagerly strapped them on as soon as they were charged with a creamy compound of gelatine and milk; and all of them were stripped to the buff . . .

Lady Charlotte took Sarah upon her knee, kissing her lusciously, and handling the dildo as if it had been alive.

'What a fine fellow!' she laughed, 'but,' she smiled slyly, 'not a bit too large to please me.' Meanwhile the fingers of Sarah were busy, nipping and pinching the clitoris of Charlotte. She glued her lips to the latter and appeared fairly to suck Charlotte's breath away. This sight was simply too much for all the men. I could not help rushing at Millicent: she drew me onto a couch and I thrust my prick into her spending cunny, her hot orgasm enhanced by her finely developed clitoris. Her bottom beneath my palms responded to my every shove and this sensation was most delicious. I responded to all her loving caresses as she clasped me firmly by the buttocks, whilst with two fingers of the right hand, she frigged both my bottom and the lower shaft of my prick at once. I thought I had never experienced anything so delectable in all my life and I could not help but notice that Dashwood had jumped upon Charlotte, Sandwich had taken Sarah, and the other men were taking the other women, led by Lord Bute. Pricks of flesh and blood are assuredly preferable to tools made of ivory.

The combination of emotions quite carried me away, what with the lovely woman bounding under me in rapture, and with our luscious kisses, the warmth and exquisite titillations of our sensual arrangements led us to such an acme of bliss that when I finally spent within her, my own nature seemed to melt into a sea of lubricity. After a few moments I entreated Millicent to let me have her stiff clitoris, which I was sure could give me further pleasure.

'Certainly, darling,' she sighed, 'as I often say to Charlotte and Sarah.' By this time, all dildoes had been cast aside and I asked Millicent if she might bring herself forward over my mouth that I might kiss her pussy and further caress that exciting clitoris of hers. This was done at once and I had a glorious view of her paraphernalia of love. There was a splendid mount, covered with glossy black hair: the serrated vermilion lips of her cunny were slightly parted and from them projected a stiff fleshy clitoris as big as the top joint of one's little finger. I opened wide the lips of her quim with my fingers, passed my tongue lasciviously about the most sensitive parts, took that glorious clitoris in my mouth, rolling my tongue around it, and playfully bit it with my teeth. This was too much for Millicent.

'Oh!' she cried. 'Oooh! you make me come, darling!' She spent profusely all over my mouth and chin. She sank down upon me, then adjusted her position. I opened my legs to give her fingers free access. 'Now it is my turn to repay the delicious pleasures I owe you,' she sighed, kissing me rapturously and sucking my tongue into her mouth, so that I could scarcely catch my breath. With her cool fingers she tickled my prick to make it as long and thick as possible, and then, directing its purple knob to her passage, she stuffed it in and closed her affair upon it, holding my throbbing penis tightly within her gripping vagina. I cannot express how delightful this conjunction was to me, for we were both so heated and excited, our spendings seemed to mingle together so as to add to our erotic fury and without separating for a moment, she rubbed and pushed about upon my dick so that the lips and hair of her cunny were titillating my sensitive prick in a most thrilling way. We consequently swam in a thrilling sea of lubricity,

UNHOLY PASSIONS

'Games, ladies and gentlemen, games!' Sir Francis Dashwood shouted. He had obviously enjoyed a very good fuck with Charlotte Hayes. We all agreed to participate and our glasses were charged. The essence of the matter was that all of us had to write our desires upon pieces of parchment and then, having folded them, drop them into a box held by Paul Whitehead, who had previously been busy fucking Dashwood's half-sister, Lady Mary Woolcott.

'Very good, ladies and gentlemen.' Paul Whitehead licked his thin lips as all ballots were slipped through his box. 'Now I draw out the first one and what do we have here? Ah! This must be from a lady, given its somewhat complex nature. The request is that Lady Mary Woolcott sits at the piano here and plays the tune of "Trumpet Voluntary" by Purcell, that everyone circulates and dances; that Lord Bute, our future chief Minister, reclines upon a sofa; and that when the music ceases, the lady nearest to him sits upon his face as everyone else takes their pleasures where they find them.'

'Of course, Mr Whitehead,' Lady Mary Woolcott smiled as she approached the piano, grinning widely as if the piece of parchment had been her affair. She began to play exquisitely well and we circulated around the room. Suddenly I recognized one of the dancing women; it was Her Royal Highness, Princess Augusta, mother of King George III. What an exquisitely pretty lady she was! As her skirts swirled around her, I wanted so desperately to fuck her! My prick was in a brilliant state of erection but she whispered to me as we danced: 'Not yet, Horby, darling, for I must see to my lover here,' indicating Bute, who had stretched himself out languidly upon the sofa earlier indicated. The piano playing of Lady Mary kept us going until, one by one, the couples subsided upon the inviting couches which stood around the room, acting without the necessity of orders. However, as the music ended, Princess Augusta whipped up her skirts and petticoats and then placed her bottom delicately upon the face of the Earl of Bute. All of us watched with interest, since Bute was caressing and kissing the back of his lover whilst this beautiful woman, her eyes languishing with love, was sighing and regarding his stiff, fine cock, which she held in her hand.

'The second request I draw from the box here,' said Paul Whitehead, 'is that you, Your Royal Highness, must kiss every gentleman's affair and then we will initiate you into the mysteries of Venus.' I am sure that this was a request made by Sir Francis Dashwood, but I was delighted by its fulfilment. Princess Augusta, all blushes, took each throbbing pego tenderly in her hand and softly kissed the velvet heads. She then returned to her seat upon the face of Bute and all the men applauded her.

'The third request,' Whitehead boomed, 'is that the Abbot does the same to the ladies.'

'With pleasure, on my knees,' Dashwood retorted: and all the ladies presented their cunnies to his lips, granting him evident delight. Excited by the matter, Bute now arose from his recumbent and indecorous posture, gently inclined Augusta backwards and put a soft pillow under her bottom, then proceeded to place himself in position. Unfortunately, he was unable to restrain his excitability, spending all over her lovely mossy mount and belly, some of the sperm going up to the alabster globes of her heaving bosom.

Bute blushed with shame and vexation whilst Augusta was crimson and gasping with excited expectation. Lady Mary, who was probably the coolest of the company, wiped all the sperm off Augusta's belly with her fingers, with which cream she lubricated her crack: then, taking hold of His Lordship's affair, she directed it properly into the longing gap of lust.

'Shove away!' Lady Mary Woolcott encouraged Bute. 'Shove, my boy. OH!' she added to Augusta: 'Heave up your bottom to meet him, dear.' She laughed; then gave Bute a good, resounding slap on the side of his buttocks. With a furious plunge, his dart of love made its second effort at just the right moment. The collision of Bute's prick and Augusta's vagina was most devastating: her defences gave way as, with an awesome shriek of ecstasy, Her Royal Highness lost all consciousness. Bute completed his conquest of the victim then lay soaking and trying to revive her sensibility by his lascivious throbbing inside of her as the ladies applied salts and other restoratives to bring her round.

She very speedily came to herself, evidently forgetting the fearful rapture of her ravishment. There was a delicious langour in her eyes as she patted Bute's bottom and hugged him to her breasts. He responded to this gentle challenge, making her revel in all the delights of coition and never withdrawing his priapus until they had mutually spent several times.

Millicent now caressed me as we lay upon our couch and the others disported themselves on the same kind of business. My own cock was still as stiff as ever and it was obvious that she longed to feel him within her but to my surprise, she positioned herself the reverse way, presenting her bottom to my face and asking me to press her fine bubbies together, so that I might squeeze them as my prick spent between her gorgeous buttocks. This was a luscious posture and I lent all my ardour to second her fancy, spending in delight so that my sperm deluged her anal canal.

Sandwich, as I recall, had Fanny Murray.

My memories of what subsequently transpired are vague, for I recall only that upon the drawing of parchment from Whitehead's box, a rule was made that if anyone had the same partner a second time, the parchment had to be returned and another plucked forth. Thus we passed a wonderful evening, refreshing ourselves from time to time with port, brandy and ices, or should one state vices? Sir Francis ensured that rare roast beef sandwiches, dripping with blood, were served, for the worship of Venus and Priapus requires continual stimulating with the most invigorating viands. Afterwards the ladies continued fairly to exhaust the gentlemen. I remained very happy with the new administration.

The stage was thus set for magnificent government. Bubb-Dodington was elevated to the peerage as Lord Melcombe. Sandwich was given a Crown sinecure with a promise of returning to the Admiralty in the following year. I was given some minor post. The way seemed to be clear for the new Patriot King, George III. Bute was an old fashioned Tory committed to this ideal, which he hoped his princely pupil would exemplify. King George III was undeniably well-intentioned but he lacked intelligence. He favoured a benevolent, authoritarian paternalism and Bute encouraged him in embracing this notion. The King genuinely wanted to improve the lot of the common people.

Meanwhile Bute ensured that his Medmenham associates were rewarded. Paul Whitehead was given £800 a year as Deputy Treasurer of the Chamber. 'Old Q', the Duke of Queensberry, formerly Lord March, was made a Lord of the Bedchamber, a Knight of the Thistle and a Scottish representative peer. William Hogarth, one of our number whom I think to be the greatest artist of our age, who painted and drew so many of us, was confirmed by the Government as 'Serjeant Painter'. Henry Fox, another member, was appointed Leader of the House of Commons.

Bute informed the King that 'most of our best authors are devoted to me'. He gave 'Dictionary' Johnson a pension of £300 a year; he patronized James Macpherson, who had skilfully faked the Gaelic epic of *Ossiam*; and he assisted that noble novelist, Tobias Smollett, who set up a journal to propagandize on behalf of Bute. It was called *The Briton*.

Unfortunately, our fellow members, John Wilkes and Charles Churchill, were so infuriated by not being patronized by Bute that they set up a rival journal called *The North Briton* which would cause us much grief in the future. More unfortunately, and unlike Wilkes, Bute did not trust the people and therefore never appeared in public without a bodyguard of prize-fighters. Still more unfortunately, the King fell asleep when Bute was explaining to him the importance of arts and letters. Our so-called 'Hell-Fire Ministry' instantly ran into difficulties.

'This new administration has begun tempestuously,' Horace Walpole told me when he served me sherry at his grotesque Gothic castle at Strawberry Hill, near Twickenham. 'My father was not more abused after twenty years than Lord Bute is after twenty days. The coins of the King are the worst that have appeared for above a century and the revenues of the Crown are being soon squandered in the purchasing of dependents. Architecture, that darling art of Lord Bute, has been contracted from the erection of a new palace to altering a single door-case in the drawing-room of St James's.' I never particularly liked Horace Walpole, finding him to be a spiteful prig, but there was some truth in his words, even though they were inspired by jealousy, since none of us wanted to make of him a Monk.

Bute was unused to the hurly-burly of practical politics, the art of the possible. He was Scottish at a time when there was much prejudice against the Scots. 'Sir, I think you are a Scotsman,' Doctor Johnson would in time growl at Boswell. 'Sir, I am indeed from Scotland,' Boswell would answer, 'but that I cannot help.' 'That, sir,' Johnson would retort, 'is a matter which a great many of your countrymen cannot help.'

On this particular night, however, I had every confidence in the regime of Lord Bute and King George III. After a mere two weeks, I was back at Medmenham and making love with the buxom blonde Sarah, in one of the Monks' cells which Sir Francis had so thoughtfully provided. I had put my arm around Sarah's slender waist and drawn her gently down by my side.

'Isn't it lovely . . . ?' I murmured. 'What a beautiful sensation the motions of your bottom give to me!' I kissed her most amorously and thrust my tongue into her mouth whilst one of my hands wandered between her silken thighs and invaded all those delicious hairy parts of the sacred vagina.

'Oh, for shame, my Lord! How can you be so rude?' she exclaimed in a loud whisper. I could judge from the heaving of her bosom that she was evidently in considerable confusion. 'Pray don't, my Lord!' she exclaimed with a sigh as my fingers found out her little clitoris between the pouting lips which her yielding legs had allowed me to titillate. 'Ohh . . .' she sighed. 'I must kiss you all over to prove my love – and certainly there, darling!' She tickled my stiff cock delectably with her forefinger. 'And you must do the same to me. My Goddess! How many women love to kiss my crack! Ah! Ah! Did you never guess, my darling, why some girls are so awfully fond of each other? It is because they are in the habit of procuring from each other all those forbidden joys which married people alone are supposed to enjoy.' She giggled.

Her giggle was wicked yet she was all atremble. My fingers were fairly buried within her slit and making her spend deliciously.

'Oh!' she cried out. 'Oh! I *must* suck it! Every pearly drop that distils from your firm cock is worth its weight in diamonds!' she shouted excitedly, throwing me back at full length on the ottoman, then falling upon her knees between my yielding thighs and gluing her lips to the purple head of my prick. Her tongue revelled in the sensation of my cock's stiff throbbing and when I came, it was with that thick, creamy emission which only real men give up.

UNHOLY PASSIONS

She enjoyed her cock-sucking immensely. How she wriggled and twisted in the excess of her excitement! There was only one problem.

'Magnificent!' I declared, only to see her mouth turn downwards at the corners. 'Here's to wonderful government!'

'It won't be,' Sarah replied, 'thanks to the man whom the King has called "that Devil, Wilkes".'

CHAPTER EIGHTEEN

'Mr Wilkes,' I said, 'what precisely is the nature of the problem?' He was supping ale in an old tavern called The Gun on the south side of the River and certainly we had a most beautiful view over the waters in the shimmering moonlight. He was sitting with the bear-like poet Charles Churchill and although Wilkes bought me a pint of good, spiced ale, their expressions were distinctly unfriendly.

'The Government,' Wilkes replied; and Churchill nodded acquiescence.

'Do you mean,' I drank a deep draught of ale, 'that you are dissatisfied? Why, gentlemen, you have been offered good jobs.' This was true.

'Wonderful,' said Wilkes, whose tone dripped sarcasm. 'Exile to India or exile to Canada.'

'It's well paid,' I replied, reminding myself to keep my temper since I was acting as an emissary for Dashwood.

'So?' Charles Churchill stared at me insolently. 'We belong in England, not in the colonies. Is this the way to treat a poet?'

'Or a Brother at Medmenham?' Wilkes added. Churchill burst into verse:

'Once on a Time, as Fame reported,
When Friar Paul Sir Francis courted,
Thus Francis answered; "You're no Novice,
"You well deserve the Jewel Office.

"A Place of Trust your faith will suit.
"You shall demand it at Laird Boot."'

'That was what I was hoping for,' said Wilkes. 'Disappointing.'
'My message to our Brother Bute is as follows,' Churchill declaimed:

'Your Manners, Morals, Virtues, Grace
Call loudly for a goodly Place.
Success attend you; I'll be blunt –
My dearest Brother there's a CUNT.'

'Come, come, gentlemen,' I endeavoured to smooth over the situation. 'I am quite sure that, given just a little time, good positions can be established for both of you.'
'Positions, sir?' Wilkes squinted at me. 'The positions have changed, in case you had not noticed. Sensible people such as Lady Mary Wortley Montague and George Bubb-Dodington, now the late Lord Melcombe, have died.' I nodded in sorrow. I was genuinely sad about the recent death of a friend who had been a highway leading into the heart of public affairs. Bute had made Bubb First Lord of the Admiralty. 'Joy joy joy to my dearest Lord,' Bubb had written delightedly to Bute, 'this is the greatest happiness I could wish for in this life.' As for Lady Wortley Montague, I had attended her funeral, as I had that of Bubb, and I was grieving for both. Dashwood had told me that Bubb, somewhat worn out by years of dieting on drink and dames and making frantic endeavours to match our scores of fucking delicate damsels, had died falling down a flight of stairs at home. The comments of Wilkes jerked me from reverie to reality. 'Bubb controlled roughly 150 allegedly independent seats in the Commons, maintaining Bute in power,' he said. 'Lady Mary Wortley Montague had influence over roughly the

same number in the Lords. What will happen now?'

'Bubb,' I replied, 'has appointed Sir Francis as his executor and has given him a legacy of £500 to erect a monument to their friendship. Sir Francis is presently constructing a six-sided mausoleum upon his lands at West Wycombe and our dear friend and Brother will be the first to be laid to rest there. Another legacy is the excellent government of our Brother, Lord Bute.' Wilkes and Churchill burst into shrieks of hysterical laughter.

'Dashwood shall pour from a communion cup
Libations to the goddess without eyes.'

Churchill murmured.

'Times have changed, sir,' Wilkes hastened to assure me. He then ordered platters of chicken legs and chops of pork and lamb to be brought to us, accompanied by bread sauce, mint jelly and apple mash. These dishes were delicious and I wondered who was helping Wilkes with his well-known debts. 'It is Democracy,' he declared, 'that is my vision of the future, not the Aristocracy of Old Boot.' His teeth chewed into a lamb chop so forcefully that the blood ran down his lean chin. 'Take our dear Brother George Selwyn. Few matters have troubled his tranquil life until the 1761 election of last year. Two of his voters were *murdered*. The agent for his rival was a man called Snell who apparently lured the intended victims into a post-chaise . . .'

'Where,' Churchill took up the story, 'being suffocated with the brandy that was given them, and a very fat man that had the custody of them, they were taken out stone dead.'

'One wonders if Selwyn rushed to see the corpses,' said Wilkes, acidly.

'I do not know,' I responded, 'for he did win the election.'

'But for how long?' Wilkes replied.

'Mr Wilkes and Mr Churchill,' I retorted somewhat

exasperatedly, 'why do we not come to the point? It strikes me that you are malcontents. Your *North Briton* journal has printed nonsensical criticism concerning Bute's Treaty of Paris which has ended seven years of war with France. The triumphs of Clive in India, Wolfe in Quebec and Hawke's naval victory over the French at Quiberon Bay have given England the French surrender of all claims to Canada, Nova Scotia, Grenada, St Vincent, Dominica, Tobago, Senegal and all lands and rights in India acquired since 1749, largely by our Vansittart Brothers, which means most of Bengal. France has furthermore agreed to cede the strategically important Mediterranean island of Minorca and Spain has agreed to cede Florida to Great Britain. I concur with Bute's statement that he hoped that his achievement of a noble peace would be inscribed upon his tombstone.'

'The sooner the better,' Churchill muttered.

'It is,' said Wilkes, 'the Peace of God – or some would say "cod" – which passeth all understanding.'

'How so?' I demanded as I called for more spiced ale.

'Cod fishing rights off Newfoundland have been surrendered to the French,' Wilkes answered smartly. 'The sugar islands of St Lucia and Guadalope have been surrendered to France. Havana, Cuba, which we have captured, is now surrendered to Spain. Our principal ally, Frederick the Great of Prussia, fighting our battles upon the Continent of Europe, has been most shamefully betrayed and abandoned as we leave him to fight his own. And you are telling me, sir, that this is "Peace with Honour"?'

'It was a tight vote, wasn't it, in the House of Commons, sir,' Charles Churchill rumbled. 'And was it not managed well? A shop was publicly opened at the Pay Office whither the Members flocked and received the wages of their venality, even to so low a sum of two hundred pounds for a Member's vote upon the Treaty. Twenty-five thousand pounds,' he snorted indignantly, 'as Martin, Secretary of the Treasury, assured me only the other day, were issued in just one morning. Lord Horby,' he smiled bitterly, 'a vast majority of Members was purchased to approve the peace.'

'Well,' I fumbled for some way in which I could make peace with *them*, 'it's done now and the consequences make for interesting discussion. But why are you circulating pamphlets attacking our goodly Chancellor, Sir Francis Dashwood?'

'Because of his useless Budget, you bloody fool, Horby!' Charles Churchill bellowed at me. 'Dashwood stated: "I am not for an extension of the excise laws but for an enlargement of them." What the fuck does that mean?' I could find no answer. 'Then he puts a tax upon cider!'

'We are paying for the war, gentlemen,' I replied, 'not for this excellent peace. The Chancellor, as I understand it, proposed to raise £3,500,000 via annuities at 4½% and a gentle tax upon cider which can be easily afforded by the farmers of the West Country and by those who sell it.' Churchill scorned my argumentation by resorting to verse.

'The King was going to Parliament
A numerous crowd was round him.
Some huzza'd him as he went
And others cried – confound him!
At length a shout came thundering out
Which made the air to ring, Sir;
All in one voice cried no Excise,
No BUTE, no Cyder King, Sir.'

'The London Mob will finish him,' Wilkes said.

'The Mob, thank heavens, does not have the vote,' I replied. 'This privilege is fortunately confined to men of property.'

'But for how long?' Wilkes demanded. 'There is a growing movement, sir, for Parliamentary Reform. In the meantime, which becomes meaner all the time, since voting is public, the muscle of the Mob is employed so as to swing elections. In London, especially, it is vital to secure the backing of the Mob, for they are a lawless lot with little to lose. If they were to riot, honest citizens might well vote for a change of regime. I know this but Bute does not.'

'I think, Mr Wilkes, that you are over-estimating your power as a demagogue,' I ventured, 'but be that as it may...'

'And it may be...' said Wilkes.

'We should all surely come to a general and genial agreement,' I continued. 'If I could secure good positions for both of you in the Government, would you not agree to become less critical?' Both men nodded. 'Good, so we're all agreed and I shall see what I can do.'

'Not so fast, sir.' The voice of Wilkes cracked the temporarily gentle silence as if it were the crack of a whip. 'We wish to enter the Inner Chapter-Room.'

Upon ensuing reflection, I wish that I had not endeavoured to be a diplomat and intermediary. If only Bubb-Dodington had been there to help me! As it was, I soon enough secured promises that Wilkes and Churchill would be taken into Government and into the Inner Chapter-Room. The consequences of my diplomatic skills were unfortunately utterly disastrous, as will be told.

On that particular night, however, I needed to stroll alone through the damp yet bracing London air. Seeing a night-watchman bearing a lamplight, I simply decided to follow him, treading my way over the drunkards, prostitutes and orphans lying in the gutter, until I came to an establishment with the following sign;

'DRUNK FOR A PENNY.
DEAD DRUNK FOR TUPPENCE.
CLEAN STRAW FOR NOTHING.'

My experience of gin palaces was limited so I decided to

expand upon it. Here was where the London Mob Wilkes desired to enfranchise spent hours of leisure. To my surprise, the interior was most enticing. There were wax candles in profusion lending a garish glitter to this place, regularly denounced from the pulpit as a 'Temple of Sin.' Mirrors reflected the flickering light and around the marble walls – or walls that purported to be so – there were exquisite portraits and engravings of gloomy landscapes. A pianist was playing delicately as upon a raised platform, a number of pretty girls were slowly denuding themselves of their clothes to raucous cries of encouragement from the spectators. Since I was not sure precisely what to order, I followed the man before me in the bar and asked for a pint of gin, which cost me one penny.

I began to feel a little dizzy after one quarter of my pint, the taste of which was not especially in agreement with my palate, and started to inspect the company further, since I wanted a woman to fuck. I noticed two wicked, sexy bitches seated upon a sofa and making eyes at me. Being well flushed with gin, I approached them and, upon receiving their smiles and acquiescence, I sat down upon the sofa between them and impudently put an arm around each of their tightly corseted waists. They both had delectably low cleavages, they were both blonde and indeed, it was hard to tell the difference between Jane and Eleanor, whom I thought to be more concerned by the quality of my clothing and the size of my purse than anything else. I urged them to neglect gin in favour of the sparkling champagne wine of France, to neglect oysters in favour of hearty beefsteak and kidney pudding, since it appeared as though they were lacking in nourishment, and to neglect a return to the slums in favour of a night in warmth and comfort.

Once I had them at my home, I gave the ladies vintage port.

'Thank you,' Jane softly whispered as Eleanor sighed, laying one hand on my thigh, most near to an important member. This action, or possibly the combination of gin, champagne and port, caused me to be so tempted by the proximity of such female charms that I fell on my knees, clasping their lovely legs as I buried my face in the lap of Jane. They appeared both to be trembling with emotion and I was equally agitated but I guessed from their looks and manner towards me that the present moment was too favourable for them to let it slip.

'Oh! Oh! For shame, sir!' Eleanor cried out. 'What liberties! Will you?'

'*Will* you . . . ?' Jane murmured as she fidgeted about since both my hands were busy. 'Ohh . . . what do you want from me?'

'Be ministering angels to my impulsive passions!' I shouted, taking advantage of Jane's confusion to gain possession of the grotto of lust. I felt her soft but hitherto tightly compressed thighs relax in their resistance and she uttered a spasmodic sigh. I then victoriously advanced my rude right hand also to feel the mossy retreat of Eleanor. 'Ah!' I sighed. 'How delicious to have possession of a double set of the loveliest charms. I shall kiss you and enjoy you by turns,' I added, enraptured by the prospect before me. Pulling up her skirts and petticoats, I threw Jane backwards on the fourposter bed and released my bursting weapon, then threw myself between her yielding thighs as I exclaimed: 'You have indeed relieved me of the duty of making an invidious selection and as I cannot restrain the heat of my passion, Jane must be my first victim!'

It was quite dark upon the bed, especially when Eleanor drew the curtains, and as my lips sought those of the lovely Jane, her entire body seemed to quiver under me and she uttered a shriek as the head of my cock first touched the lips of her cunny. As if I did not know that she had long ago lost her virginity! Eleanor then took my affair within her hand and her touch added to my excitement. She kept drawing the foreskin back and took care to present the head rather above the proper entrance to the vagina, to make me think that the resistance I felt was genuine, but it gave me great pleasure and made Mr Pego spend all over the entrance of Jane's longing quim. At last, after great simulated difficulty, they let me fairly in and I asked Eleanor still to keep her hand there so as to stimulate my exertions. Thence I spent more excitedly within her than without her, whilst the dear girl was a constant flood of lubricity and seemed to melt with lust, clinging to me with all the tenacity of her voluptuous force.

At last, notwithstanding Jane's entreaties to go on, *on*, ON! I managed to withdraw.

'Jane, darling,' I said, 'I will still give you pleasure with my tongue.' Thence I made her give way to Eleanor, who eagerly slipped off some of her skirts and petticoats to give me, so she said, a greater freedom: but in reality it was for her own greater enjoyment. Her pussy was quite wet with the spendings which had flowed in sympathy with our enjoyment. Jane quickly arranged herself over Eleanor's pretty face, so as to present her own excited cunny to my lips.

Eleanor had an extraordinary gift of contraction in her vagina. It took hold of my cock, like a delicately soft hand with a frigging motion as she wriggled and met my thrusts. I grasped and moulded her beautiful breasts with both hands, for she held me convulsively to her body. Our conjunction was so exciting that I spent again under the touches of her hand then, steadying myself, I revelled in lust and lasciviousness for more than an hour, having both these sweet ladies gasping, sighing and sometimes, when they spent, giving vent to shrieks of pleasure and endearment. Eleanor was quite as excited as Jane, whom I discerned to be frigging the other girl's bottom-hole with her tongue and rousing all her lustful propensities to the utmost. I do not quite recall how we finished for there seemed to be no end to it but we eventually awoke from a loving lethargy. I gave them gold sovereigns and they went back to the slums, but not for long, since upon account of my recommendation, they were soon earning many more golden sovereigns in the employment of Mrs Charlotte Hayes.

Jane and Eleanor were both there and looking well at the next fateful meeting at Medmenham Abbey. The same was true of Charles Churchill and John Wilkes. Dashwood had sent word that matters of State detained Sandwich and himself and that in the meanwhile, Paul Whitehead would be, as was customary, Steward of the proceedings. Whitehead duly ensured that we were all served with sherry, the choice being the dry *fino*, the salty *manzanilla*, the medium dry *amontillado* – that glorious 'sack'' that Falstaff extols in Shakespeare's plays – or the sweet and creamy *oloroso*. With our beverages were served anchovies, sardines, pilchards, sprats, smoked trout and poached salmon. Meanwhile Whitehead proposed that we play a game, and the prize for the winner would be a platter of fried whitebait followed by baked whiting. I was not quite clear regarding the rules but his game was most enjoyable.

Lady Clarissa Hyde presided at the piano where her brilliant execution helped to hide the excitement engendered by the lascivious motions of the dance. As far as I could see, Paul Whitehead was the referee, indicating when the ladies and the gentlemen should change partners as we went through the figure. As I understood the matter, it was quite within the rules to elevate the ladies' skirts and to give their bottoms a fine smarting spank, which the ladies repaid by sharp little flicks on the extended cocks of the men. We all soon grew tremendously excited over our quadrille and it was apparently part of the rules for Whitehead to kiss all the ladies' palpitating cunnies. The ladies, for their part, could scarcely

UNHOLY PASSIONS

restrain themselves sufficiently to allow him this liberty.

It was not quite clear why and how as we twirled in time to the piano trilling of Clarissa, but some men – possibly for not keeping time – were ordered by our referee to lie upon sofas and various women were then ordered to sit upon their faces. A death worse than fate? I doubt it. For my own part, and I do not know what error of dancing I may have committed, I was ordered to sit down, unbutton my britches and expose my rampaging cock. To my delight, the beautiful Arabella Marchmount was ordered to kneel down and suck it. Her licks were exquisite. It was a delight to poke my prick within her prim lips, come in her mouth and to send my shower of sperm gushing all the way down her deep throat.

By the time this game finally ended, Lady Clarissa was still playing the piano with her bottom upon the face of one of the Vansittart brothers. Every woman in the room was either sucking the cock of a man or else having her bottom licked by a man, apart from Paul Whitehead who was both having his cock sucked by Jane and licking the arse of Eleanor. After we had all come to our great satisfaction, he announced that all of us had won and that the prizes would be presented to everybody.

The whitebait and the whiting may be counted amongst the most delicious fish that I have ever tasted.

I was subsequently relaxing with a glass of sherry and speaking pleasantly with John Wilkes and Sir Henry Vansittart, which latter told me that he had brought a baboon in a basket from Bengal as a present to the Club, when our Abbot and our Prior entered, both Dashwood and Sandwich alike roaring out warm greetings to ladies and gentlemen, Brothers and Sisters. Both of them were visibly in a very good mood and why should they not be? With Bute as Prime Minister (he was having his cock sucked by Charlotte Hayes with consummate skill), we were running the country.

ANONYMOUS

'Ladies, gentlemen, Brothers, Sisters!' Dashwood roared. 'Today there will be two innovations in terms of our rules. Firstly: *all* may enter the Chapel of the Inner Chapter here. Secondly, we will be essaying an experiment in Magick and the Prior is in charge.' Little did I then know of the dreadful consequences to which this experiment would lead.

'We shall,' Sandwich said with a wicked gleam in his eyes, 'invoke Satan.'

CHAPTER NINETEEN

All preparations were duly made in order for the experiment of Sandwich to be conducted. I was curious about the matter and noticed that John Wilkes ensured the basket of Sir Henry Vansittart was carried into the Chapter-Room.

For my own part, since I do not believe in Christianity, I have always found satanism to be infantile. The ladies, however, were finding it to be exciting and were whisking their dresses in pleasurable anticipation. I agreed to participate as I would in any scientific experiment.

The logistics were arranged by Sandwich and Dashwood took a passive part. We donned our robes and entered the Temple to see that gorgeous buxom blonde, Sarah, spread-eagled upon the altar with her legs apart, proudly displaying her gorgeous quim. Sandwich then proceeded to chant the Catholic Mass backwards and I became as bored as if he had chanted it forwards. Certainly matters became more interesting when he withdrew to place his arm around Fanny Murray and handsome Sir Henry Vansittart, on leave from governing Bengal, stepped forward to fuck this lovely woman. Sarah writhed and wriggled upon the altar in a manner that could grant a pulsating erection to any healthy man.

Now Sandwich insisted upon a parody of Holy Communion. A wafer was placed within her cunny. When it was well-soaked by her juices of lust, this was placed within a chalice of wine with the utmost solemnity and passed around for all of us to eat and drink. Actually, the wine was excellent and the wafer was delicious.

'Hail Satan!' Sandwich cried out, standing manfully with his arms upraised before the altar, 'We have honoured you. Now come down and appear before us!'

It was at this point that John Wilkes, sitting at the back, tore open the mysterious basket of Sir Henry Vansittart.

'Come, Satan, come!' Sandwich screamed. 'I *dare* you to come among us if you dare!'

It was at this instant that Wilkes cackled with laughter as Sir Henry Vansittart's baboon leapt out of its basket and, being enraged by its long confinement, sprang at the back of Sandwich and tumbled him to the ground.

'Aargh!' Sandwich shrieked, turning to see this fearsome form. 'Mercy! Be off! Oh, for the love of Jesus ...' He fell to the floor with the baboon sprawled over him, squawking out his fear. Whitehead, Vansittart and I rushed to his assistance to pull this creature away from him. The baboon scratched and fought and we needed more strong men to subdue it and force it back into its basket as Sandwich lay quivering in shock upon the marble floor and Wilkes and Churchill remained convulsed with laughter.

'Brother John and Brother Charles ...' Dashwood had turned quite white with inner fury though he spoke calmly, 'would you kindly leave the stage?'

Wilkes and Churchill duly departed, sniggering like schoolboys.

They had made a farce of the meeting and it was all so embarrassing for all concerned that I left as soon as I decently could. Perhaps the worst aspect of the matter was that most of the ladies had found this outrageous incident to be most amusing and had visible difficulty in containing their mirth. Dashwood declined to speak with anyone and left even before

I did. The consequences of this matter were to be horrendous.

It had been a fiasco, a term we receive from Signor Fiasco of Italy. He is an impresario who promotes Opera, a word which can be translated as meaning 'The Works'. Unfortunately, on every single occasion whereby an Opera was presented by Signor Fiasco, the scenery fell down, the curtains collapsed, the prima donna had a bad sore throat, the tenor was belching and the baritone was farting. Hence one calls a disaster a *fiasco*.

Wilkes and Churchill proceeded to mock Bute's Ministry in their publication, *The North Briton*, causing the London Mob to riot against the regime of 'The Boot and the Petticoat'. Bute could take neither the repercussions of this rioting nor the acidity of Wilkes and Churchill. Wherever he went, he was publicly hissed and stones were thrown at his carriage. This upset him dreadfully since Bute genuinely felt that he had exercised his abilities so as to benefit the finances and foreign policy of our nation. He promptly proceeded to solve his own financial problems by marrying the daughter of the coal magnate, Edward Wortley Montague, which brought him a dowry of one million pounds.

'I wish to retire from the World before the World retires from me,' Bute stated as he resigned from office and I have not seen him since.

Lord Grenville, no friend of Wilkes, was appointed Prime Minister by King George III. Dashwood, was relieved of his duties as Chancellor and created Lord le Despenser, the premier Baron of England. Lord Sandwich, vowing vengeance upon Wilkes for what he regarded as being a betrayal of shared ideals, was reinstated in his beloved position as First Lord of the Admiralty. No offer of office was made to Wilkes, who went wild.

Number 45 of *The North Briton*, edited and largely authored by Wilkes and Churchill, was issued on 23 April

1763. It damned the Government as a group of degenerate and corrupt time-serving hacks who were looting the nation for their own grubby ends. The Government replied by issuing a General Warrant for the arrest of the publishers, editors, authors and printers, indeed all those connected with *The North Briton*.

'Those few,' Wilkes responded, 'those very few, who are not afraid to take a lover of liberty by the hand, congratulate me on being alive and at liberty.' This man then proceeded to arouse the London Mob once again. The address of congratulation had to be presented to the King customarily by a delegation representing the City of London: and these men were booed and hissed by the Mob all the way to St James's. Wilkes was promptly arrested and imprisoned in the Tower of London. The authorities had to release him in May 1763, since he had fought back legally and *Wilkes's Case* has established the illegality of a General Warrant. The Government can no longer arrest or imprison anyone suspected of subversive activities without even naming him or her.

The London Mob saluted Wilkes with fireworks and a procession, and cries of 'WILKES AND LIBERTY!' rang throughout the streets of London.

For my own part, I could hear these cries from the street as Sandwich and I proceeded to the notorious brothel of Mrs Theresa Berkeley.

'I shall *crush* that insolent man!' Sandwich said to me. 'I shall employ all the resources of the Government to *smash* Wilkes. I have challenged him to a duel. Will you be there to witness it in Hyde Park?'

'Of course, Sandwich,' I replied, 'so that I can see fair play. But meanwhile let us see what Mrs Berkeley has to offer us.'

To my astonishment, I was informed as we entered the Mayfair establishment to partake of good manzanilla sherry wine, that the victim of tonight, at the price of a thousand guineas to spectators, would be our new Prime Minister, Lord Grenville. Mrs Berkeley, all resplendent in a fine dress of silvery silk imported from Bombay, bade us to wear masks and be seated. It looked at though her beautiful breasts would burst out of her dress and her bottom showed signs of endeavouring to split her skirt seams. Grenville, who was surprisingly slim, was marched into the drawing-room by three beautiful young girls: I recognized Sarah the blonde; Millicent the brunette; and Charlotte the red-head. All three were pointing to a fine *Berkeley Horse* which one knew at Medmenham Abbey and which was now being wheeled into the centre of our lady's chamber. It was a thing somewhat like a common pair of steps, only covered with red baize and provided with a cushioned footboard on which the victim could stand, whilst his hands were well stretched above his head, so as to allow only of his standing on tiptoe. Grenville stepped forward gallantly and was instantly secured by his wrists to the topmost rings of the horse.

Mrs Berkeley, grinning with delight upon having our Prime Minister at her mercy, tightened the cords unmercifully, causing Grenville to expostulate with her at the painful tension.

'That is nothing, my boy,' said Mrs Berkeley. 'Do not cry out before you are hurt. Wait until you feel the rod tickle and warm your posteriors. It will do you good for it is the most invigorating thing in the world.' All her girls were now furnished with beautiful bunches of long, thin, elegantly tied-up birches.

'Now, sir,' said Sarah, stepping to the front, 'mind you answer my question under pain of severe punishment. I am told that you are against the Medmenham Monks. Now, my Lord, what do you say to *that*?' She gave his bottom a smart cut, which made him wince with pain and left a long red mark across the white skin of his manly buttocks.

'My God!' Grenville exclaimed. 'You punish without waiting.' Before he could speak further, all the ladies attacked him with their rods, raining a perfect shower of painful cuts upon his helpless bottom.

'Answer!' they shrieked gleefully. 'Answer!! ANSWER!!!'

'No prevarication!' Mrs Berkeley screeched as the Prime Minister's noble bottom jerked, writhed and wriggled beneath female birching. 'Don't spare him! Cut away, ladies!'

'Hold!' Lord Grenville gasped. 'Hold!! Don't kill me!' His bottom was scored all over and little drops of blood trickled down from where the skin was broken.

'Well, my Lord,' Millicent lisped, 'pray excuse our virtuous indignation if you are not really against the Monks of Medmenham. But how about a Government you intend to build for them, eh?' And she cut him with several deliberate strokes as she was speaking, each one making him quiver under its smarting force.

'Oh!' Grenville squealed. 'I shall try...'

'But my Lord,' Millicent said, 'allow me to drive all foolish thoughts from your mind. Can you not think of better applications for Government money? Will you promise me not to make of yourself a fool?' She was cutting harder and harder at every moment until he fairly howled with pain.

'Ah! Oh! Damme!' Grenville expostulated. 'How cruel of you, Madam! Ah! Let me off now! I will do everything I can for you!' The red-headed Charlotte stepped forward, swishing her petticoats and swinging her birch.

'Beg my pardon instantly, Lord Grenville,' she demanded, 'or you shall feel what cruelty really is like. Cruel indeed! To a young lady who is only doing her painful duty.' Catching hold of a fresh rod, Charlotte slashed his bleeding bottom with all her might. Grenville writhed his body about in dreadful pain yet his fine cock stood out rampantly in front, in a most outrageous state of stiffness, the head quite purple from the extraordinary pressure of blood which distended it.

'Ah!' Grenville cried out, 'ah! oh! oh! I do beg your pardon. I trust that you will forgive me and let me off now...' he groaned in agony. Mrs Berkeley now marched forth into the centre of the floor, swishing her birch.

'I have only a trifling thing to ask you now that you have apologized,' she said coolly and calmly. 'My duty is far more painful and disagreeable to me than it can possibly be to you. Bodily suffering cannot for a moment be compared to anguish of mind.' This remark did not prevent her from furthering her cuts into his raw-looking posteriors and looking delightedly around the spectators for encouragement. 'Will you help the Temple?'

'*Oh!*' Grenville was gasping in pain. 'Oh! Yes! That I will! Fifty thousand from the Government if you let me down at once...' he sighed. 'And good places for good placemen!' There was a general clapping of hands all round.

'Enough! Enough!' the women cried out. 'He's a good boy now.' Sandwich and I proceeded to tumble respectively Sarah and Millicent, lashing into them most unmercifully as they laughed and shrieked out:

'Keep the game alive! Keep the game a-LIVE!' Mrs Berkeley had meanwhile let down poor Grenville, who was into her in a trice, to the dear lady's great delight, both of them frequently spending and screaming with ecstasy.

I threw Millicent across my knee and made her bottom smart beneath my loud slaps. She screamed and struggled desperately and at last endeavoured to equalize measures by grasping my stiff cock. She was sitting by now with her slim buttocks upon my lap and she placed my pego right up into her vitals. I clasped my arm around her, taking the globes of her bosoms within each hand and moulding them delightedly with my fingers as she rose and fell upon my shaft, leaning back her head so as to meet my kisses and give me her tongue.

This was a delicious position since my spendings shot with extraordinary force into her quim and her own love juices fairly drowned the hair around the roots of my pego. At last we all stopped temporarily from sheer exhaustion. Mrs Berkeley gave Grenville quite an amorous kiss as she led him to a sofa, pretending that she did it to put him at his ease. We all followed her example, Millicent excitedly returning my embrace with ample interest and ardour, her hot burning lips sending a thrill of desire throughout my frame.

Pretending to wish to cool myself a little, I walked Millicent into the next room, which was only lighted by the brilliant moon, and we opened the window, which looked out over a lovely garden, and then sat in a rather dark recess to enjoy the slight breeze, which was loaded with the perfume of flowers and had a soft, sensual effect upon my excited nerves as I longed to enjoy my young partner once again. Despite the lasciviousness of her quim, her manner was so prim.

'Dear Lady,' I addressed her, 'did you but know the intense pleasure which your lips have afforded me, you would hardly think that my kiss was thrown away. I expect you just did it in fun.'

'Silly man,' she laughed in a whisper, 'I shall give you another here in the dark.' She kissed me again in a most amorous manner, clasping my heaving form to her bosom with a shiver of delight rushing through her trembling frame.

'What makes you throb so?' she asked in a most innocent manner, laying her left hand carelessly upon my right thigh as if, watching her smirking mouth, she hoped secretly to make an important discovery. Nor was I displeased when she touched my engine of love through my britches, prodding it gently as her face remained seemingly unconscious of anything untoward.

'Oh, lady, you have driven me mad!' I cried out, ripping

UNHOLY PASSIONS

open my britches to expose my rampant pego. I had let my love dart loose and it now stood throbbing within Millicent's hand. 'Oh, darling! Oh, Millicent! What pleasure!' I gasped out, kissing her enrapturedly and taking liberties with her gorgeous bubbies which my hands moulded and pressed.

'What am I doing?' Millicent squealed suddenly. 'Pray, Horby, do not be so rude,' she replied hastily, dropping the hold of my affair and pretending to want to free herself from my embrace. But my hands went swiftly under her skirts, forcing their way once again to the very shrine of love itself. I was far too impetuous to heed her faint remonstrances and in spite of all she could do to keep her thighs closed on this dance, my venturesome hand soon took possession of her heated cunny.

'If I die I must have you, darling lady...' I sighed as I suddenly forced her quite back on the sofa and whisked up her skirts and petticoats.

'Ah! No! No! I shall faint. How your violence frightens me!' She tried to smother her desires by simulating helplessness and then feigning unconsciousness. 'Frailty, thy name is Woman!' as Shakespeare has it: or is this really quite the case? Show me a man who declares himself to *understand* the Nature of Woman and I shall show you a conceited liar. Nevertheless, the fact remains that ever since this occasion, Millicent and I have been very close friends and recently, at my request, Millicent wrote to me her own account of what followed:

'I promised myself a rare treat by allowing you to think I really had fainted which, no doubt, would have urged you to take advantage of my most secret charms.

'"She's quite gone, the darling!" I heard you say to yourself as you gently patted my relaxing thighs. "I'll kiss it first." Then I knew you were kneeling between my legs and I felt your fingers gently parting the lips of my quim. I could virtually *hear* you thinking: *How I must have excited her; she's been spending!* Then I felt your lips right between my nymphae as you kissed me rapturously, just on my excitable little clitoris. What a thrill of desire it sent through my frame as it made me literally quiver all over with emotion, so that I could scarcely refrain from clasping your head within my hands or squeezing your dear face between my thighs.

'This only lasted a few moments, which seemed to be awfully long in my excitable state, for my cunt was spending and throbbing under the voluptuous titillations of your velvety tongue. Heavens! How I wanted to feel your prick inside of me again! I could not have feigned my fainting state another instant. The moment my lips were in the act of parting to implore you to fuck me at once, you started to your feet, pushing my thighs as wide apart as possible; and directly I felt the hot head of your cock placed to the mark. Slowly and gradually you pushed your way in whilst I contracted my usually tight affair and made it as difficult as I could for you to achieve possession: yet you did! How you kissed my lips, calling me: "Darling lady, dear Millicent, oh! you love! what pleasure you give me!" I felt you spend a torrent of your warm essence right up to my vitals and then you lay still upon me, exhausted for the moment by the profusions of your emission.'

And how does a man such as myself remember what followed? As I recall, Millicent was apparently in a state of inanimation yet without opening her eyes, she made her cunt nip and contract on my throbbing prick. Her quim was soaking around me in such a delicious manner that I was aroused from my lethargy and recommenced my movements and I could not resist saying:

'You love of a girl! Even in your fainting state, the love pressure of your cunt responds to the smart action of my prick.

What a pleasure it would be if I could but arouse you once more to sensibility!' I thence kissed her over and over again rapturously, quickening my stroke until my blood was so fired that she suddenly threw her arms around my neck and her amorous kisses, responding to mine, silently assured me of the delight I was affording her.

I had a wonderful fuck. I hope that Sandwich did. We both needed it in view of what was to come.

CHAPTER TWENTY

Gentle reader, tonight I sit down to dine, after which I shall continue with my Memoirs. I shall have four glasses of sherry wine: the dry *fino*, the salty *manzanilla*, the delectably balanced *amontillado* and the sweet and creamy *oloroso* before I retire to my late supper of turtle soup, two baby lobsters, two baby chickens, a roasted sirloin of beef done rarely with Yorkshire pudding and gravy, accompanied by fresh garden peas and buttered spinach; then I shall gorge myself on ripe Stilton cheese with Devon creamery butter and thin captain's biscuits followed by apples, pears, and tangerines. There will be German hock, red wine from Bordeaux and from Burgundy, then vintage port wine and after that, brandywine from the Cognac region. Possibly I may take a pipe of opium or hashish since it is rather hard to understand the matters I am about to present to you. I refer to the ensuing correspondence, meanwhile reflecting that whilst *eating* on one's own is a pain, *dining* on one's own is a pleasure. What actually happened 1763–64? Take this letter from Sandwich:

Dear Horby,
It was very good seeing you at Mrs Berkeley's. I have since succeeded in my aim of destroying that revolting traitor, John Wilkes. I can suffer injury but I cannot suffer insult. Can you? Wilkes is a liar. His journalism is cheap and nasty. As he said to our dear late Brother,

Thomas Potter: 'Give me a grain of truth and I will mix it up with a great mass of falsehood so that no chemist will ever be able to separate them.' Our King is outraged about the fact that Wilkes has called him a liar in print and so the officers of the Law have raided the offices of The North Briton *and have come away with incriminating evidence. I trust that I may count upon your vote not only to expel him from the Club for his recent outrage but also to expel him from Parliament.*

Now take this letter from John Wilkes MP.

Dear Horby,
It was very good seeing you at Medmenham Abbey and I hope that you are not too upset by my merry practical joke. Unfortunately Sandwich has become positively ape-shit about the matter, if you will excuse my French. He challenged me to a duel and we both shot our pistols into the air. Honour was satisfied, or so I had thought, but it appears that Sandwich is endeavouring to hit me below the belt now. Good old Dashwood, now Lord le Despenser, has tried to make peace and although his milk punch is divine, I cannot be fobbed off with the offer of some minor post in Bengal. The former Sir Francis endeavoured to explain to me that the Establishment can do much more harm to me than I can do to the Establishment. For my own part, I endeavoured to explain to him that the voice of the People is the Voice of God.

Sandwich, of course, thinks that power should be held by an exclusive élite. Before our duel he declared:
'Sir! You will die, if not by my shot, either on the gallows or of the pox.'
'That, sir,' I replied, 'depends upon whether I embrace your principles or your mistress.' I wonder that he did not

have the wit to kill me in that duel, since he was quivering with fury. I had thought, nevertheless, that after our duel honour would be satisfied. Evidently not. Sandwich is now endeavouring to prosecute me for seditious libel and to have me expelled from Parliament. You, my Lord, if I may say so, without intent to flatter, have always struck me as being a gentleman who values truth above all things. I hope, therefore, in these coming, trying times, that I may count on your support.

Then I have a letter here from Dashwood:

*Dear Horby,
I very much regret the fact that there is a quarrel between Sandwich and Wilkes. I have tried to talk peace to both of them but they are both so dreadfully intransigent. It is awful when my Brothers quarrel for I feel like a piggy in the middle. You are friendly with both men: may I ask you kindly to do what you can?*

That was why the following day found me visiting a scruffy newspaper office in Clerkenwell to see John Wilkes and Charles Churchill.

'Look, chaps, don't get me wrong,' I told them. 'I have to admit that I found your satires to be most amusing. But it's just a little too much, y'know; over the beam and all that. Surely all these untidy differences of opinion can be sorted out satisfactorily . . . ? Ah, yes, I think I will,' I murmured as I accepted a glass of claret from Charles Churchill. 'I don't quite see the nature of the problem, however. After all, let's be reasonable.' Then I was suddenly startled by a noise coming from the streets outside. It was the London Mob roaring: 'Wilkes and Churchill! WILKES AND LIBERTY! RAH! RAH! RAH!'

'Lord Horby, I have no quarrel with you personally,' said the bear-like Charles Churchill, 'but a man must speak the truth. We want Democracy!'

'Democracy?' I was horrified. 'Why, that's just Mob Rule!'

'WILKES AND CHURCHILL! RAH! RAH! RAH!' the London Mob was roaring outside as they looted, pillaged and plundered.

'No, no, sir,' said Churchill. 'Democracy is One Man, One Vote.'

'Impossible, sir!' I expostulated. 'One can't give stupid, illiterate brutes a share in the Government of our nation!'

'Then what are they doing in the House of Lords?' asked Churchill.

'Mr Churchill,' I sighed, 'I think that you are being deliberately difficult.' I turned to Wilkes. 'Jack, surely you don't share the views of your estimable friend here?' Wilkes fidgeted awkwardly.

'I'm afraid that I do, Horby,' he replied at last.

'Well,' I said, 'that's rather absurd, isn't it? Correct me if I'm wrong but I had thought that we were all members of a Club dedicated to the establishment of a Patriot King.'

'That is what I had hoped for, Horby,' Wilkes replied, 'but I have been disappointed, quite honestly. One just sees the same old faces in the same old places doing the same old things in the same old ways.' The chanting of 'WILKES AND CHURCHILL' grew louder as I fidgeted uncomfortably.

'Forgive me, Jack,' I said, 'for finding this argument to be slightly preposterous. Let's face it, you owe your present Membership of Parliament to the present system. Why upset your own interests? As for you, Charles,' I turned to Churchill, 'your poems would never have been published without the present system of patronage. The system as it stands works reasonably well and with benefit to both of you. Why rock the boat?'

UNHOLY PASSIONS

'The people of this country,' Churchill replied, 'presently have no say in its Government.'

'True enough,' I answered, 'but it would probably be ten times worse if they did.'

'Horby,' Churchill demanded, 'what do you want from us?'

'Oh, nothing very much, gentlemen,' I replied. 'Simply pulp all remaining issues of *The North Briton* Number 45 and tone down the contents in future issues. Is that really too much to ask? Then,' I smiled, 'life can be made easy for the pair of you. The Club may have lost power but we retain our influence.'

'And if we do not accept your kind offer...' Wilkes queried.

'Well, it would be rather awkward, really,' I returned.

'Meaning?' Churchill demanded.

'Obviously you'll have to leave the Club,' I responded. 'Further animosity will do no good for the patronage of your poetry, Charles, or your Parliamentary career, Jack. And there could be more serious consequences. Look, gentlemen, we have known each other for some years now and I am simply trying to be helpful.'

'Are you threatening us?' Churchill snarled.

'Me personally?' I returned. 'No, certainly not. But His Majesty's Government may be.'

'Would ye kindly leave the stage?' Churchill requested.

'Sorry...?'

'I believe in clean democracy, not in corrupt oligarchy,' Charles Churchill declared. 'And I'm prepared to state whatever needs to be stated in favour of that belief. If England does not like it, then so much the worse for England. Those are my terms. I do not care to exist on any other.'

'I agree with Charles,' Wilkes murmured.

'I'm sorry to hear it, Jack,' I murmured in return. 'Well, the social occasion was pleasant. Pity I couldn't persuade you to listen to reason.' I took my hat and stick. 'Good day, gentlemen.' I was about to go when six strong men kicked down the door and burst into the room.

'Ye're both under arrest, Wilkes and Churchill!' the first officer yelled.

'Who are you?' Wilkes retorted coolly, 'a burglar?'

'No,' said this bruiser with unpleasing features, 'we are His Majesty's Officers of the Law, so just shut yer mouth, sunshine.' He smiled unpleasantly as he produced a legal document. 'You had better come quietly, Mr Wilkes and Mr Churchill, since this is a Warrant for your arrest and for the search and seizure of any properties relevant to prosecution.'

'May I see this document, please?' Wilkes responded, waving to an agitated Churchill to be calm. The officer handed over the documents with a toothy grin. 'Why, this is perfectly preposterous. There is no name on this Warrant. Warrants of this nature have been declared illegal in the High Court of Justice, in case you did not know. This is illegal.' He put it inside his coat pocket. 'I shall keep it for future reference, if you don't mind, but meanwhile you are in severe breach of the Law of the Land and since your company is so unpleasant and uncouth, I must ask you to leave.'

''Ear 'im, lads?' the first officer declared. 'Did you 'ear 'im? Wot a joker! Ha! ha! Mr Wilkes, you can 'ave it the easy way or the 'ard way though I'd prefer it the easy way. Just 'and over all copies of *The North Briton*, Number 45 . . .'

'You must be joking, officer,' Wilkes retorted. 'Don't you understand? What you are doing is totally *illegal!*' Outside, the London Mob were chanting 'Wilkes and Churchill!' and 'Wilkes and Liberty!'

'All right, then, Mister Wilkes,' said the first officer, 'I see it's going to have to be the 'ard way. Right. Pile in, lads.' Two officers stormed at Churchill's desk and Churchill proceeded to flatten the pair of them with his fists. One assailant had his

UNHOLY PASSIONS

nose mashed and sank to the floor, crying softly; and the other had his jaw broken with an audible *crack!* and, sighing softly, expired into unconsciousness. At a signal from their sergeant, the three remaining officers drew their bludgeons and rushed forward to savage Charles Churchill.

'Stop it! Stop it! STOP IT!' Wilkes yelled as the officers of the law hit Churchill with iron bars. Wilkes and I rushed to Churchill's assistance. The latter had clobbered one of the officers but the blows of the other two had made him stagger backwards, bloodied but unbowed, yet suddenly it was as though his heart had seized up and he coughed, spasmed, spluttered and collapsed into the arms of Wilkes, who cradled him in his arms.

'Well, get up, lads,' the sergeant commanded his bruised and bloodied men. 'Get the *North Briton*, all the printing plates and all the papers.' I protested but it was of no use as the officers rummaged through the household, wrecking everything.

'Live, Charles, please, LIVE!' Wilkes was saying to Churchill. 'You can, you *can*, you CAN!' He glared at the bruised officers who were wrecking the printing works. 'You swine . . . you disgusting, fucking swine!'

'Oh, don't take it like that ,sah!' said the sergeant. 'After all, we're only doing our job . . .'

'Doing your job . . . ? MURDERERS!' Wilkes screamed.

'Shut yer mouth, Wilkes,' the sergeant sneered, 'ye're under arrest.'

'FUCKING MURDERERS!' Wilkes roared. The officers seized him and appeared about to club him. I was just rushing to intervene when the London Mob burst through the broken door.

'Whassis, then?' the leader of the Mob demanded.

'Get out of here!' the law officer shouted. 'And don't you dare mess with the Law!'

'I wasn't talking to you, wanker,' the Mob leader replied. 'Got a problem, Jack?' he asked Wilkes.

'Yes,' Wilkes replied. 'My friend Charles Churchill here is half-dead – and *they* did it to him.'

'Wot?!' the man looked stunned. 'The bastards went for Charles Churchill . . . ?' He turned to his gang. 'Wot yer reckon about that, lads?' A deep growl of anger came from the London Mob.

'Rip 'im to pieces, lads!' a woman's voice shouted from the back. And the London Mob proceeded to produce knives and cudgels so as to take the law officers out into the street, break their bones and slit their throats to a chorus of loud cheering from the women.

'''Urts, dunnit, I know,' said the leader of the Mob, who told me that his name was John Bull. 'Felt that way when my best mate got killed by the bastards.'

'Yes, thank you . . .' Wilkes muttered. 'Truly appreciated . . . but please help my friend here . . . ?'

'Certainly!' said John Bull. 'We always liked Charles Churchill round these parts and we didn't mind you either, Jack Wilkes. Liz! Molly!' Two women instantly appeared. 'Get our friend Charles Churchill to the 'ospital.' The women obeyed with alacrity but I fear it was too late since Charles Churchill died in the following year. (It says something for his poetry that the Royal Navy – under Sandwich – dipped flags in salute: *Editor's note*). 'I know you're in grief but so are we,' said the beefy John Bull. 'You couldn't perhaps say a few words out there to my Mob, could you? After all, we're trying to 'elp you out . . .'

'All right . . .' Wilkes gritted his teeth as Churchill was carried out to hospital on a stretcher, 'all right.' The London Mob cheered as Wilkes strode out of the house to cries of 'Speech! Speech!'

'Ladies and gentlemen . . .' Wilkes began.

UNHOLY PASSIONS

'There ain't no ladies 'ere,' said some tart and everyone laughed.

'Maybe not, Madam,' Wilkes retorted smartly, 'but there are men and women, thank God – or should I say thank Goddess?' Everyone laughed. 'I would like to thank you all for your help.' The Mob looked attentive. 'Oh, yes, you helped me and I shall never forget it. Unfortunately, help came too late to save a splendid man from injury. I refer to my great but disgracefully injured friend, Charles Churchill! What a man he was!' Wilkes roared to applause, 'and what a good friend he was to me!'

'And to us!' a woman shrieked out.

'YEAH!' the Mob roared.

'What a fantastic man!' Wilkes declaimed. 'Always willing to box with the toughest men of England!'

'Oh, don't I know it!' a beefy bruiser shouted out. ''E broke my nose one night!'

'He is also England's greatest poet,' Wilkes continued softly and now the Mob looked solemn and respectful. 'Now, maybe Poetry means nothing to you . . .'

'We like it as long as we don't 'ave to read it!' some woman shouted.

'All right, Madam,' Wilkes returned smartly, 'but *I* like it. Many people like it. And England's greatest poet has had his influence in making this country into a better place.'

''Ow?' an unshaven rough at the front demanded. 'Look, I liked Chas Churchill as a bloke and I've 'ad many a good pint wiv 'im, but wot I'm asking is: 'ow did 'e make this country into a better place? I mean, all I can see is the rich getting richer and the poor getting poorer and the Government doing a Robin Hood in reverse, know wot I mean?'

'Oh, yes, indeed, sir – I agree with you,' Wilkes replied. 'And this is why we must never forget Charles Churchill. What did he stand for, we ask, as he quivers upon a hospital bed?

Obviously it is *for the right of every man to be himself!* But can anybody else tell me what else he advocated?'

'Screwing women!' a tart cried out.

'Indeed,' Wilkes answered, 'and what else?'

'Boozing!' a man shouted. 'By Christ, he could put it back!'

'Certainly,' said Wilkes. 'And what else?' There was a long pause. 'Has anybody here ever heard of something called DEMOCRACY?' The Mob all looked a little puzzled and many scratched themselves. 'Well: that is something for which Charles Churchill has battled all his life. And what has he fought for? DEMOCRACY means: ONE MAN, ONE VOTE.'

'Give over, mate,' a strong young man interjected, 'we ain't even got a bleeding vote.'

'Yes!' Wilkes shouted back. 'That is how it is now. And it is wrong! You, me, everybody ought to have a say in how our country is governed. The rich oligarchy is just robbing you blind – and they are passing laws to keep it that way. What I am saying and what Charles Churchill was saying before – let us say before his enjoyment of health was rudely interrupted...' the London Mob was now howling with macabre laughter, '... is that *you* should have a vote, a say, a power in what happens to your country, which is also mine.'

'YEAH!' the London Mob roared. 'WILKES AND LIBERTY! RAH! RAH! RAH!'

'You're talking such shit,' said a sour old man when the cheering had died away.

'You are entitled to your opinion, sir,' Wilkes responded, 'but since I am serving your interests, I trust I may count on your vote...?'

'I'd rather vote for the Devil,' the sour old man grumbled.

'Fair enough,' Wilkes retorted, 'but if your friend isn't standing...?' The Mob roared with laughter. 'But a serious moment, please, ladies and gentlemen. Charles Churchill, my great, dear friend and a friend of many of you, was alive – and now he may be dying. They tried to murder him – and this disgusting outrage was done by those who oppress you! He fought for your rights – and he may even die for them. Let us never forget that. Let us always honour his memory. Above all, let us never stop fighting for our right to have a say in the governance of *our* country.' The Mob roared out its approval. 'I pledge myself before you now always to honour his memory, in present sickness or, I hope, in future health. Dead or alive, *I* shall preserve his legacy! I shall always fight for his greatest ideal. And what is it?'

'Fuckin' liberty!' some tart cried out.

'Indeed, Madam,' Wilkes replied. 'One needs a woman to tell one that,' he added genially, as the Mob just laughed, plainly and simply. 'Madam, you have encapsulated the matter with exact precision. LIBERTY!' he roared. 'Yes! GIVE ME LIBERTY OR GIVE ME DEATH!'

'WILKES AND LIBERTY!!!' the London Mob roared as Wilkes and I returned into Churchill's house. I heard that, later that night, the London Mob went on the rampage, destroying some buildings and looting, pillaging and plundering. They also overturned the carriage of George Selwyn when he was on his way to White's and left him lying, mud-soaked, in the gutter.

I know that night that I saw Wilkes sobbing out his heart before a portrait of Charles Churchill etched by William Hogarth.

'Accident has made me a patriot, Horby,' he said. 'Please be a good chap and lend me a thousand guineas.'

I don't know why: but I did.

CHAPTER TWENTY-ONE

I needed to get away from these men for a time and to enjoy the company of women. It struck me that I could have a good time at the brothel Mrs Charlotte Hayes had established at the Haymarket and so that is where I went. Charlotte greeted me warmly.

'My dear boy . . .' she murmured as she placed her slender arms around my neck. Her amorous kisses responding to mine silently assured me of the delight I was affording her. I was not expecting her to lead me into an orgy but this is precisely what she proceeded to do. We passed into a chamber festooned by chandeliers and wicked murals copied from those of Pompeii. 'Here they are, the sly ones,' Charlotte laughed. 'Why, Sarah is the hottest one of the lot, for, see, she has got Sir Thomas Stapleton well into her.' I could see that the front of Sir John Dashwood-King's britches were undone whilst the flushed face of Lady Betty Germain and the delighted manner in which she clung to her partner, William Hogarth, assured me that she at least was on the best of terms with him: meanwhile Millicent was sucking the cock of Sir John Dashwood-King.

'Don't the ladies,' Charlotte observed, 'appear so loving with their damask cheeks and sparkling eyes? Oh, Horby! You seem to be dreadfully confused and especially by the appearance of Lady Betty Germain. Don't you understand that, occasionally, she *likes* to work in a brothel.' And with that, she hurled me to the floor, threw her long legs around me so as to squeeze my hips with her thighs and took my stiff prick within her hands; this ecstasy left me helpless before an assault. 'It's this naughty fellow, my dears,' Charlotte squealed, 'who has taken liberties with me, and aroused my passions to the highest degree.' Before I could comprehend the happenstance, I had been rudely seized, hurled and bound upon a patented Mrs Theresa Berkeley rocking-horse. 'Ladies!' Charlotte Hayes commanded, 'slap his bottom well for me and make him now complete my pleasure, my own greedy lustfulness!'

When I state 'a patented Mrs Theresa Berkeley rocking-horse', I do not actually refer to that ingenious mechanical contrivance, even though my wrists had been bound behind my back. I mean that I was now being forced to fuck the blonde Mrs Charlotte Hayes whilst enduring a spanking from her most delectable assistants. I struggled hard to free my wrists as Charlotte's thighs held me tightly and all the ladies slapped my bottom without mercy, making me fairly bound in the saddle, so to speak, to Charlotte's great and visibly evident delight, more especially when she found me swelling up to quite unnatural stiffness, until my prick was virtually breaking her quim, for I was furiously fucking with all my might, crying out for the ladies to leave me be and let me go to it properly.

The noise of the slaps upon my bottom seemed to give Charlotte intense delight and it was a most delicious session of fucking until we both came together, quite frantic with delight, as our mutual essences were commingled at the same moment.

'There, don't let me catch you slipping away to have a wank!' Lady Betty Germain exclaimed as she gave me a tremendous slap, which fairly made me bound under her hand in spite of my exhaustive spend. 'It spoils half the fun, when some are so sly,' she added, 'when they are more inclined for the sport than anyone.'

My wrists were untied: and we then refreshed ourselves

with sparkling wine from the French Champagne district, meat jellies, dressed crab, oysters and other reinvigorating delicacies, including slices of rare roast beef dripping with blood. The ladies laughed and bantered with us, threatening us with a forthcoming party game. Charlotte wrote all the names of the ladies on slips of paper, which she said she would hold out for the men to draw their prizes, adding that all ladies present must submit to being fucked again. Sarah, Millicent and Lady Betty all squealed and protested their innocence then looked so gleeful when asked to assist in stripping we cavaliers quite naked.

'I hope that you enjoy the sight of these jewels and beauties,' Charlotte declared.

'These are all finely formed young fellows,' Lady Betty observed, 'but the splendours of Horby's penis assuredly carry off the honours of the evening. Why, it is more than eight inches long and very thick with it!'

'The others have mighty tools too,' Millicent lisped. Sarah nodded eager acquiescence.

'Now, there shall be no deception or cheating,' said Charlotte. 'I've a novel idea as to how the lots shall be drawn.' She drew up her skirts and petticoats until she could show us the beautiful lips of her luscious cunt, just peeping out between the slit in her drawers, as her long, lissom legs were wide apart: then drawing Lady Betty close to her side, she gave her four slips of paper.

I saw the ladies whispering and Lady Betty proceeded to place a slip within the vagina of each woman, finishing with herself. The gentlemen then had to kneel down in front and each one drew his paper from her mouth. This was jolly good fun. Charlotte looked as if she would have liked to be fucked by all four of us instead of merely having a lot drawn from her gap, which was so tickled as I drew out the paper that she actually spent under the novel excitement.

Dashwood-King drew Millicent; Hogarth drew Lady Betty Germain; Sir Thomas Stapleton had Charlotte; whilst I was lucky enough to have the handsome Sarah, she of the beautiful buttocks, who had been eyeing me with a most amorous leer, which you may be sure did not in the least offend me. Millicent and Sarah were now told by Charlotte to fit themselves with a couple of most artistically moulded dildoes of a very natural size, which Lady Betty Germain said her own husband had procured for the purpose of having his lady wife bottom-fuck him occasionally whenever he wanted extra stimulation.

The ladies were by now divested of everything excepting the pretty boots and stockings, which I always think look far sweeter than naked legs and feet. But our interest centred for the time being, upon Sir Thomas and Charlotte since we were all eager to see the working of his fine prick in her splendid cunt. He was in a very rampant state of anticipation, so she laid him at full length on his back on a soft, springy couch. Then, stretching across his legs, she first bent down her head to kiss and lubricate his fine prick with her mouth before placing herself right over him and gradually sheathing his grand instrument within her longing cunt, pressing down upon him, with her lips glued to his, as she seemed to enjoy the sense of possessing it all. I motioned to Charlotte's writhing bottom with my finger and the slender Millicent, understanding my ideas, at once mounted up behind her mistress and brought the head of her well-creamed dildo to the charge against her brown-wrinkled bottom-hole. Millicent clasped her hands around Charlotte, with one hand feeling the fine shaft of Sir Thomas whilst the fingers of the other were tickling the fine clitoris of our mistress of ceremonies. It was a delightful tableau and it excited us all when they plunged into a course of hair-raising fucking. The willowy Millicent was as excited as either of them as she vigorously dildoed her mistress and kept her hands stimulating both of them in front. Lady Betty now attacked Millicent from behind with *her* dildo, delighting her – with frigging combined.

How they screamed with delight and spent over and over again! It is impossible to describe . . . but Sarah had taken my stiff prick in her hand and we were now kissing and indulging in every possible caress. My cock throbbed in her grasp as she repeatedly drew back the foreskin, until at length, fearing that I might spend over her hand, she sank back on a sofa and drew me upon her, guiding my affair to her longing quim, whilst I clasped her around her voluptuous body and kissed her more ardently than ever. I could see all that was going on around the room. Charlotte was still riding furiously on Sir Thomas, stimulated by the double exertions of Millicent and Betty. I watched with delight the frenzied joys of Millicent as she handled and felt how Thomas was going in front, whilst Betty's dildo almost drove her to distraction by its exciting movements within her wiggling bottom.

William Hogarth now drew Lady Betty back onto a sofa as Dashwood-King did with Millicent.

'Dear Betty!' Hogarth exclaimed excitedly, 'can you not pity my unrequited love, won't you even favour me with a smile as I look at your face?' She smiled as he took her hand and covered it with impassioned kisses, growing quite impetuous, with one arm around her waist, whilst he covered Betty's blushing face with the most ardent bites of love. I could see his other hand wandering over her prominent bosom and her satin thighs, then, taking one of her delicate hands, he forced her to feel his standing cock. The mere touch visibly sent a thrill of desire throughout her whole frame as she sank backwards in an assumed faint.

Kneeling down by Betty's side, William kissed her legs all the way up and, parting her thighs, opened the slit until he enjoyed a fair view of her pussy.

'What a sweet little slit; what soft silky down it is ornamented with!' I could hear him sigh as he pressed his lips to her Mons Veneris; then we could see her shudder at the feel of his fingers parting the lips of her cunt with the greatest tenderness so as to enable him to kiss the little button of love. She pressed his head down with her hands as she spent over his tongue with a deep drawn sigh of pleasure. 'She is mine,' he murmured, 'how she likes it ... the touches of my tongue, painted upon her, have made her come!' Suddenly she laughed with unashamed delight. 'I thought a few delicate kisses, bestowed in the most sensitive place, would revive you.'

At that moment, Mrs Charlotte Hayes produced a small book from a drawer and passed it to me.

'This,' she said, 'will show you the most delightful avenue of rapture and open up to your ravished senses heavenly bliss of which you have hitherto had no conception.' Sarah promptly snatched the book from my eager fingers and, retaining hold of my priapus in one hand, she showed me with her other a series of splendid little illustrations, all of them demonstrating the way to enjoy bottom-fucking. She could see that I was tremendously excited and I lost no time in placing her on her hands and knees. Then, anointing her tight little bum-hole with some scented ointment from a box passed to me by Charlotte, I made Sarah push her voluptuous arse well out behind, with her long legs wide apart so as to give me every facility. Having also anointed the stiff shaft of my prick, I commenced my assault.

'Ah!' she shrieked out. 'Ah! No, NO! I can't bear it.' The tears were fairly starting in the blue eyes I could see reflected enticingly in the looking-glass opposite as she felt the first advance of my engine forcing its way through the tightened orifice. 'Ohhh ... the pain is like a number of needles pricking my parts all at once ... I am relaxing ... *ohh*!' Her sphincter muscle certainly was. I frigged her deliciously in front all the while, pushing so firmly and getting in with such a gentle manner behind that Sarah seemed to love me more and more with every movement and to long for me to complete my task and her enjoyment, as if the very pain was a precursor to some extraordinary bliss. I was not disappointed. 'Oh! the pain!' she squealed. 'Sir, your movements stir me up to the *highest* pitch of excitement!' I did not withdraw until we had both spent in rapturous ecstasies, screaming with delight from excess of enjoyment.

Meanwhile, it seemed to be time for changing partners in that Sir Thomas was licking the quim of Millicent, she who was orginally paired with Sir John Dashwood-King, who now arose in a fury and rudely seized her back, a demoniac glare in his eyes, so unnaturally brilliant did they look just then.

'Ha!' he exclaimed in a husky voice, 'my little beauty here has been tongue-frigged and has been spending. Suck my prick or I'll kill you, you little bitch!' he added savagely. 'Do it!' he snarled as he reversed himself over her and plunged his head between her thighs, where he at once commenced to lick her quim most deliciously, to judge by Millicent's expression. For her part, she nestled his rather long prick between her bubbies, pressing them together with her hands so as to make him frot her there. She readily took his prick into her mouth, causing Sir John to become quite furious in his gamahauching.

'Spend, spend, why don't you come, you little bitch?' he growled, growing visibly more outraged until Millicent shrieked out, writhed about and deluged his mouth with quite a profusion of her creamy emission, which appeared to cover all his face as he paused to draw breath. 'A devilish good spend, that,' he murmured, then: 'Now suck my prick again!' he declared with renewed fierceness, turning around and presenting it full in her face. Millicent took his throbbing prick within her long, delicate fingers, stroking the shaft softly as she titillated the purple head with her tongue.

'Oh, John, it is *tremendously* distended,' she cooed, 'and as hard as iron.' At an instant, the cock of Sir John spurted spunk all over her prissy face, after which he momentarily expired within her slender arms. We all took claret and fruit cake as we enjoyed the sight.

'Sir John!' Lady Betty suddenly said sharply with a meaningful glance at both Charlotte and Sarah. Instantly these two ladies rushed forward to bind his wrists and ankles with thongs of leather and Dashwood-King was too astonished to resist.

'What is the meaning of this outrage?' he spluttered, his body thrashing about in its tormented writhings but his limbs unable to wrestle against their bonds.

'Sir John,' Lady Betty said in a voice so gentle that I knew that what was coming might be excruciating, 'do you not remember our bet?' He shook his head furiously. 'It was a bet made at the Club, yes, at the Abbey. You solemnly swore to me that you would never come over a woman's face on pain of the Sisterhood coming over *yours*. I have seen you do that and now you must pay.'

'I don't recall this bet,' Sir John muttered through gritted teeth.

'I do,' said Sir Thomas, who was probably still mildly irritated by the way in which Sir John had snatched Millicent from him. Charlotte, Sarah and Millicent all nodded eager acquiescence.

'Ladies,' said Lady Betty, 'let us withdraw and adorn ourselves with suitable garb appropriate for this most auspicious occasion.' Mrs Charlotte Hayes rang a bell and a maid entered to conduct Sir Thomas Hogarth and myself to another drawing-room, where we were served with crusted port and almonds. Civilized conversation accompanied this interlude and we all agreed that a bet has to be paid. A bell rang to introduce another maid, who conducted us into the room we had previously inhabited, only in the meantime it had been tidied and somewhat rearranged. The maid motioned us to our seats.

Sir John Dashwood-King lay in the centre of the room, upon his back, his wrists bound behind it, his ankles entwined. He was naked and one could not but notice his rampaging penis. On the sofa opposite us men sat four lascivious and exquisitely dressed ladies, clad in silken gowns, whose petticoats rustled and crackled each time one of them turned a peeping ankle, which was often. Their breasts threatened to split their bodices. I noticed a copy of the Rokeby Venus now hanging upon the wall above the fire-place, displaying, indeed boasting of her beautiful buttocks.

'Ladies,' Lady Betty announced, 'whenever there is sexual insolence, as there has been in this instance, I think that a woman's place is upon a man's face.' That said, she stalked over to Sir John and squealed, 'HOOP LA!' as she lifted her dress and petticoats and hoops to place her bottom upon his facial features. It was quite a stately emplacement. 'Sir John,' she laughed raucously, 'is being taught the pleasures of *queening*. Uh ...' she sighed, 'how pleasant it is to force a male to tongue me.' The ladies smiled prettily in their pleasure. 'It is almost as if one were sitting upon a lavatory seat. Of course I agree with the Magick of Sir Francis Dashwood and I agree with the books of Sorcery and Witchcraft which he bought in Venice and now keeps in his library. Uhh ... do that again, Sir John.' Her bottom twitched with pleasure visibly expressed upon her gleeful facial features. 'We hereditary witches and bitches know of the use of the Four Elements: Fire, Water, Air and Earth. We know how the colours correspond with them and also the weapons of Magick. This is why I am wearing silken scarlet and for the magical weapons, the Wand, the Cup, the Sword and the Disc, I take the *Wand*!' That said, she grasped Sir John's rampant pego within her hand and squeezed it so lasciviously, as her bottom pressured his face, that his rampant cock spurted all over the Persian carpet. 'What appalling behaviour, John!' Lady Betty exclaimed, rather frivolously. 'You will now experience the pleasures of the *Cup* that is Water, and this is most appropriate since you have spilled your seed upon the carpet of Charlotte.' With that she arose, arranged her skirts and moved back to her seat, where she gladly accepted a glass of port from the maid.

Charlotte arose, dressed in navy blue. She stepped around the fulminating figure of a man, smiled sweetly and uplifting her skirts, placed her bottom upon his face. One could hear Sir John's groanings as her hips writhed: then there was a strange sound of gurgling. Charlotte sighed as this occurred, then arose and walked back to the sofa.

Sir John was spluttering as Sarah arose, tightly swathed in yellow, which suited her long, blonde hair. She giggled as she lifted her skirts to place her voluptuous bottom upon his face and she continued to giggle as she wiggled it.

'Air,' Lady Betty announced. 'Yellow is the colour and the *Dagger* is the weapon.' Sarah promptly produced a knife from a sheath hanging between her breasts and as Sir John was forced to pleasure her arse, applied its tip to his testicles. This action caused Sarah to spend copiously and shudder all the way down her spine. 'And now,' said Lady Betty, 'it will be Millicent in black to represent the *Disc* or *Coin* of Earth.' Sarah withdrew to her seat by the ladies as Millicent approached Sir John.

I have never seen a black skirt tied so tightly upon a woman. I am not quite sure how Millicent managed to pull it up beyond her hips but, in any event, she placed her slim bottom upon the face of Sir John and she did not so much wiggle, like Sarah, as *wriggle*, doing so all the while with a self-satisfied smirk upon her face, having placed her seat upon him so delicately.

UNHOLY PASSIONS

How the ladies laughed with joy when she came!

He had spurted in her face: and as she arose, his face was soaked and dripping from the juices the ladies had spent upon him in such rich profusion.

CHAPTER TWENTY-TWO

Charles Churchill's fame in life was enormous: his eclipse after his death was rapid. His prestige as a poet was no longer there to protect his friend, John Wilkes, upon whom a savage assault was unleashed. With the full consent of King George III, who hated the man he called 'that Devil Wilkes', Lord Sandwich assailed him in the House of Lords. I had tried to dissuade him from this course of action.

'Ruthless men call for ruthless measures,' Sandwich had replied. Through a rather dirty individual, a most unpleasant pervert, the Reverend John Kidgell, Chaplain to the Earl of March, later Duke of Queensberry – 'Old Q' as we knew him at the Club – Sandwich had been able to lay his hands upon a copy of *Essay on Woman*, a witty parody of Alexander Pope's *Essay On Man*. Sandwich was especially outraged, or professed to be so, since it mocked his mistress, Fanny Murray with:

'Awake, my Fanny, leave all meaner things
This morn shall prove what rapture swiving brings.
Let us (since Life can little more supply
Than just a few good fucks and then we die)
Expiate free o'er the loved seat of Man;
A mighty Maze, for mighty Pricks to scan...'

I tried to dissuade Sandwich from pursuing this matter since firstly, when it was read out at dinner at Medmenham Abbey, Sandwich had been among the first to hear it: and he had roared with laughter. Secondly, although Wilkes may have assisted in the composition of some lines here and there, we all knew that the author was the late Thomas Potter. Unfortunately, Sandwich could be quite implacable in revenge. He felt that Wilkes had insulted him and betrayed the Club. Smacking his thin lips salaciously, his beaky nose plunged within this wretched book, he proceeded to read out its more salacious passages to the House of Lords.

'My Lords,' he said, 'there cannot be a more revolting, repulsive and more obscene document than this – and it was written by a Member of the House of Commons, Mr John Wilkes. His Majesty King George III has sent a King's Message to Parliament stating that Mr Wilkes is the "author of a most seditious and dangerous libel..." His Majesty the King was quite right since, by a vote of 273 to 111, the House of Commons has decided that Number 45 of *The North Briton* is: "a false, scandalous and seditious libel, containing expressions of the most unexampled insolence and contumely towards His Majesty, the grossest aspersions upon Parliament and the most audacious defiance of the whole Legislature." Does a depraved and vicious rake such as Mr Wilkes deserve a place in the Houses of Parliament?'

(*Editor's note*: The *Essay on Woman* texts may be viewed courtesy of the Home Office, where Sandwich lodged copies.)

I could barely believe the hypocrisy of the speech of Sandwich, even though he had indeed been injured and insulted. He gloated over the Frontispiece, an engraving of a stiff penis with the caption 'Saviour of the World', when he knew full well that we had worshipped that principle at Medmenham. To my stupefaction, he pretended to be a Christian, as did so many others.

'"Say first," he quoted, "of Woman's latent charms below,

UNHOLY PASSIONS

"What can we reason, but from what we know?"'

That seemed to me an eminently reasonable proposition but the majority of Lords and Bishops pretended to be shocked, especially when Sandwich hinted at what we all knew: that Lord Bute had given Princess Augusta advice on the architecture of the pagoda in the Royal Botanical Gardens at Kew and that this pagoda was subsequently known as 'Bute's Erection'. The matter grew more squalid when Sandwich quoted again:

'Presumptuous Prick! the reason wouldst thou find;
Why formed so weak, so little and so blind?'

'I don't quite believe this performance,' I murmured to Dashwood, with whom I was sitting. 'He is reading out with obvious relish the verses which used to delight him in the company of the Medmenham Monks. He is condemning without reserve the alleged "obscenities" and "blasphemies" of these verses despite the fact that the Beefsteak Club is about to expel *Sandwich* for obscenity and blasphemy: and everyone here knows that.'

'I never thought to hear the Devil preach,' Dashwood remarked loudly enough for everyone to hear.

Lord Lyttleton, who had abandoned the consolation of being a rake for the austere rigours of Christianity, implored the House of Lords to hear no more: but when their Lordships insisted on further salacious verses, he did not leave the Chamber. The Bishop of Gloucester indignantly declared that 'the blackest fiend in Hell would not keep company with Wilkes'. I then saw him rub his hands together with joy and place them deeply within the pockets of his britches as Sandwich read out:

'The grasp divine, th'emphatic, thrilling squeeze,

The throbbing, panting breasts and trembling knees,
The tickling motion, the enlivening flow,
The rapturous shiver and dissolving, *oh!*'

Despite my vote against the Motion, the House of Lords resolved that the *Essay on Woman* was 'a most scandalous, obscene and impious libel'. The next question concerned the identity of the author, who, Sandwich claimed, was Wilkes. Lord Mansfield properly moved for the right to hear Wilkes in his own defence and the motion was carried. Wilkes had two days to prepare his case but these were spoiled by duels. After all, it would suit our oligarchy if, for our convenience, he could be shot. To this end, Wilkes was challenged by one Mr Talbot, whom he had insulted in his paper, and he accepted the challenge, even though he was so short-sighted that he would miss a barn door at five paces with a blunderbuss. Talbot was the same and missed.

Instantly, this was followed by another duel. One Mr Martin, Secretary to the Treasury and a friend of Talbot, had been called 'treacherous, base, selfish, mean, abject, low-lived and dirty', in *The North Briton*. Martin had responded in the House of Commons by calling Wilkes 'a cowardly, malignant and scandalous scoundrel'. Wilkes promptly challenged Talbot to a duel, which took place at dawn in Hyde Park and I was there to see it with my dear friend, Lady Clarissa Hyde, as we took stirrup cups of hot punch in her carriage after a night of frenzied love-making. I was pleased to see that Wilkes had George Selwyn for his second: though Selwyn always did like the sight of death. Mr Martin's second looked like some fellow he had hired at an eel-and-pie shop.

'Horby, darling,' said Lady Clarissa, 'can't you stop it?'

'That is just not possible, my dear,' I replied.

'It is so stupid,' she said. 'Wilkes is a good man, despite all his many faults, and both men could get killed.'

'I know, Clarissa, I know. But, you see, serious insults have been exchanged and it *is* a matter of honour.'

'*Men!*' Clarissa exclaimed exasperatedly.

The wind blew and autumn leaves littered the ground as Selwyn and the unknown second, presumably some government hack, conducted the ceremonies with the utmost formality. Eventually, Wilkes and Martin were standing back-to-back and, at a command from their seconds, they proceeded to tread the doleful dozen paces.

Wilkes was the first to turn and, cocking his pistol, he aimed it straight at the heart of Martin, who had yet to realize how his pistol worked. There is a possibility that Wilkes may have been taking shooting lessons and a possibility that he could have killed Martin but, having demonstrated his point, he acted like a gentleman, flicked his wrist, discharged his pistol into the air and let it fall to the ground. Honour was assuredly satisfied, and I could see that Selwyn was about to say so; obviously Martin would do the same.

I could not quite believe what I witnessed then; and nor could Lady Clarissa. Slowly and deliberately, Martin aimed his pistol at Wilkes and pulled the trigger. The pistol ball struck Wilkes in the groin and he fell to his knees. Martin threw his own pistol upon the turf, turned his back and walked away, his jackal of a second running hot upon his heels.

George Selwyn was much possessed by death and saw the skull beneath the skin: but he was disgusted by Martin's grossly ungentlemanly behaviour. Naturally, Lady Clarissa and I rushed to the assistance of Wilkes, as did Selwyn, and we put him in Clarissa's post-chaise, took him to Guy's Hospital and ensured that he received every possible assistance. Fortunately, the wound had neither killed him nor maimed him; it had merely slowed him down for the time being. As he was recovering, Selwyn, Lady Clarissa and I devoted our time, energy and influence to ensuring that Martin would never be received again in any place of good repute, which led a year later to the dismissal from the Government of a functionary who had outlived his usefulness. One gathers that he died in a brawl within some abominable gin palace he was known to frequent after the disappearance of his patronage and I say: good riddance! I cannot bear poor conduct in a matter as noble as The Duel.

Wilkes, I am glad to say – for he acted honourably in all duels – recovered sufficiently to visit France. It was no use my endeavouring to intervene on his behalf. Sandwich *was* implacable in revenge. Dashwood said that he thought the action of the Government to be wrong but refused to do anything more.

'You know, Horby,' he said to me over the port at White's. 'I *do* feel that Wilkes has insulted the Monks. He has insulted my vision. I did actually try to see his point of view and was even in a position to offer the bloody man the Lieutenant-Governership of Bengal but he spurned my offer. He genuinely seems to think that *Democracy* is the system of the future and that he will be its leader in England. Myself, I doubt it, but I shall remain neutral.'

This he did: but meanwhile the Establishment, from the King, to the Lords to the Commons was resolved to crush Wilkes, especially since the London Mob had rioted once more with the cry of 'WILKES AND LIBERTY!' On 20 January 1764, the House of Commons passed the motion: 'That the said John Wilkes Esquire be, for the said Offence, expelled from this House.' This 'said offence' was, of course, his 'false, scandalous and seditious libel' in *The North Briton* 45 against the King and His Majesty's Government. The resolution robbed Wilkes of the protection of Parliamentary privilege, which enabled his enemies to have him tried in his enforced absence before Lord Mansfield in the following month. Wilkes was found Guilty of seditious libel against King George III (which lunatic is still our King as I write this) in *The North Briton*: and Guilty of seditious libel against that notoriously dirty old man, the Bishop of Gloucester, in the *Essay on Woman*, which he had not even written. He was declared to be an outlaw and would face arrest and imprisonment if ever he returned to England.

Lord Chesterfield was his usual sardonic self over the matter when I saw him to arouse his ire over a flagrant breach of natural justice. 'Thank heavens, sir,' he declared as he took a pinch of snuff, 'that we have a Wilkes to protect our liberties and a Sandwich to safeguard our morals.' He declined to take any further interest in the matter and probably continued with writing his celebrated *Letters to His Son*, which, as Dr Johnson later stated, taught: 'The manners of a dancing master and the morals of a whore.'

For my own part, I was somewhat depressed as I returned home and, in order to succour myself, I ordered my butler to bring me a bottle of vintage port, pipes of briar, clay, meerschaum, tobacco from Virginia, Carolina, and Yenidje from the shores of the Caspian Sea: and the opium and hashish which the Vansittart brothers had brought me from India. Opium induces a calm and slightly drowsy contemplation of matters: hashish can be exceedingly enlivening for one's sensibilities. As I smoked a series of pipes, I contemplated the extraordinary letter I had received from my dear Arabella Marchmount:

My darling,
I miss you tremendously as I write to you from Paris, a city abundant with philosophes, *writers of pamphlets and journals, including Voltaire, Rousseau and Diderot; yet there is an attraction similar to that of London.*

After a while, attending dinners and the theatre can prove to be rather exhausting, what with the formality

*and displays of pomposity. The French call it a
fanfaronade. Occasionally I want to remove myself yet I
feel that there is a rising insurrection in this city, an
incipient rebellion about to break out, which will
culminate in an open resistance to established authority.*

*My travel over to France was absolutely miserable.
The ship pitched and tossed with every wave and I often
found it essential to retire to my cabin: and how I did
suffer violent bouts of nausea! Later I was able to
converse with my fellow passengers and I was especially
attracted by one, even more than a bee seduced by the
nectar of a honeysuckle with its fragrant yellow and pink
flowers. Is it possible for an eternity to be greater than
infinity? That is the way I wanted my voyage to be, yet
one feels that one has come to the end of the Universe
only to discover the most uninteresting sands of Calais.
Meanwhile I looked at this man. How is it possible for a
man to be so physically unsightly? And yet I would not
consider him to be ugly, repulsive or odious.*

*He wore a mulberry wool court suit decorated with
silk flowers, the petals made of coloured glass sequins
from Venice, and there were cambric frills on the shirt
front from above the waistcoat.*

*John Wilkes is not only a rebel but a young buck with
charm and wit. He charmed me into his arms and into
my cabin, claiming to have won a gun duel. There is
something appealing, attractive about a man who can
appear to be so arrogant yet so modest at the same time.
He fascinated me; yet I felt that under present conditions
and considering the rough sea, seduction would not be
possible.*

*'Do you think that we will ever arrive in France
safely?' I enquired.*

'I hope so,' he replied. 'I have never known there to be

such a choppiness of the waves.' And then he kissed me. At least, he tried to kiss me and I believe that he actually wanted to kiss me upon the lips but the boat lurched and reeled, in consequence of which his ardent kiss landed upon my left brow. He laughed and then he took my hand within his . . . and suddenly the sea was as tranquil as the breath of a new-born baby who has been suckled so gently upon his mother's breast. The waves were quiet yet I had felt embraced by the salinity of the sea breezes, which have curative powers, and also by the salty John Wilkes. I requested the Steward to bring us tea with brandy, which was done soon enough, then the door of the cabin closed and we were alone together. Then he undid the top three buttons of his suit and his jabot, his delightfully frilly shirt, spilled out of his coat. I then proceeded to open the lower buttons and slowly removed his boots and britches.

His member was so ready for me and I took it into my hands: and how it did pulsate and throb! I looked at the veins upon his erection, veins that convey blood from the heart; and I sucked upon his organ, his mighty reed. At first I kissed upon the tip of his tremendous tool and then I allowed my tongue to flicker up and down his erection. How excited he became as my saliva lubricated the underside of his stiff penis and I proceeded gently to suck upon each testicle, each one larger and harder than the size of chestnuts, encased by skin and hair, hair of soft curly ringlets that tickled upon my palate. That man has balls!

As his organ penetrated down my oesophagus, I felt a vacuum building up within my throat and I found it essential that I should breathe through my nose. Warm steam exuded from my nostrils, gently to tickle his scrotum.

'I can contain myself no longer!' he roared: and I drank of his spumy white spunk that had such a saline taste. John Wilkes lay back and closed his eyes but did not slump nor 'sink into a bag'. I watched his eye-lashes gently flutter and could see, beneath the frail skin of his eyelids, a blueness and amber contained within the iris of his eyes. I felt as though I had telescopic vision. Even in a mild slumber he could not hide his squint and I wondered if his life was equally oblique.

Gradually I removed my clothing, lazily dropping the items upon the side of the bed, a four-poster in a first-class cabin. Our ship was four sails to the wind as Jack Wilkes discarded his garments, then closed the canopy. The embers in the brazier prepared by the Chief Steward were dying down. There was an occasional crackle and flicker from the coals: ah! but what a delight it was to be between the sheets and under the eiderdown with my nostrils inhaling the sweet scent of lavender water; a cologne of distilled lavender, ambergris and alcohol.

'My beautiful Arabella . . .' he sighed, 'I never realized the beauty of a blue and silver gown . . .' and he stroked my velvet trimmings and gathering of lace upon the hem of my skirt. As I lay upon my back, he raised my skirt, removing it over the top of my head and he then requested that I turn over. Slowly he unlaced the stays of my corset to find that I wore a petticoat embroidered in gold upon brocaded white silk. 'Madam, how painful it must be for you to wear such a stiff-bodied gown; yet I detect a fine delicacy upon your petticoat and gown . . . perhaps it is the work of James Hargreaves?'

'You are correct,' I replied. (Editor's note: James Hargreaves was to revolutionize the business of weaving

UNHOLY PASSIONS

with his invention of the *Spinning Jenny*.)

'Was he your lover?' John Wilkes asked. 'Did he not design this petticoat especially for you?'

'I think not.'

'Then why are these initials embroidered around the hem of your petticoat? Perhaps there might be more underneath . . . or has he designed further initials upon your inner thigh?'

'I assure you not, sir. You may see for yourself.' I did not feel it necessary to make of my pubes a masquerade. He kissed upon my quim and sucked upon the lips of my labia, the folds of my tender pudendum, the corolla, petals of a flower, a cornucopia of abundance; and his teeth gently nibbled upon the funnel-shaped red and violet scented flowers of my petunia; and then his tongue penetrated me to taste my nectar . . . or as the French would say, my bonne-bouche.

This was just an hors d'oeuvre, a little something to whet the appetite before the main meal. For from within me I could feel a pulsation and a tightening of my muscles and then a relaxation, a release of tension upon reaching that uncontrollable state of orgasm whereby the cream from my vaginal channel flowed profusely down my thighs. My lover responded by drinking the opalescence of my juices.

'Now my love, my darling Arabella, is it not about time that I enter you so that you may receive the full benefits of my throbbing organ? There has been enough sexual stimulation between the two of us but now I would love to ravish your beautiful body! There is a treat within. Jump up quick on your hands and knees, you darling little whore . . .' And he gave me a couple of tremendously smarting smacks upon my buttocks, loud enough to have been heard a long way off. Turning up *my rump as desired, I found it was only a fancy of his for entering my cunt that way.*

'Ah, no, no, no, you surely shan't do that to me?!' I cried out in mock protest.

'Nonsense, you randy little bitch,' he replied. 'Shove your arse out and let me get in or I'll serve you out dreadfully and pitch you out of the window and into the sea and say that you committed suicide through over-excitement!' I felt the head of his prick, like a cannon, forcing its way within my tightly contracted quim. At last he plunged within and, withdrawing his hands from my mount where he had been teasing the hair to increase my pleasure, he placed both his arms around my neck. Beginning slowly, he fucked my vagina most voluptuously, until with a scream of delight, I spent again in perfect ecstasy as I felt the delicious hot spendings shooting within the warm, wet walls of my inmost recess. Wilkes sighed audibly but retained his stiffness and did not give up possession of my person until we had come together a second time.

'Jack,' I said, 'although your prick is handsome, I think it is said that your face is less than pretty. How do you manage to succeed with so many women?'

'It is simple, Arabella,' he smiled. 'I like to think that I treat women like ladies.'

'I wish you well, Jack,' I responded, 'but for how long can a man defy His Majesty's Government without being either imprisoned or killed?'

'That, Madam,' he answered gravely, 'is what I am trying to find out.'

We both had separate friends to meet us at Calais though I would be quite happy, remembering the rocking and rolling of the boat, to see Jack Wilkes again in Paris. The poor man is

now an outlaw. Horby, you have some influence. Please do something to help him. I look forward to seeing you soon.
  All my love,
  Arabella.

As I lit another pipe and took another glass of port, I reflected that certainly John Wilkes had *something* going for him.

CHAPTER TWENTY-THREE

'I never could get a set speech by heart,' Baron le Despenser, formerly Sir Francis Dashwood, lamented to me at his principal house in 1765 over copious quantities of sherry. 'I am not a man who can operate effectively unless I can write my own part. And I have proceeded to do so, Horby, in my own inimitable fashion here at West Wycombe Park.' As I knew, Dashwood had made himself popular in the locality by providing employment in having a road built to his house, using the chalk from a nearby cave.

His house was intended to be a representation of all he loved, showed in a sermon delivered in stone, supplemented by all the arts and crafts of the painter and interior designer. It was obvious to me that he had worked feverishly to have the house his father had left him remoulded after his own design. (*Editor's note:* it was recently featured in *Hello!* magazine and it is unfortunate that its creator was not mentioned.)

'My father,' Dashwood continued, 'built this house in the Queen Anne style in 1710. It is, or was, exactly the sort of house a wealthy businessman turned squire might have been expected to build.' I nodded, since my father had also come from a mercantile background. 'Now look around. Isn't this a finer repository for our revels than Medmenham Abbey?' I looked around and admired an harmonious synthesis of contrasting styles. The north front embodied a polite English classicism, with two stone lions, Ionic columns and stone steps to the main door. The south front was somewhat more exotic. From here I saw a beautiful view of a lawn and a lake from beneath a double colonnade. In one drawing-room there were busts of gods, emperors and philosophers; and paintings of members of the Club as executed by William Hogarth and other sundry artists. In the next room, the central section of the ceiling was decorated by a fresco featuring Bacchus and Ariadne.

'This was painted by our Brother, Giuseppe Borgnis,' Dashwood told me, 'and completed after his untimely death in 1761 by his son Giovanni. This Graeco-Roman theme is repeated in the next room – look! This main drawing-room is principally adorned by a picture of Psyche being admitted to Olympus, after an original by Raphael. Now, the dining-room here ... more sherry, Horby – the ceiling is after Caracci and reiterates the theme of Bacchus and Ariadne. One does not have to be overtly intelligent to discern that Bacchus represents drinking, fornication and the male probing for lust after truth: yet Ariadne represents the thread of that truth. The East Wing, built in 1754, y'see, is after the manner of an Ancient Greek Temple. The West Wing was built under the supervision of that fine architect Nicholas Revett, and it is a reconstruction of the Temple of Bacchus which I saw in Smyrna, Turkey.'

Again and again I found the theme of Dionysus/Bacchus, a wild male, mating with the Goddess of Truth. Around the house, further delights existed. There were woods of oak, beech and birch. There was a menagerie of monkeys, snakes and rodents. The lake contained four sailing vessels, including a fully rigged sixty-tonner. There was a greenhouse which boasted exotic insect-eating plants standing before a circular pond, which was home to the golden and silver fish of India. This was only the start of a series of remarkable buildings. Down the hill, Dashwood had had constructed the Church of

UNHOLY PASSIONS

St Lawrence, and I had never seen a church quite like this one.

'The ceiling is a copy of that in the ruined Temple of the Sun at Palmyna,' Dashwood murmured. Flowers abounded: and these are, of course, living symbols of female sexuality. I noticed four port-holes at north, south, east and west. We then climbed the stone steps to a golden globe above this church. 'This once more symbolizes the Sun,' Dashwood told me, 'and it can seat a maximum of four people to enjoy it.' At this instant, we were joined by the Steward, Paul Whitehead, who brought us tankards of marvellous milk punch, wonderfully intoxicating, and who then pointed out to me the beauties of the garden we could see beneath from our vantage point within the globe. All the flowers below us had been enchantingly planted so as to portray the wondrous shape of the female form, the view of which exquisite arrangement was only possible from the golden globe atop the Church; we contemplated for a time in delighted silence.

Upon descending the steps and leaving this remarkable Church, Dashwood showed me the Mausoleum.

'Again it is the worship of the Sun,' he informed me. 'It has six sides and six is the number of the Sun. Good old Bubb-Dodington left me money in his will to contribute towards its construction. I had his ashes buried there in 1762 and those of my dear, late and sorely lamented wife a year later.' This hexagonal building was beautiful to behold. 'Let us look at the caves,' said Dashwood, wiping away some tears from his eyes. We entered a series of dark caverns, accompanied by Whitehead who was bearing an oil lamp. 'I have spent over a million pounds on the construction of these artificial caves to express my beliefs,' Dashwood continued. 'Since I wish to be the soul of discretion, here I employed Cornish miners rather than local labour.' I was led for roughly two hundred feet into the very centre of the hill, and as Whitehead held up the lamp, I saw 'XXII – F' inscribed. 'F' was obviously Francis but I asked after 'XXII'. 'Why, Horby,' he replied, 'twenty-two are the letters of the Hebrew Alphabet from which the Magick of Qabalah derives, and from which communion of Man with God proceeds.

'My labyrinth,' Dashwood went on, 'is based upon all the wisdom from the East which my learned colleagues have brought me. Do you know of Tantra?' I shook my head. 'It is an Eastern philosophy of theory and practice which unites Man and Woman in sexual ecstasy, thus bringing forth the finest forces of their spirit. My caves represent the Tantrik World Egg, the ovum, bisected twice and once through the centre, by the sperm: and this symbol dates from 2000 BC.' He then led me through a tunnel that led to a chamber roughly forty feet in diameter, with four alcoves precisely positioned at north, south, east and west, just as the port-holes had been positioned in his Church. 'Beyond this,' Dashwood's voice boomed throughout the caves, 'there are passages laid out to the left and right so as to form a triangle, which is the Tantrik symbol for the sacred vulva. Probably you do not yet understand the matter, my dear Horby. But never mind: let us proceed.' We passed on to an artificially created river.

'The River Styx, sir!' Dashwood declared. 'This is the River of Death. Sex and Death are the only interesting Mysteries in Life.' I noticed that Paul Whitehead was preparing a rowing boat, tethered by the side. 'Ah, and here is Charon who will row us across the River of the Dead.' Whitehead duly did row us over these black waters, enabling me to see a chamber carved out of rock. 'Here,' said Dashwood, 'and carved into the wall and half-hidden by pebbles at foot-level, you find an ovoid representation of a vulva. Here is a bas-relief key, roughly 5½ inches long, the average length of the modern male penis.' I looked, I saw and I marvelled at the matter.

'These caves, Horby,' Dashwood said, 'are hardly a good

place for holding an orgy. They are cold, draughty, hard and uncomfortable for this purpose and in any case I have an ideal home appropriate for the matter. These caves were constructed for the celebration of the English Eleusinian Mysteries. Interested?'

'Yes,' I answered, 'providing that you can explain to me what these are.'

'You die,' said Dashwood, 'so as to be reborn and refreshed, but after another manner.'

'Yes,' I replied, 'I am interested.'

'I was sorry to learn,' Paul Whitehead said as, having emerged from the caves, we plodded up the hill to the house, 'that Charles Churchill died recently. I always did enjoy his verses.'

'He was cruel, though, Paul,' Dashwood reminded him. 'Look at how he satirized our friend and Brother Sandwich!'

'Oh, I know,' said Whitehead, then quoted Churchill:

'Nature design'd him, in a rage,
To be the Wharton of his age,
But having given all the sin,
Forgot to put the virtues in.'

'Too hard, Paul, too hard!' Dashwood laughed as we essayed the final steep climax of the hill. 'I wish my friend Sandwich every possible success in his crusade against corruption in the docks, though it will make him plenty of enemies. Let us face the fact that four factions are presently struggling for power and influence. The few hundred Whig families who have run England for over half a century want to carry on doing so. Our dear King George III wants to curb their powers, wanting a regime of benevolent paternalism, based upon the alleged Divine Right of Kings, with a right to curb freedom of speech, in which he is supported by the Tories. The third factor is the emerging movement of Democracy, which John Wilkes has personified.'

'Wilkes is finished,' said Whitehead. 'He is just an outlaw and an exile.'

'I am not so sure,' Dashwood responded. 'We have yet to evaluate this matter and movement. There is, of course, a fourth factor: the Independents. How do you feel about that, Horby?'

'It depends on what you mean.'

'Well, I'll give you my views gladly,' Dashwood answered. 'Great Britain should be ruled by a wise élite. This élite should represent true aristocracy rather than mere oligarchy and its purposes are best served if there is a Patriot King upon the throne. This élite should practise a religion based upon the truths of Nature and this should be done in the most exquisitely aesthetic surroundings, preceded and followed by the finest wines and feasting and sexual satisfaction, with women admitted upon equal terms. This religion, essentially pagan in nature, is based upon the worship of the male and female principles in Life and this is sacred, not sinful: this includes practices taken from the Orient, the Knights Templar, the Renaissance Hermeticists and the Rosicrucians designed to enhance human intelligence and human evolution. Anyway, if our political objectives cannot be achieved *overtly*, they can be achieved *covertly* – and underground, so to speak. But enough of that, sirs. I believe that some delightful guests await us.'

Dashwood was absolutely right for as we entered the second drawing-room, there were two women dear to my heart, Lady Clarissa Hyde and the Hon. Arabella Marchmount, accompanied by the lascivious Lady Betty Germain.

After our sherries, we proceeded to the dining-room in order to enjoy one of Dashwood's eccentric but delicious dinners. He declared that there would be a feast of fish and so served us *a*nchovies on toast; *bouillabaisse*, a most appetizing

UNHOLY PASSIONS

fish stew of Provence; *c*rawfish; baked *d*ab; smoked *e*el; baked *f*lounder; *g*ougones of whiting; *h*ake in herb sauce; *i*nk of squid to be eaten with crusty bread; bottled *j*alapeño peppers from Mexico to enhance all flavours; *k*edgeree, an Indian dish made of smoked herring and rice; *l*obster with a new sauce called *m*ayonnaise; *N*iersteiner wine from Germany; *o*ysters; *p*laice fried and served cold in oil; *q*uenelles of pike; *r*ed mullet, lightly grilled; *s*ardines from Portugal, lightly fried; *t*errine of salmon with *t*oast; *u*nusual fish such as the sea-*u*rchin; *v*ictorious fish, as in the cases of fried slices of shark in lemon sauce; *w*hitebait, neatly fried in breadcrumbs; then an e*x*traordinarily fine Dover sole. After which, for our pudding, a *y*olk of egg will be whipped with warm wine to make the delicious *z*abaglione. 'Ha! ha! Dig in, ladies and gentlemen! And do excuse my humour!'

We did indeed dig in and every dish was delicious. The occasion was made all the more delightful by Paul Whitehead, who organized the servants for the pouring of the wine. He ensured that each of the many varieties, whether it was Niersteiner, Bernkastler Riesling, Gewuerztraminer, white Burgundy or white Bordeaux, was served at just the right moment to complement any particular dish. He noticed also that some like to drink red wine occasionally with a fish course and so lost no time in ensuring that light claret was served to those of this persuasion. I thought it a pity, during this otherwise superlative dinner, that Sir Francis had not chosen to serve potatoes, since these go exceptionally well with fish. These were a tremendously expensive luxury in my grandfather's day but, owing to trade and the development of agriculture, have become cheaply available even to the poorest. I gather that the pie shops have developed a novel way of chopping and cooking this vegetable: they call it 'chips'. I really must try 'chips', even if it means visiting some Cockney shop, since it is obvious to me that deeply fried potatoes, neatly sliced, could go rather well with fried fish.

'What is the best thing to do after dinner?' Dashwood demanded. 'I say: let's make love!' With that, he fell to his knees and, swivelling about, twisted Clarissa's body around so that he could get at her cunt. It was obvious how delightful the thrusts of his tongue were to her in her excited state. She wriggled about in ecstasy and, getting one foot upon his prick gently, she rolled it on his thigh and under her sole, making it quite enormously stiff and at the same moment she appeared to faint away from an excess of emotion.

I thought that he was going to fuck her properly now since his engine was so rampant but instead of that, he turned his back on her. Being passed a fine, light birch rod from Arabella, made of three or four twigs only, elegantly tied up with blue and crimson velvet ribbons, he commenced to flagellate her body. How his light switch seemed to weal the flesh of her tender bottom at every stroke! It was in vain that Clarissa cried out for mercy as tears rolled down her cheeks. Sir Francis, the leading Baron of England, only seemed to be the more delighted and jeered at the effects, telling Clarissa first how rosy her bottom looked.

'Now, you bitch!' he snarled, 'it's getting fine and red and it is glowing deliciously! Spanking good fun, eh?' At last the rod was used up, the splinters lying all about the floor, whereupon Dashwood threw it aside and assaulted Clarissa's quim, visibly more and more delighted in forcing his entrance, to which Lady Clarissa made mock protest but to which she willingly acceded. It was clear to me that she was soon forgetting everything under the influence of his ecstatic moves and either she fainted or else she successfully pretended to faint. Obviously she was enjoying herself.

For my own part, I made Arabella lie down on a sofa, ignoring Clarissa in her role as chaperone, and tied a bandage over her eyes, fastened her hands and feet so that she could not

UNHOLY PASSIONS

move and then, lifting all her clothes up, I tickled and frigged her with my fingers until she was quite beside herself with unsatisfied desire and begged me to fuck her.

'It really is a damned shame to tease you so, my sexy little bitch,' I laughed, for then she could feel more of my fingers deep within the depths of her vagina. Suddenly I pounced upon her, ramming her with my rampant penis, and, throwing my arms around her beautiful, nubile body, my stiff cock filled her longing gap in a manner which, it seemed, she had not felt before. Arabella spent in an ecstasy of bliss, murmuring her thanks in endearing terms for the pleasure I had afforded her by such a delectable proof of my manhood.

Presently a strange hand seemed to be feeling my prick whilst thrusting a pair of fingers into the quim of Arabella alongside my still vigorous engine.

'Ah! Oh! Oh!! Who is that!' Arabella screamed from under the skirts which I had thrown over her face. I saw the joke and withdrew, smiling at Clarissa.

'Ha! Ha! Ha!' Dashwood roared. 'She no longer knows who is fucking whom!' With that, he whipped the blindfold from her face. 'Ha! She pretends to think that I have been fucking her when she must have known that it was Horby all the time!'

'No,' said the Honourable Arabella Marchmount. 'Pricks do differ, Dashwood, and we ladies *can* tell the difference. However, it is a pleasure to have all the obstructions removed from my face so that I can see that it is you on top of me, with your prick in full possession and just beginning to run a second course.'

''Yoicks! Tally Ho!' Dashwood yelled out as he fucked away.

'Kiss her!' Clarissa cried out. 'Pout your tongue in her mouth, my dear sir! Fuck! Fuck away! Or it will be the worse for your arse . . .' murmured Her Ladyship, who was handling his balls with one hand and slapping his rump furiously with the other. 'See how she pretends to be ashamed? It's quite delightful, Arabella, to observe that you can still *blush!*'

'Ohhh . . .' the dear girl sighed and protested against any supposed outrage, but the smooth motions of Dashwood evidently made her forget everything. He spent a second time and, keeping his place, renewed the love combat with unabated vigour. Discerning that Arabella was becoming quite carried away by her feelings as she responded to his manly attack with all her naturally voluptuous ardour, he released both her hands and feet so that she might thoroughly enjoy herself.

'Hold tight, Francis!' Clarissa cried out. 'Arabella is so high spirited that you'll become unseated: but the little devil needn't think that she is having this treat all to herself!' Saying this, she flung herself upon the soft Persian carpet and tickled the stiff shaft of Dashwood's prick, quite exciting me by the lascivious movements of her gorgeous bottom. I could no longer restrain myself and joined her there, where we amused ourselves by kissing and toying with each other's parts, until my handsome teacher, notwithstanding the previous hard work of the evening, was in a most rampant, impatient state and she would fain have cooled my ardour within her longing cunt were it not for the enchanting sight before us.

His Lordship's hard cock was now battering against the tight, dark, wrinkled nether hole of Arabella's rounded, pearly-white bottom. Instantly Clarissa dashed to protect Arabella, raised her skirts and encouraged Dashwood to lick her cunt. I turned my head suddenly to glance around the chamber, for Paul Whitehead and Lady Betty Germain had become quite uncharacteristically quiet. One glance revealed the obvious reason for the matter. Paul was so eager for work that he had scarcely entered Betty's quim before his fingers went busy with lubricant upon her bottom. Whitehead then directed his tool so cleverly to the mark that almost immediately she responded by coming in response to the fullness of his insertion: though that was always the way of the delightful Lady Betty!

'I want a man,' she was murmuring, 'who rogers me right up to the roots of his hair!'

'Ah!' Paul responded, complying with her request, to her evident satisfaction, 'I revel in the delicious sensations and pleasures to which my lady love treats me!'

Dashwood was sucking excitedly now at the beautiful bottom of Arabella.

'Beautiful...' we could hear him murmur in a half-choked voice as Arabella's buttocks writhed with pleasure. Clarissa and I chose to fuck slowly with one another as we watched this intriguing sight. 'Fuck!' Dashwood continued as he temporarily arose from the cleft to kiss each beautiful buttock. 'Go on quick!' he suddenly exclaimed, then, pulling up his head, he thrust his throbbing dick straight between the bum cheeks of Arabella. 'Ah! Aargh! SPEND! Spend...' Clarissa and I could see Arabella's eyes to be full of kindled fire as Francis shot his juices within her arse cheeks.

'Where the bee sucks, there suck I,' Dashwood murmured. Meanwhile I turned to see that Paul Whitehead and Lady Betty had changed positions and that Whitehead's stiff prick had shot its juices into Betty's voluptuous mouth: indeed, the drops of thick, creamy spend fairly oozed from her lips as she still sucked with great gusto. My own prick was now stiffening into a more than manly state and I proceeded to fuck my dear Clarissa's cunt with fury. We spent almost simultaneously and her spendings were so wild, what with the heaving of her nubile body, that I swear I might have been flung away from her, had I not clung to her neck.

Dashwood and Arabella clearly did not intend to remain idle and enacted another exciting scene before our eyes as Clarissa and I recommenced a lazy, slow fuck. Francis wetted the head of his prick and Arabella's bum-hole with spittle and soon enough drove his great machine through the narrowest gate of Paradise.

For my own part, I continued to fuck Lady Clarissa, who used her vagina for gentle, squeezing movements. These movements were indeed heavenly, blissful! I never before felt such an acme of pleasure, especially when she inserted an elegantly manicured forefinger into my behind; and the sight before me, the soul-stirring movements aback made me groan in an agony of delight in our mutual emissions. A perfect frenzy of lust appeared to possess Dashwood as he fucked Arabella time and time again, to her greatly evident delight.

I think that possibly certain matters regarding Dashwood are put best by his friend, John Hall Stevenson, who assisted Laurence Sterne of *Tristam Shandy* fame and who also founded the Club of the Demoniacs at his Yorkshire 'Crazy Castle'. I empathize with Stevenson's: *A Query into the Strange Events which Took Place under West Wycombe Hill*, which venue he had attended:

'Where can I find a cave to muse
Upon his Lordship's envied glory?
Which of the nine dare to refuse
To tell the strange and recent story?
Mounting, I saw the egregious Lord
O'er all impediments and bars,
I saw him at Jove's council board
And saw him stuck among the stars.'

CHAPTER TWENTY-FOUR

'What the people of this country want, as I do,' Colonel Henry Luttrell declared at a public meeting when addressing the electors of Middlesex, 'is Constitution, Restitution and PROSTITUTION! ... sorry, PROSPERITY!'

'Boo!' roared the audience. 'Sit down!' some cried out. 'Go home!' others shouted. 'We want Wilkes!' was the yell that came from others, and now John Wilkes mounted the platform. He had come back to England and dared King and Parliament to do their worst, backed meanwhile by the Society of the Bill of Rights which paid the debts of Wilkes on account of the fact that he was their most powerful spokesman. The Government had moved cautiously, fearing the wrath of the London Mob, and Wilkes was not arrested. The London Mob had welcomed him with joyous cries of 'WILKES AND LIBERTY!' However, they did not have the vote and so his endeavour to be elected as a London MP was a failure.

He had promptly been elected MP for Middlesex by a large majority, only to be expelled by the House of Commons. This raised a vital constitutional point. Did the House of Commons have the right to expel a Member duly elected? The London Mob rioted once again and Wilkes promptly pulled another move. He surrendered to the authorities, fought them via the Courts and had his conviction for outlawry quashed on a technicality. Then, in confronting two charges of which he had been convicted in 1764, he waived his privileges as an MP at that time and accepted a sentence of two years of imprisonment and a fine of £1,000. The London Mob rioted once again and the Government had to let Wilkes go.

Wilkes had not only aroused the Mob: he had activated the emerging middle classes, who had no love for the Whig oligarchy and who desired a more powerful political presence. Meanwhile their champion slogged on quite relentlessly, demanding a full pardon and a restoration to his former position, in a war which Wilkes relished. He published savage attacks on the Government for its use of the military against rioters. A petition to the Commons complained of the illegality of the proceedings undertaken against him. Having been expelled, though elected on 3 February 1769, Wilkes promptly won re-election for Middlesex two weeks later. The House of Commons resolved that Wilkes was incapable of being elected to serve in Parliament. The reply of Wilkes was to win *another* election as MP for Middlesex on 16 March: and, once again, the House of Commons had the temerity to expel him. I was therefore present to see Wilkes debate on the hustings with his utterly inept opponent, Colonel Henry Luttrell, on 13 April 1769.

'Ladies and gentlemen,' Wilkes began.

'The ladies don't 'ave a vote!' some tart shouted out.

'I hope they will some day since I am all for it, Madam,' Wilkes retorted. 'I want DEMOCRACY!' How the people cheered! 'I will promise you nothing that I cannot deliver. Make no mistake about me. I do know what I stand for and what I stand against. I am against the over-privileged *few* governing the country and swindling the under-privileged *many!*' How the electors cheered him!

'Don't listen to this fraudulent fool!' Colonel Luttrell shouted, his face quite empurpled with rage. 'He is just spouting airy-fairy nonsense. Now, if *I* am elected, beer will be a penny a pint!'

'That's no bloody use, mate!' a strong man shouted as two waggons drew up by the hustings. 'Wilkes is giving it to us for free!'

'Shut up yer face!' a woman yelled at Colonel Luttrell as assistants in the waggons commandeered by Wilkes proceeded to serve good, free beer to the crowd.

'Don't listen to my opponent!' Wilkes roared as everyone helped themselves. 'He is just the same as the rest of them. He will promise you cheaper beer -- and once he is elected, the beer will be watered and the price will be doubled!' The crowd laughed and cheered as I noticed that some Officers of the Law had mounted the stage and were approaching Wilkes.

'Mr Wilkes . . . ?' said the first officer.

'Haven't I seen you somewhere before, sir?' Wilkes responded. 'Really, we can't go on meeting like this.'

'You're under arrest, Mr Wilkes,' the first officer said, flourishing a document beneath his nose. 'And this time I think you will find that *this* is a specific legal charge, naming both you and your alleged crime.'

'May I see it, please?' Wilkes replied and the first officer handed it to him. Wilkes promptly addressed the increasingly restless crowd, holding the document in the air. 'And now you see, ladies and gentlemen, for yourselves, just how disgustingly suppressive the system is!' He spat upon the Warrant and threw it to the crowd, who tore it to shreds. 'I promise to fight for Liberty!' The officers grabbed Wilkes by the collar. 'I promise to fight for DEMOCRACY, for *your* right to make it *your* country . . . aargh!' The first officer had grabbed him in a choke-hold.

'We going to allow this, lads??!' a rough bellowed.

'NO FUCKING WAY!' his mob roared.

'Right, lads, pile in,' the mobster ordered.

'Yeah, that's right!' a woman screeched. 'Smash 'is face in!'

'Kill the pigs!' the women yelled as the men pounded the

ANONYMOUS

Law Officers to pulp. They crawled away, bloody and bowed, being given a few added kicks from assorted tarts.

'Thank you, good people, thank you,' said Wilkes, dusting off his coat. 'And don't let these bastards grind you down!' The crowd cheered him. 'There's life left in Great Britain yet . . . but you have seen just what I'm talking about! It is the oppression of the poor by the rich.' The crowd roared for him. 'It is Robin Hood in reverse. It is robbing the poor to feed the rich. And many of you do not even have a vote in the matter!' The crowd cheered him. 'Am I going to stand for it? Are *you* going to stand for it?! Say *NO* NOW!' he roared.

'NO!!!' the crowd bellowed.

'Thank you, ladies and gentlemen.' Wilkes doffed his tricorne hat in a stylish, sweeping bow to his audience. ' I know that my faith in the British people is right!'

'Wilkes and Liberty . . .' the crowd chanted as the electors made their way to the boards to record their open votes, 'Wilkes and Liberty: WILKES AND L-I-B-E-R-T-Y!!!' The mob without votes jeered and threw rotten eggs and stinking vegetables at all electors for Colonel Luttrell.

Two hours passed. Then the Returning Officer, a sober, bespectacled, conscientious elderly man announced:

'The result for the votes cast in this constituency of Middlesex is as follows: for Colonel Luttrell – three hundred and sixty-seven votes.' The Mob booed and hissed. 'For John Wilkes – three thousand and fifty-six votes.' The crowd yelled its approval. 'I therefore declare Mr John Wilkes to be our newly elected Member of Parliament.' The crowd cheered and chaired Wilkes as Colonel Luttrell glowered at them.

'Wilkes and Liberty! Wilkes and LIBERTY!' the Mob chanted. Unfortunately, the House of Commons resolved once again that John Wilkes should be expelled from Parliament, a motion carried by two hundred votes for and five against. Colonel Luttrell therefore took the seat of Wilkes in a

UNHOLY PASSIONS

disgusting defiance of Democracy. Wilkes responded by going to the authorities and demanding that he be arrested. This was duly done and he was flung into the Tower of London. Instantly, the London Mob rioted, wrecking all before them in the names of 'WILKES AND LIBERTY!'

I was staying at the town house of Sandwich at the time, where he was entertaining his gorgeous mistress, Fanny Murray, and the Mob was howling for his blood. Fanny stepped out onto the pavement to confront the Mob.

'Good people, desist,' she said, but she had to duck to avoid the stones thrown at her.

'Whore . . . *Whore!* WHORE!!!' the Mob chanted.

'Yes, all right, I am a whore!' Fanny retorted. 'But as Nell Gwynne said: "I am the *English* whore, not the French one." But let me tell ye something . . .' The Mob went uncharacteristically quiet. 'Ye might not agree with the views of my man Sandwich but he has his honour. And if it were not for me, there'd be ten men, armed to the teeth to shoot down you lot . . . but I don't want that since yer cause is just. Of course I know Jack Wilkes. And even my man, who fought a duel with him, has called him a gentleman. Believe me, good people, I will do my all to get Jack Wilkes out of prison.'

'Go for it, Fanny!' the women yelled out.

'Go for it, Fanny!' the Mob roared out. 'Yeah, leave her alone. She's all right!' They then went away to tear down more buildings and, no doubt, to beat up some other people. Fanny returned upstairs to see Sandwich crouching concernedly at the open window looking out and down into the street, a blunderbuss in one hand and a pistol in the other. I was backing him up with a brace of flintlocks.

'Are you all right, my dear?' Sandwich enquired.

'Does it look as if I am not?' Fanny responded.

'If any man,' said Sandwich, 'had harmed a hair of your gorgeous head, I would have blown him away.'

'Probably enjoy that, wouldn't you?' Fanny said heavily.

'Oh, for heaven's sake, what's the matter?' Sandwich expostulated. 'You spoke incredibly bravely in front of the scum of the earth.'

'We're not the scum of the earth . . .' Fanny retorted through gritted teeth. 'Johnny, you're a good, brave man in yer way but you just don't see certain things.'

'What things?' Sandwich retorted irritably.

'The London Mob could have taken this place apart and killed all three of us, guns or no guns,' Fanny explained patiently.

'Horby and I would have fought to the death!' Sandwich snarled.

'Yes, that is what it would have been,' Fanny responded calmly. 'Now, Johnny, I want ye to do something for me, if you would be so kind.'

'Fanny,' said Sandwich, 'you are not only very beautiful, you are also very brave. I genuinely admire that. Name it and it is yours, m'dear.'

'Get Jack Wilkes released from prison.'

'What?' Sandwich was outraged. 'Never!'

'Then would ye kindly leave the stage?' Fanny requested. 'And never darken the doors of my house again.' There was a long pause as Fanny and Sandwich stared into one another's eyes.

'Ahem,' Sandwich coughed. 'Didn't realize that you felt so strongly about the matter concerning that bloody rascal . . . very well . . . I'll see what I can do!' Fanny rushed to embrace him.

'Oh, Johnny!' she cried out, 'ye're such an angel!'

'I'm a completely cold bastard, actually,' Sandwich responded, after which he went to bed with her and I went home.

Sandwich kept his promise to Fanny; and Wilkes hit back as usual through building upon his 'democratic' power base in London. Having become a City Alderman in 1769, he was made a sheriff in 1771 and Lord Mayor in 1774. That was the year in which he was once again re-elected as the MP for Middlesex. This time, the House of Commons did not dare to expel him, even though he was standing for a radical programme. The Bill of Rights, embraced and proposed by him in 1771, in concert with his growing army of supporters, called for shorter Parliaments, more votes for more people and the abolition of boroughs in the pockets of the oligarchy. 1771 was also the year in which he established the freedom of printers in their reporting of Parliamentary debates and secured them from arrest by invoking the judicial privileges of the City. As a Magistrate there, he frequently showed himself to be conscientious and enlightened.

Having established the right of a democratically elected Member to take his seat in the House of Commons, no matter how much the oligarchy might dislike him, Wilkes always spoke in favour of Parliamentary Reform and consistently defended the rights of the American colonists, as Dashwood came to do. His enormous popularity with the common people made of this former outlaw a man of civic respect.

'Sir,' Wilkes said to me when released from prison, 'I consider the voice of the people to be the Voice of God.' There was so much to like in the character of this man, I reflected, as I gave him good claret at my home. Certainly he had wit, even though his friends feared that his drinking might lead to his drowning, like the Duke of Clarence in a butt of Malmsey in Shakespeare's *King Richard III*. For my own part, I shall never forget that wonderful evening I enjoyed with Jack Wilkes at an Aylesbury inn just after he had defeated Colonel Luttrell at the polls though before the Government went for him and he defeated them. His jests at my expense were annoying me mildly, as we sat drinking mulled spiced ale in the best inn that Buckinghamshire could offer.

'Don't you think that King George III is a rather decent chap?' I enquired.

'Nay, sirrah,' Wilkes responded sharply. 'Once you invited me to play cards with him and I declined, for I can't tell the difference between a king and a knave. Really, my dear Horby, you *are* sometimes Whore-be.'

'Huh! Your jokes!' I snorted disgustedly. 'I won't be your butt!'

'With all my heart, sir,' Wilkes returned, 'since I never did like an empty one.' Obviously I took his hint and ordered another pint of tawny port for both of us. 'Are there any girls here for us to fuck, sir?'

The fact was that, on this particular night, we were escorted to our respective bedrooms by the daughter of the landord. Upon our way up the stairs, we passed a portrait of John Wilkes, so similar to many that were being hung in public places throughout the country in favour of Wilkes as the Champion of Democracy and of votes for the working man. We were guided well by an extremely attractive, buxom wench who, as I knew, happened to be married to a handsome man. Perhaps celebrity was going to the head of Wilkes since he put an arm around her waist and said:

'Now, my pretty dear, are you to be let with the room?'

'No, sir,' she replied, 'I am to be let alone.' She turned to point at the portrait of Wilkes. 'There you 'ang, sir. Everywhere but where you should.' Wilkes cackled wickedly in reply and entered his bedroom. I entered mine to read the letter I had received but not yet read from Lady Clarissa Hyde:

Horby,
Have I ever told you before that you are my favourite cousin, yet I sometimes wonder about your alleged

UNHOLY PASSIONS

affection for Arabella? She has an outstanding knowledge of Ancient History, the Prehistoric, the Celtic remains, and megalithic burial chambers, yet she suffers from the mégrim, a melancholia of ill-founded fears. Yet now she is much more beautiful, divinely tall, with a Goddess-like quality. Is it no wonder that Sir Francis was so attached to her? He gave her a proposition in his customary sanguine manner, hoping that she would accept the idea that they might go in search for the Holy Grail through the act of coitus; and Arabella found a need, a deficit that could not be completely satisfied.

'Would you like to come with me,' I invited her, 'to the Isle of Mona, Ynys Mon, *as it is known by the Welsh. I think you would perhaps know it as the Island of Anglesey.'*

'How do we get there? Is not the crossing dangerous and fraught with difficulty? And where shall we stay?'

'We shall stay at Beaumaris and it is there that my grandfather has purchased a property facing upon the sandy beaches of the Menai Straits and right next to the Beaumaris Castle, which was built during the reign of King Edward I. Our journey might be rough but I hope you will appreciate the beauty when we arrive.' Arabella kissed me upon the lips and hugged me.

'Thank you for inviting me and I so look forward to meeting your grandfather,' Arabella responded. 'Is this not the island that was invaded by Suetonius Paulinus, slaying the Druid priests and destroying the sacred groves?'

'Agricola completed the conquest several years later,' I replied, 'and I hope for an easy journey across the waters.' We travelled by carriage to Bangor and, perhaps to the disappointment of Arabella, were not held up by handsome highwaymen. I hired a sedan chair so that we

ANONYMOUS

could cross the Lavan Sands in comfort in order to take the ferry. Once aboard, Arabella tucked her arm into mine and I could feel the tension underneath her skin.

'What if there is a bull with mighty horns there?' she lamented. 'Might he want to attack me?'

'I fear not, as you are of the wrong species,' I murmured. Eventually a rickety carriage brought us from the boat to my grandfather's house. The oil lamps flickered as the old man opened the door.

'Welcome.' He kissed me gently upon the cheek. 'I thought you would never arrive . . . Arabella, what a pleasure to meet you!' and he stretched out his frail, elderly hand in greeting. 'Before my wife and I retire for the night, can I offer you both a negus? And there is more gently heating up upon the stove. As I am getting on in age, I find it necessary that I retire for the evening. Two beds have been prepared for you upstairs and first upon the left. Arabella, Clarissa, I am tired so please excuse me.' We both drank up our cups and then retired to bed. I put on my nightgown and watched as Arabella put on hers. Her back was turned towards me as she unlaced the stays of her corset, one similar to mine, and we both climbed into our separate beds. The candles flickered and went out and there was silence. I arose to open the curtains to reveal the moon and the stars.

'Clarissa . . . ?' I noticed that suddenly there was a noise from outside that sent shivers up and down my spine as I looked upon the castle. 'Clarissa, I am cold and frightened and cannot go to sleep.' I sat down next to her upon the bed and stroked her hair and kissed gently upon the nape of her slender, swan-like neck; and then lay down next to her, under the eiderdown, as even I felt something eldritch within the air and sprang up to relight the candles. How can I describe the sounds that

night? There was the crackle of dying embers, one could actually hear the snoring of the elderly from the nearby bedrooms, there was the lowing of cattle and the splashing of the waves, drawn by the moon, lapping upon the shingle of the beach. I enfolded Arabella within my arms. Her nightgown was so silken and I unlaced the front and touched upon her breasts.

'There is nothing more by which to be intimidated,' I murmured as I lay down next to her. At one touch, her hair fell down almost to her waist in ringlets and I kissed her locks, inhaling that scent of the altar of rose petals that is usually contained within a pouncet-box in order to intensify the perfume. Her lips were rosy red, cochineal, paying a compliment to her lily-white, ivory complexion; there appeared to be an unguent upon her lips to ensure that they were soft and kissable. I suspect that this contained spikenard (an ancient and costly aromatic ointment from India, believed to have aphrodisiacal qualities). The candles again flickered as if the winds from the north had entered without an invitation to quell us into darkness.

We were not idle whilst this exciting scene was enacted. Arabella instinctively wetted my cunt and my bum-hole with spittle and then proceeded to drive her tongue through the narrowest gate of Paradise. Its movements were indeed heavenly, blissful. I never before felt such an acme of pleasure, the sight before me, the soul-stirring movements behind; and our mutual emissions almost made me groan loud enough for the fish to hear, in an agony of delight.

A perfect frenzy of lust seemed to take possession of my body. I could discern that the clitoris of Arabella was now finely tuned and I alternated between kissing and sucking it. I threw myself upon Arabella's quim, taking the breath out of her by my sudden pressure upon her belly.

'Damned hellish BITCH!' she shouted as I fixed my stiff index finger within her bottom-hole in triumph, nipping and squeezing and, I must confess, wriggling the forefinger of my right hand upon the proud erect nipples of her breasts. She sighed and, as I moved upwards to kiss her full lips, her fingers took possession of my hot, raging cunt. I could feel that she, for her own part, was thoroughly enjoying the matter as her clitty stiffened more and more every moment under the delightful movements and pressures to which I treated her.

I frigged Arabella until her eyes started from her head from excess of emotion and she spent as the firm round globes of her bosom heaved in rapture.

'I have never felt anything quite like this before . . .' Arabella sighed gently. 'My quim is so extended by the excess of lustful excitement that I am gorged to repletion and yet I feel that I want more, more, MORE! Uh . . .' She seemed to be semi-delirious, 'Had I been cunt all over . . . I should have wanted every hole well filled by a good stiff one. Ah! What a delicious movement! Ah! ah! if I could but die like that! I seem transported to another world . . . my senses are leaving me . . . I am indeed in Paradise!'

'I am delighted, my darling,' I replied. 'I am going to give you a real taste of what sex is like. Here!' I reached beneath the bed and strapped on a leather dildo. 'I want you to tickle my bottom-hole and gamahauch my cunt. Won't that be a delightful conjunction, my love?'

'You frighten me, Clarissa dear,' Arabella whispered. 'What is a dildo? Will it hurt?'

'Exactly like a man's affair, Arabella!' I laughed. 'Although it cannot shoot a delicious, soothing emission

UNHOLY PASSIONS

into you at the ecstatic moment,' I softly explained. 'Now let me straddle over your pretty face and present my cunny to your sweet pouting lips for a sucking kiss. You will like it. It will excite you so to the unmistakable joy the dildo will give when it once gets in,' and I suited the action to the words by placing myself over her.

Her blood was on the boil. She thrust her tongue eagerly into my longing cunt which instantly rewarded her by a copious spend which Arabella seemed to relish as much as any epicurean gamahaucher would have done, with her legs spread lasciviously wide apart. Opening the lips of her spending cunt gently with my fingers, I now cunningly frigged her with my thumb until Arabella became so excited that she began to bite me and wiggle about in such an extraordinary way as well as to moan and sob:

'Oh! Ah! shove, SHOVE! Do push your thumb in further, Clarissa, darling . . . I feel that I must have it . . . Ohh . . . OH! Ah-huh! O! Pray don't . . .' I continued to force the way of my thumb deep within her vagina. I pressed my cunt upon her mouth so that she could not scream and I intensely enjoyed the pain that I put her to, for she was awfully tight yet I was not to be denied.

With my dildo strapped on duly before me, I changed my position and now pushed and rammed into her in lustful fury until I had the whole of it within her sheath. I then rested for a few moments, moving the dildo within its tight receptacle until the natural lubricity of her nature asserted itself once more and answered with a wanton heave of her pearly-white bottom to every thrust of mine. There seemed to be no satisfying her greedy cunt now that it had a taste of matters.

We broke off to laugh, kiss, eat prawns and drink hock followed by port and brandywine before resuming our lubricious and lascivious languors and raptures. Also, there was game pie, to which Arabella did ample justice.

I drank glass after glass with Arabella. My veins were on fire, consumed by my longing to enjoy further so handsome a young girl. As soon as Arabella had finished her repast, I requested her to sit by my side on the ottoman and, just as she was in the fact of sitting down, I drew her upon my lap, saying with a laugh:

'What a pretty dear you are . . . kiss me.' My lips met hers in a long-drawn osculation which made her quiver all over with emotion as she lay on my bosom. 'Do you truly have a sweetheart, dear girl?' I asked.

'Many,' she replied, 'but Horby is my dearest.' I pondered upon that, Horby, and I think that you should do so too. As it was, I declared indignantly:

'And you have been putting yourself about! This is intolerable!' Seizing Arabella – and I admit, Horby, what a lark! – I flung her over my lap and proceeded to administer chastisement with my hand, giving the matter some thought and some well-orchestrated percussion. 'You impertinent little hussy!' I snapped at her as my hand came down hard and she squealed. 'I shall make your bottom smart!' It was fun to see how undignified Arabella looked once I had whipped up her skirts and petticoats to expose her beautiful bottom to my censorious gaze. How she blushed as I pulled down her drawers to expose a very pretty, white-skinned bum which was soon rendered rosy enough from the hand-slapping she received from me. 'I shall give you your just deserts for your impudence,' I said sternly.

She is a rather plucky girl and disdained initially to cry out overmuch although I saw two or three big tears roll down her crimson shame-face under my infliction of

UNHOLY PASSIONS

chastisement – and I could also feel that her clitty was as stiff as a poker.

Arabella begged hard to be let off, and I was merciful, though gleeful as I watched her adjust her clothes. I laughed and joked about her gorgeous, scarlet glowing bottom as her face flushed. After that, we kept it up until five o'clock, kissing, licking, sucking, stroking and indulging in every fancy of which we could think.

She is the one for you, I feel. Oh! I would that you were my manly champion in this combat of bliss! Would to Heaven that I might die in spending as I felt your very soul shoot into my vitals, but alas! it cannot be! We can only make love between us now and again yet still, if there is bliss in the world to be, I feel assured of an everlasting fuck.

All my love,
Clarissa

As I snuffed out the candle and stretched out my legs in the bed, to bump and scorch them upon a stone hot water bottle, I wondered just where the Democracy lay.

CHAPTER TWENTY-FIVE

'Horby, would you like to come with me and see a charity school for the poor, of which I am a patroness?' Lady Clarissa Hyde, that delightful woman, asked me. I gave her my eager assent and so we travelled by my post-chaise to see the school she patronized, which was near Clapham Common. 'The pupils are exceedingly curious to know all about the secret pleasures of lust,' she remarked casually as the braces upon the horses jingled. 'Since it is a school of mixed sex, obviously boys and girls soon become very intimate and tell each other all their secrets.' I had learned *so* much from Clarissa and was eager to learn more. 'The boys and girls of adolescence are exceedingly curious to know all about the secret pleasures of love and no doubt they often talk over the subject, particularly at night, all the time fondling and playing with each other's private parts, which of course is strictly forbidden though, on occasion, one takes no notice of the matter. I am only seriously concerned if there has been violence against girls.'

I knew that many wealthy women liked to give much money to charity schools and I was about to see why. The Headmistress, a tall, angular woman with a snappy, cut-glass voice that terrified her pupils, was clearly in her turn terrified by Clarissa, who could withdraw her funding at a moment's notice. She demanded an interview with the Girl Head Prefect, which request was gladly granted. The Headmistress vacated the study for which Lady Clarissa had paid. There was a tremulous knock upon the door.

'Come,' said Clarissa as I took a pinch of snuff. I sneezed into my multi-coloured silken handkerchief as the Head Prefect entered, since she was so uncommonly beautiful. (These days I find it very irritating to be of middle age. You give a young girl of startling prettiness your most ravishing smile – *and she smiles back* because she thinks that you are a friend of her father.) Jane had long blonde hair, thrusting breasts and a voluptuous bottom. She was dressed in a fussy white blouse with frills and a grey, bell-shaped skirt, the clothing of which emphasized the excellence of her fine figure. Clarissa addressed her sternly.

'Do you ever hear any name for the little chink between your legs, Jane?' Clarissa asked, getting to the point in her inimitable manner.

'Yes, Ma'am. "Cunt". One of the girls wrote it the other day on her slate. She said that was what the boys called it.'

'And what do they call their own things?'

'Pricks, Ma'am.'

'Why do they call them "pricks"?'

'I suppose, Ma'am, it is because they prick our cunts.'

'Would you like to have your cunt pricked?' Clarissa enquired gently.

'Yes, Ma'am, I think I would like it now,' Jane answered innocently, 'since, to be truthful, my cunt feels so very hot.'

'So it is, no doubt, my dear,' Clarissa responded graciously, 'and mine is just the same. Oh, Jane!' Clarissa then got over her and rubbed her quim against that of Jane, who was visibly thrilled by Clarissa's attentions and held the cheeks of her bottom through her skirt. 'Jane, did you ever notice the lump between the legs of Mr Blakeley? The resident tutor?'

'Yes, Lady Clarissa, that is his prick. Every man has that, though some have it larger than others.'

'And have you seen it swell out when he talks to the girls?'

'Yes, Ma'am: especially when he leans over us to make us hold our pens right. Perhaps he is then thinking of our cunts.'

'Thank you, Jane.' Clarissa arose. 'It would be a pleasure to make love to you further – and later.' She swished the skirts of her dress. 'But there are more important administrative matters to be resolved first. Could you please send me all girls with claims of sexual abuse by Mr Blakeley?' Jane arose, smoothed down her skirts, curtsied to us and left the room.

A series of delectably pretty girls entered the room, curtsied humbly to Clarissa and myself and then proceeded to make their depositions against Mr Blakeley, all of them accusing him of sexual molestation and of the unnecessary application of corporal punishment. Clarissa and I listened intently. Apparently this was all done in the name of Christianity.

'Horby,' Clarissa said over dry sherry when all the girls had gone, 'give me a thousand guineas.' Clarissa knew that I always carried two purses, one of a thousand guineas and one of five hundred guineas; so I handed over the former. 'Congratulations, Horby, you have just given a most generous donation to the school and are hereby appointed a governor. Do you not think that these orphans must be helped without cruelty? You have just given me the wherewithal to buy out one of the Christian governors and your entry makes it possible for me to out-vote the Church on all meetings of the Board of Governors. Let us now examine Mr Blakeley.'

I did not like the look of Mr Blakeley when he entered the room. He struck me as being a cringing cur, a bully and a coward. He was a short, thin fellow with an unpleasant countenance, the type who looks as though he has just farted and is trying to blame it upon somebody else. In the course of Clarissa's admittedly severe interrogation, the ghastly Mr Blakeley writhed and squirmed like a worm upon hot coals.

'Mr Blakeley,' she addressed him severely, 'you have not managed to answer any of my questions to any degree of satisfaction. However, I like to think that I am of a merciful disposition and therefore I shall give you a choice. Either you can be dismissed without references, in which case I shall ensure that you will never obtain a stipend in teaching *anywhere*: or you can choose to reform yourself and submit to punishment.' Mr Blakeley swallowed. 'I gather that you are very keen on corporal punishment for recalcitrant pupils. I am reliably informed that you call your canes either "Big Willy" or "Little Willy". Which one would you prefer for your own chastisement?' She glared at this cringing wretch with her cold, azure eyes and he shivered before her gaze. 'Well?'

'Little Willy,' he mumbled.

'Very well.' Lady Clarissa seized the bell which the Headmistress had left upon the desk before her and rang it resoundingly. Instantly all pupils ran to assemble before her, the boys in long grey shorts cut to the knee, which rather reminded one of a skirt. She regarded the pupils pleasantly. 'We have a very naughty boy here before us,' she informed them. 'I refer to Blakeley. BLAKELEY!' He nodded his submission and attention. 'I do not appreciate what you have done to punish the pupils in my charge here and so, therefore, *you* will be punished.' The pupils were barely able to contain their glee. 'Now, Blakeley, go and fetch Little Willy. Go on, go fetch, fetch, fetch . . .' Clarissa laughed as the shame-faced fellow left the room in search of his cane. 'Jane!'

'Yes, Madam.' Jane, the gorgeous Head Prefect, stood to attention.

'I want you to bring me a dress, a corset, stockings, drawers, shoes and plenty of petticoats for Mr Blakeley – I am sure that among the girls there are clothes to fit his build – and bring them back here.' The girls could barely contain their mirth as Jane carried out the instructions of Clarissa. Even

UNHOLY PASSIONS

their Headmistress, who was not unpopular, smiled upon the matter. 'Have you heard,' Clarissa asked me, 'of the Society for the Promulgation of Petticoat Government?'

'Yes,' I replied, 'and there seems to be a Society for the Promulgation of just about everything these days.'

'Wait and see,' said Clarissa, as Mr Blakeley re-entered the room bearing a cane. 'Give me that cane!' Clarissa snapped. 'Now kneel and kiss my boots!' He did so. 'Oh, but you have forgotten to lick my high heels ... do so, or your whipping will be worse than your wildest nightmares.' Blakeley obeyed. 'No! Not that way, you fool! *Suck* my heel!' There was a deep sigh of satisfaction among the boys and girls as he did so. 'Now bend over!' He obeyed. Her victim was stretched out upon the flogging block. 'Ah, Horby, do you not see what I am doing? I have armed myself with a very light cane, made of rattan, which will sting awfully.' Her victim squealed as she lashed his twitching bottom with three cuts. Mr Blakeley begged piteously for Clarissa to forgive him. 'What a little coward you are!' Clarissa laughed. 'I should have thought that such a bold molester of young people would have more spirit and I have hardly touched you yet. Why, you would abuse my pupils directly if I don't beat it out of you now.'

'Ohh ...' Blakeley moaned, 'my arms and legs are so dreadfully stretched and my poor behind still smarts from the three whacks you have given me. Oh! Have pity! Have mercy! Dear Lady Hyde ...'

'I will not listen to such childish nonsense,' Clarissa snapped at him. 'You are both an abuser of my pupils and a dreadful liar, Mr Blakeley. Will you ... ?' Swish! '*Will* you ... ?' *Swish!* '*Will* you?!' SWISH! 'Will *you* ever do it again?' As she gave the man these stinging cuts, her cane hissed through the air and she flourished it before each stroke, which made the sound rather more effective.

'Ah!' he cried out. 'Ah! Ah-r-r-re! I can't bear it, you're

thrashing me with blows that are red-hot...! Oh! Oh! I promise that I shall never, *never* do it again!' His bottom was finely streaked by thin, red lines, the pain being increased by the strain upon his wrists and ankles as he could not restrain his writhing at each cut.

'You don't seem to like it, Blakeley,' Clarissa smiled cruelly. 'But it is for your own good, you will thank me for it later and I fear that it hurts me more than it hurts you.' Swish! 'You have only had seven yet. How you do howl, you silly boy!'

'Aargh!' This was quite a prolonged shriek from Blakeley, whose bottom was now well-whaled. 'You're killing me!' Swish! 'Oh!' *Swish!* 'Oh! I shall die soon!'

'You will have a dozen strokes of the cane,' Clarissa answered him, caning, counting and cutting deliberately until she called 'Twelve!' Then, giving a little pause as if finished, she let the victim compose his features with a sigh of relief; and then just gave him another whippy lash, exclaiming: 'Ah! Ha! Ha! Ha! You thought I had done, didn't you, Mr Prig? It was a baker's dozen you were to get, yet I always give thirteen as twelve for fear of having missed one and like to give the last just as you may think that it is all over.' Blakeley sighed and quivered. 'Jane!' Clarissa threw down her cane and addressed the beautiful Head Prefect. 'Bring your assistants and untie this fellow.'

I watched with fascination as the girls released Mr Blakeley from his undignified posture.

'Step into your silken drawers!' Clarissa commanded him and he obeyed. These white, laced drawers were pulled up tightly upon him by Jane as his bottom burned all the while from the lashing it had received. 'Now, Jane, lace him into a tight female corset here.' This was done as Blakeley gasped. 'Blakeley, step into your petticoats... ah, good. Now, Jane, kindly attach the stockings to the suspenders of his corset...

yes, and girls, kindly assist Mr Blakeley in donning his light blue satin dress . . .' The girls giggled and took great pleasure in obeying Clarissa's command. 'You are now all frilled and petticoated, Mr Blakeley.' How the boys jeered and how the girls cheered! 'You are furthermore demoted. You will only teach the girls. If, after six months, they can inform me that you are teaching well, than I shall restore your britches to you and also your classes with the boys. But for the ensuing six months, you will be in petticoats and you will *never* be allowed to administer corporal punishment again. Only *I* can do that here. Now curtsey to me, Mr Blakeley, curtsey to all the boys and girls here – ah! good boy – curtsey to your learned Headmistress – no! that is not the way to curtsey at all, you fool! You *sink* down on one knee as you spread your skirts . . . ah! much better!' Clarissa turned to the Headmistress. 'Kindly keep me informed of his progress.'

As we travelled back into town by post-chaise, Lady Clarissa kindly invited me to dine with her. I explained that few prospects could please me more, which was true, but I was otherwise engaged to meet James Boswell in order to enjoy a dinner he had arranged whereat both John Wilkes and Dr Samuel Johnson would be present.

I did not know James Boswell that well but he had always struck me as being a most charming gentleman, who had that unique knack of being able to meet the most outstanding individuals of our time, such as Voltaire, Rousseau, General Paoli (who liberated Corsica) and of course, Dr Samuel 'Dictionary' Johnson. He also liked drink and women as much as I did and so it was a pleasure entertaining him to sherry in my home prior to the occasion he had arranged. He was quite a handsome, well-dressed man with much charm and wit, I found.

'It is possible, sir,' Boswell informed me, 'that there are still people in England who do not adore Dr Johnson. These must be removed at once, if possible, by persuasion.' I nodded acquiescence since I was most impressed by Johnson's *Dictionary*, his poetry, his essays, his prose and his novel *Rasselas*, which states essentially that one can be wealthy and powerful yet a spiritual ache may still make one's life empty and cause one to cast all riches aside in order to seek out truth.

'Now my dear friend, Dr Johnson, detests the reputation of John Wilkes,' Boswell continued, 'as being a rake and a dissolute, dissident radical. It is my intention, Lord Horby, and after much diplomatic manoeuvring, to bring Wilkes and Johnson together at the table of the pleasant Mr Dilly. Two men more different could perhaps not be selected out of all mankind. They have even attacked one another with some asperity in their writings; yet I live in habits of friendship with both. I can fully relish the excellence of each since I have ever delighted in that intellectual chemistry, which can separate good qualities from evil in the same person.'

'Quite agree,' I murmured. 'More sherry, Boswell?' He gladly accepted my offer.

'Yes, I was persuaded,' Boswell resumed his discourse after quaffing half his glass, 'that if I had come upon him with a direct proposal: "Sir, will you dine with Jack Wilkes?" He would have flown into a passion and have answered: "Dine with Jack Wilkes, sir!? I'd as soon dine with the Devil!" In consequence, I have been somewhat surreptitious in persuading Dr Johnson to attend Mr Dilly's dinner where he will inadvertently meet John Wilkes . . .'

Mr Dilly, to whose home by Leicester Square we travelled in my phaeton, was a pleasant, thin man who welcomed us in from the cold with hot milk punch. After a time, Wilkes arrived and then Johnson. The latter was a large, bear-like man with clumsy movements, dressed in clothes that he seemed to have bought ten years before. Now, James Boswell, Johnson's

UNHOLY PASSIONS

greatest friend, has of course written a magnificent life of him for he recorded his friend's every saying. For my own part, I can only recall a few words of Johnson that night. When I congratulated him on his *Dictionary*, he snorted indignantly and said:

'Bah! Sir, a lexicographer is merely a harmless drudge.' When John Wilkes congratulated him upon the excellence of his writing, he replied: 'Sir: no man other than a blockhead ever wrote but for money.' When Mr Dilly praised his patriotism, Johnson replied: 'No, sir. Patriotism is the last refuge of a scoundrel.'

'Congratulations, sir,' said Boswell, 'you have tossed and gored several people, as is your custom. I had hoped recently to calm your irascible temper by taking you to see the Giant's Causeway of the Outer Hebrides. Sir: was that not worth seeing?'

'Indeed, sir,' Johnson muttered grumpily, 'but not worth *going* to see.' He drank a pint of milk punch and called for more, gladly supplied by the pleasant Mr Dilly. 'I am pleased, sir,' he said, 'that there are no women present tonight, much as I enjoy female company. I am pleased to see an evening of *men*, since I find this fashion for those idle blue-stockinged women who prate to be tedious. A woman preaching is like a dog walking on its hind legs. It is not done well but one is amazed that it is done at all. However,' he smiled, 'I admit that if my dearest wish for pleasure were to be fulfilled, I would spend my time driving briskly in a post-chaise with a pretty woman.' He scowled and glowered at Wilkes, who of course spent much of his time doing precisely that. Mr Dilly implored us to go in to the dinner his cook had prepared and Johnson acceded to his request. Here, Wilkes charmed him.

Wilkes placed himself next to Dr Johnson and behaved to him with so much attention and politeness that he gained upon him insensibly. No man ate more heartily than Johnson or loved better what was nice and delicate. Wilkes was very assiduous in helping him to some fine veal.

'Pray give me leave, sir,' he said; 'It is better here – a little of the brown – some fat, sir? – a little of the stuffing – some gravy? – let me have the pleasure of giving you some butter – allow me to recommend a squeeze of this orange – or the lemon, perhaps, may have more zest...'

'Sir, sir!' Johnson cried out, 'I am obliged to you, sir!' Bowing slightly, Johnson turned his head to Wilkes with a look for some time of surly virtue but, within a short while, of genial complacency.

'Some claret, Dr Johnson?' Dilly asked him.

'Certainly, sir,' Johnson answered. 'Ah! Of course, claret is for boys. Port is for men. But he who aspires to be a hero must drink brandy!'

'There will be much port and brandy later, Dr Johnson.' Johnson snorted his approval. I noticed that when he ate, it was as though he had not eaten in the twenty years until he had established his literary success and reputation. His veins bulged and sweat stood out upon his forehead.

'Dr Johnson,' Mr Dilly asked him, 'you have contributed and are contributing so much to English Literature. One also gathers that in the past you have had to suffer hard times. May I ask you why, given your most estimable talents, you never saw fit to enjoy patronage?'

'Oh, upon my arrival on London I did endeavour to secure that, sir,' said Johnson, 'but when I had once addressed Lord Chesterfield I had exhausted all the art of pleasing which a retired and uncourtly scholar can possess. I had done all that I could; and no man is well pleased to have his all neglected, be it ever so little. Years have now passed since I waited in Chesterfield's outward rooms, or was repulsed from his door; during which time I have been pushing on my work through difficulties, of which it is useless to complain; and my works

UNHOLY PASSIONS

have been published without one act of assistance, one word of encouragement, or one smile of favour. Such treatment I did not expect, for I never had a Patron before.

'Is not a Patron, Mr Dilly, one who looks with unconcern on a man struggling for life in the water, and, when he has reached ground, encumbers him with help? The notice which Chesterfield might have been pleased to take of my labours, had it been early, had been kind; but it has been delayed till I am indifferent, and cannot enjoy it; till I am solitary and cannot impart it; till I am known and do not want it. I hope it is no very cynical asperity, not to confess obligations where no benefit has been received, or to be unwilling that the Publick should consider me as owing that to a Patron, which Providence has enabled me to do for myself.'

'Ha! ha! Excellent, sir!' Wilkes laughed heartily. 'May I help you to some more roasted sucking pig, sir?' Johnson, chewing with enjoyment, nodded his assent.

'Thank you, Mr Wilkes, for I look upon it, sir, that he who does not mind his belly will hardly mind anything else.' He ate heartily.

'And tell us, Dr Johnson,' the pleasant Mr Dilly enquired gently, 'how you would define this new word, *Net-work*, which appears to refer to communications between England, France, Prussia, Austria and the American Colonies?'

'Sir,' Johnson replied as fruit, cheese and port were served, 'I should define the word as being anything reticulated or decussated, at equal distances, with interstices between the intersections.'

There was a long pause as this information sank in.

'Ha! ha! Excellent, sir!' Wilkes laughed as he took port with Johnson. 'What a golden example of your otiose prolongation of polysyllabic vocables!' Johnson laughed and we discussed the state of the World over brandy. I only recall a few of Johnson's aphorisms.

'Human life,' he stated, 'is everywhere a state in which much is to be endured and little to be enjoyed.'

'Such as being on a ship?' I suggested.

'No, sir!' Johnson bellowed. 'Being on a ship is being in a gaol with the chance of being drowned. Many men who are married will find their fate to be similar. Marriage has many pains but celibacy has no pleasures. As for a second marriage, it is a triumph of hope over experience, yet, and let us face it, no man is a hypocrite in his pleasures. To be happy at home is the ultimate end of all human ambition, I believe, though it remains for many men, sir, that a good tavern is the highest throne of human felicity.'

'Dr Johnson,' Mr Dilly enquired, 'I have just read an article which had criticized your essays about Shakespeare. This notable French critic states that Shakespeare neglects to observe the Aristotelean Unities of Drama, for he states in *The Spectator*: "It is unrealistic when witnessing Shakespeare's *Antony and Cleopatra*, for the spectator to believe that he is in Rome at one moment and in Alexandria at another".'

'Sir,' Johnson growled, 'the spectator is no fool and does not believe himself to be in Rome or in Alexandria, but *in a theatre!*'

I could see that Johnson's friend, Oliver Goldsmith, that excellent dramatist with *She Stoops to Conquer*, novelist with *The Vicar of Wakefield* and poet with *The Deserted Village*, had sense in saying of Johnson: 'If his pistol misses fire, he knocks you down with the butt-end of it!'

Johnson responded by calling Goldsmith 'an inspired idiot': yet he composed the inscription upon his friend's tombstone which reads: 'He touched nothing that he did not adorn.'

Dr Johnson and John Wilkes took a hearty leave of one another and of James Boswell, Mr Dilly and myself. As we passed out into the street, Boswell climbed into his fast cabriolet, Wilkes climbed into his even faster gig, I climbed into my phaeton and Dr Johnson was obviously resolved upon walking a few miles to his home.

'Sir!' I cried out as the horses of Boswell and Wilkes galloped away, 'Dr Johnson, can I not assist you? Perhaps I can ensure that you are driven to your home . . . ?'

'Most kind of you, sir,' he answered gruffly and ascended the steps to my carriage, 'but only on condition that we go via the Embankment.' I did not know why he wanted to essay this particular expedition, but since the man fascinated me so much, I gladly assented to his proposition.

'And what did you think of Jack Wilkes, Dr Johnson?' I enquired as my driver whipped up the horses.

'Did we not hear so much said of Jack Wilkes,' Johnson returned, 'we should think more highly of his conversation. Ah! My thanks to you, sir!' he exclaimed, since I had produced a flask of brandy, from which he proceeded to drink deeply. 'Jack has great variety of talk, Jack is a scholar, and Jack has the manners of a gentleman. But, after hearing his name sounded from pole to pole, as the phoenix of convivial felicity, one is disappointed in his company. He has always been *at me*: but I would do Jack a kindness, rather than not. The contest is now over.' For my own part, the best verdict was given by the goodly James Boswell regarding the meeting of Johnson and Wilkes a year later.

'I was struck,' Boswell wrote in his inimitable manner, 'with observing Dr Samuel Johnson and John Wilkes Esq., literally *tête-à-tête*; for they were reclined upon their chairs, with their heads leaning almost close to each other, and talking earnestly, in a kind of confidential whisper, of the personal quarrel between George the Second and the King of Prussia. Such a scene of perfectly easy sociality between two such opponents in the war of political controversy, as that which I now beheld, would have been an excellent subject for a picture. It presented to my mind the happy days which are foretold in Scripture, when the lion shall lie down with the kid.'

'Most kind of you, sir,' Dr Johnson said to me meanwhile as my horses clip-clipped their way towards the Embankment. He stared eagerly at the streets of London. 'Indeed, sir, look at this variety. When a man is tired of London, he is tired of life!' I looked at this extraordinary man and wondered. The gossip of the servants, for which I paid, had informed me that Johnson was in love with Mrs Thrale, wife of a wealthy brewer, with the consent of Mr Thrale, and that rather than fuck her, he asked to be bound and fettered, with which request Mrs Thrale gladly complied. Well, each to his own taste is what I say. We continued on our way to the Embankment as I wondered as to what his designs were. I love the sight of the River Thames, dear old Father Thames, but the Embankment was notorious for thieves, rogues, robbers, beggars and prostitutes. Did Dr Johnson want a prostitute? I cannot say that I was worried since my expert driver, Mark Ardonne, carried a blunderbuss and was also an expert shot with his brace of pistols. The carriage stopped shortly after Charing Cross. Muttering to himself, Dr Johnson dismounted and proceeded to walk along the Embankment.

'There 'e goes!' men and women cried out. 'There goes the great Doctor Johnson!' I ensured that Ardonne and I covered him but it was not necessary. Johnson was simply looking at the urchins, boys and girls, who were sleeping roughly upon the Embankment, probably after a pint of gin. I know what I saw. This man simply walked among them, quietly slipping coins into their beds, then quietly returned to my carriage.

'What have you been doing, Dr Johnson?' I enquired.

'Nothing,' he muttered in reply.

'But, Dr Johnson, I saw you slipping coins into the bags

which serve as beds for the poor homeless boys and girls of London.'

'Possibly so, sir. I have, if you must ask, given a few coins to the young ones, since they will wake up to find, to their delighted surprise, that they have the means by which to buy breakfast.' He smiled ruefully. 'I am hardly a rich man but earlier in my life, I endured a period of horrendous poverty and I know what it means to be young, ambitious and starving, sir! A few coins can give a boy hope.'

'Hope makes for a good breakfast but a bad supper,' I remarked, 'as Henry Fielding has said.'

'Indeed, sir,' Johnson replied, 'and I have breakfasted on hope and supped on despair all too often. Perhaps I owe my continued existence to odd acts of kindness years before from a passing stranger.'

'Some wine, Dr Johnson?' for I always keep a few bottles and glasses in my carriages. He assented happily.

'Few people,' he murmured as the horses took him home, 'have the intellectual resources to forgo the pleasures of wine. They cannot contrive how to fill the interval between dinner and supper.' I asked after his opinion of our present leading politicians. 'Why, sir,' he replied, 'Grenville is dull, naturally dull; but it must have taken a great deal of pains to become as we now see him. Such excess of stupidity, sir, is not in Nature. As for Lords Rockingham and North; sir, there is no settling the point of precedency between a louse and a flea.'

CHAPTER TWENTY-SIX

'The secret of seducing a woman is quite simple, gentlemen,' Sir Francis Dashwood addressed us in his home at West Wycombe, on this occasion serving Dublin Bay prawns accompanied by wine from Alsace. 'Treat all the duchesses as chambermaids and all the chambermaids as duchesses.' I looked around at the gentlemen gathered. A few of our Club had died but on this blazing hot day of 2 August 1770, a number of the Club's members were still in being and thriving. Sandwich was still there and restored to his former and dearly beloved position of First Lord of the Admiralty. He was presently encouraging Captain Cook to go exploring: Cook discovered the Sandwich Islands and proceeded to discover Australia, all the while supported by Sandwich.

'I shall be,' Dashwood informed us, 'Join Postmaster-General. As such, I wish to expedite swift transmission of information via a Penny Post.' (*Editor's note:* Baron le Despenser proposed this matter but it was not accepted until the days of Sir Rowland Hill and the Penny Post of the 1840s.) 'I intend to develop diplomatic relationships with interesting revolutionary groupings in France, Germany and the Colonies of America.'

'You remind me, sir,' Sandwich smiled, 'of Shakespeare's Mark Antony.'

'Perhaps so, sir,' Dashwood retorted, 'but lend me your ears.' Sandwich smiled again. I regarded my fellow members.

Of course, Paul Whitehead was there, looking as cadaverous as ever. Dashwood had assembled quite a number. There was George Selwyn, MP; Sir Thomas Stapleton; Sir Henry Vansittart on leave from governing Bengal well; Dr Benjamin Bates; Sir John Dashwood-King; the Earl of Orford, Horace Walpole's half-witted half-brother; the Duke of Kingston, the Marquis of Granby; 'Old Q', the Duke of Queensberry; William Hogarth, the great artist; Joseph Banks, the great scientist; and John Hall Stevenson, fine patron of the arts and later one to enshrine what he had learned among us in his 'Crazy Castle' in Yorkshire. There was also of the company one Benjamin Franklin from America, a pleasant bespectacled man of wide and deep learning.

'Listen to me, gentlemen!' Dashwood roared. We did since we all knew that nobody could tell this Baron to shut his mouth. 'Although I do not want John Wilkes to be a member of our Club any longer, given the fact that he has betrayed it to the journalists and has caused us to abandon Medmenham Abbey and go underground, as you shall see; he and his London Mob have nevertheless spoken some sense in terms of what is coming in our times.'

'And just what,' Sandwich asked, '*is* coming in our times?'

'Revolution,' Dashwood replied, 'and Democracy. No, sir!' he exclaimed as Sandwich snorted disgustedly. 'Whatever your quarrels or mine with Jack Wilkes, he has actually shown us the future. Does a sane man swim *against* the stream? You will see Wilkes defending the rights of the American colonists in the House of Commons: and you will see me defending the rights of the American colonists in the House of Lords. If the Government fails to see sense, then I shall concur with my friend Benjamin Franklin here and declare for the right of a newly-formed United States of America to secede from the British Empire and formulate an independent country with the highest of ideals such as we have always sought to uphold in our Club.'

'That policy is doubtful and full of daring,' Sandwich said. 'Are you seriously proposing, Francis, that the American Colonies *break away* from us?'

'Yes, I am,' said Dashwood, 'if the British Empire will not see sense. We have tried our religious and political ideals here in England, gentlemen, and we have in consequence been forced to go underground. In America, a young country, there is the possibility of the ideals being established as espoused by Francis Bacon in *The New Atlantis*. (*Editor's note:* these ideals were in fact espoused in the American *Declaration of Independence*, the *Constitution* and the *Bill of Rights*.). (*Translator's note:* Yes, they were: and these ideals have been most shamefully betrayed, albeit to my own subsequent advantage.) 'Moreover,' Dashwood declared, 'Benjamin Franklin and I here will be rewriting *The Book of Common Prayer* so as to give people a good religion.'

'Sir Francis,' I protested mildly, 'I had thought that you had no patience with Christianity.'

'The common people need a religion,' Dashwood returned, 'and that is why the new *Book of Common Prayer* for America will make Church services short and endurable and all references to anything other than Divine worship and ethical benevolence will be cut.' (*Translator's note:* this was done and this Book is still used in Episcopalian churches, though it is customarily attributed to Franklin.) 'As the ancient Chinese curse has it: "May you live in interesting times." Hah! No choice about it at all, gentlemen. We do.'

'And France?' Sandwich enquired.

'Face the fact, Sandwich,' Dashwood urged him, 'that France is ripe for revolution. I know this from our Brother – or is it sister? – the Chevalier D'Eon. I do not think that there will be a revolution in England because the squire *likes* to go to the inn and speak with the workers. There will be a revolution in France because the French aristocrat despises his peasants and labourers in a manner that would be considered deplorable in England. Have you not read the tale of Voltaire? Possibly he is the most intelligent man of our century; or else it is Dr Johnson. "My Lord, I must live," a French peasant pleaded when his Lord raised the rent. "I fail to see why," this arrogant bastard replied. And *that*, Sandwich, explains why there will in time be a bloody revolution in France. But enough of politics, gentlemen, let us proceed to matters of religion.'

We drank up our cups, changed into our robes and followed Dashwood down the hill to the caves he had had carved out of the rock and stone. The blazing orange sun was setting as we walked and I recall reflecting on what we had added, were adding or were about to add to the sum of human knowledge and experience.

'We shall be crossing the River Styx, the River of Death,' Dashwood announced.

I wondered about the possibility of dying here, now, and at this moment. Certainly in our clubbability, which included leading women, we had contributed substantially to the artistic, scientific and cultural life of England. We had realized that it was possible for a grouping of extraordinary people to come together in exquisite surroundings in order to raise the consciousness of those present, assisting us to evolve.

'After this, it's back to the library,' I overheard Dashwood saying to Sandwich. 'You must read my books on Tantra. Believe me, the techniques really work. These days I can go ten hours without coming, and this delights the ladies.'

'Ten hours?' Sandwich laughed. 'Myself, I prefer ten seconds.'

'Ha!' Dashwood roared with laughter. 'A grope and a squirt is it for you, sir? Or five and a half seconds of squelching, possibly?'

'Both,' said Sandwich, 'if I have little interest in the girl. And neither, sir, if I do!'

What paradoxes there were between us! Although our endeavour to have Great Britain governed well by a Patriot King, backed by a loyal élite, had turned out to be a failure, this had inadvertently provoked the rise of Democracy in England and this was evidently spreading so as to enflame the torches of LIBERTY! EQUALITY! FRATERNITY! to spark off Revolutions in both the American Colonies and in France.

Certainly Dashwood had preserved a holy tradition received from predecessors and which I hoped would be passed on to successors. (*Translator's note:* Aleister Crowley is probably the most notable twentieth-century exponent of this philosophy in action.) Definitely I concur with the view of Dashwood, that sex between man and woman is holy, sacred, sacramental and religious: in addition to being jolly good fun.

The Friars of Sir Francis had restored pagan worship and occult rites graced by fine art. One hoped that they might found a legend to inspire those to come after them. Nevertheless, I *was* nervous as we entered the caves, those spaces where perhaps apes became men. Within a few yards, one was conscious of the fact that we were no longer subject to the blazing August heat and the further we descended, the colder the chill became. We wound our ways through seemingly endless catacombs, then we stood by Dashwood's artificially-created River Styx that was flowing quite fast. Benjamin Franklin, who was carrying a walking cane, professed that this was a magick wand that would enable him to calm these troubled waters.

In my opinion, Benjamin Franklin – and 'franklin' means free man – was an extraordinarily talented individual. His earlier experiments with a kite concerning the effects of lightning and the resulting advance in comprehending the application of electricity had gained him a justly earned reputation among men of science in both America and Europe. He waved his magick wand over the waters, muttering and chanting mysterious incantations, and the waters became still; and many gasped.

'It is *electricity*, perhaps, gentlemen, that may have done this. What *is* electricity? We are starting to learn about how it behaves,' he said in his even, measured tones, 'but I ask you, what *is* it? Does anybody know?'

'Mr Franklin . . . ?' There came a thin, piping voice from the back. It was that clown, Horace Walpole's brother, the Earl of Orford.

'Yes, sir,' said Franklin, 'please tell us what electricity is.'

'Um – I th-thought I knew what it was, P-professor,' the Earl of Orford stammered, 'but I f-fear I h-have f-forgotten.'

'Just my luck!' Franklin exclaimed. 'There was only one man on this goddamn planet who can tell me what Electricity is . . . and he has forgotten.'

'Mr Franklin,' I said, 'I do not think that you stilled the waters of the River Styx by means of Electricity. I also do not think that you stilled the waters by means of Magick. I think that you stilled them because concealed in your walking cane, which you called your Magick Wand, you had copious quantities of oil.'

'Why, you are quite right, sir.' Benjamin Franklin smiled at me. 'I applaud your keen powers of observation. Of course it was a trick which *appeared* to be magical, but I wanted to demonstrate the method of Science.'

'Quite rightly so, sir,' Dashwood stated solemnly, 'but now allow *me* to demonstrate the method of Magick. Let us initially essay that in silence.'

There was a boat tethered by a post. With a wicked grin, Paul Whitehead stepped into this boat and seized the oar as though he were truly Charon, rowing us across the River of the Dead. As we were waiting to enter this boat, I stared at

UNHOLY PASSIONS

Franklin who made a most favourable impression upon me. In later years, of course, he would be one of the principal architects of the American Revolution and Constitution; and as the American Ambassador in Paris during what the Americans term the War of Independence, his bringing of France into the conflict proved to be decisive in gaining victory and independence for the young United States of America.

Whitehead rowed the boat across the short distance which led to the very heart of the caves. Upon alighting, Dashwood had us ushered within and bade us stand in a circle illuminated by thirteen tall, black candles, placed in candelabra fashioned in gold so as to show writhing serpents. Dashwood proceeded to invoke the Powers of the Four Elements: Fire, Water, Air and Earth, all of them crowned with Spirit. There was a beautiful statue of the Goddess of Love here and before Her, he raised a candle for Fire, a chalice for Water, a small brazier of incense for Air and a gold coin for Earth. Then he began his strange and unearthly chant:

Thee I invoke, the Bornless One
Thee that didst create the Earth and the Heavens.
Thee, that didst create the Night and the Day.
Thee, that didst create the Darkness and the Light.
Thou are ASAR UN-NEFER – Myself made Perfect –
Whom no man hath seen at any time.
Thou art IA-BESZ – the Truth in Matter.
Thou art IA-APOPHRASZ – the Truth in Motion.
Thou hast distinguished between the Just and the Unjust.
Thou didst make the Female and the Male.
Thou didst produce the Seeds and the Fruit.
Thou didst form Men to love one another and to hate one another.
Hear me, and make all Spirits subject unto Me; so that

every Spirit of the Firmament and of the Ether: upon the Earth and under the Earth, on dry land and in the water; of Whirling Air, and of rushing Fire, and every Spell and Scourge of God may be obedient unto Me.'

We stood in silence for some minutes and I could swear I felt fire hot enough to sizzle one's bones, succeeded by water which gave succour to ever pore of my skin. Then I felt as though I was blown about by a rushing mighty wind and then I sat as if I were a stone statue of Earth. At this instant, it was as though the Grace of God descended upon us in the form of a Dove.

Eventually Dashwood gave the signal that we should leave, which we did in a solemn and reverent silence. Upon crossing the River Styx again, I felt as though I had died and experienced rebirth. Whitehead now stepped out of the boat and plucked a flaming torch from the wall so as to lead us elsewhere, through what appeared to be an eternally winding labyrinth. In the distance I discerned braziers of glowing coals and we entered the chamber within the caves to see Lady Clarissa Hyde spread-eagled upon a stone slab, her nubile body quite naked, and surrounded by all my favourite women. There was my darling Arabella Marchmount; Lady Vane; Lady Betty Germain; Miss Fanny Murray; Lady Mary Woolcott, Dashwood's half-sister; Mrs Charlotte Hayes; and there were Millicent and Sarah, too.

To my amazement, Dashwood cast off his robe to reveal himself, despite his years of middle age, as being still a strikingly fine figure of a man.

'The Way to Succeed!' he declared. 'And the Way to suck Eggs!' He took a deep breath then proclaimed: 'This is the Holy Hexagram. Plunge from the height, O God, and interlock with Man! Plunge from the height, O Man, and interlock with Beast! ABRAHADABRA . . .' he chanted after which he flung himself upon Clarissa, placing his face so that he was licking her cunt and simultaneously thrusting his cock deep within her mouth. 'Ah!' he cried out. 'The Holy Hexagram! The Red Triangle is the descending tongue of Grace; the Blue Triangle is the ascending tongue of prayer. This Interchange, the Double-Gift of Tongues, the Word of Double Power ABRAHADABRA! – ARARITA! – is the Sign of the GREAT WORK.' He sighed in ecstasy. 'For the GREAT WORK is accomplished in Silence. And behold is not that Word equal to Cheth, that is Cancer.' He appeared to be quite delirious though I think that we all were as we felt the divine light of the white spirit descend among us: and Francis and Clarissa came to a simultaneous orgasm which made both their bodies writhe.

'This Work,' Dashwood gasped, his mouth wet with the copious spending of Clarissa, 'also eats up itself, accomplishes its own end, nourishes the worker, leaves no seed, is perfect in itself. Little children, love one another!'

We certainly had no difficulty in accomplishing *that*.

'This beautiful mound,' Dashwood continued eagerly, 'is covered with such a profusion of dark hairs; and the swelling lips . . . how deliciously they pout, while the glowing red chink between is most luxurious and inviting. I must kiss it. Oh! how sweetly it smells!' He warmly kissed her cunt, then, opening the lips yet again, he sucked her clitoris and pushed his tongue into the hot recess.

'Ah!' Fanny Murray shrieked out. The touch of the tongue of Sandwich was clearly making her quim thrill. 'O!' She writhed. 'The touch of your mouth makes my cunt thrill and when I feel your tongue moving around my clitoris and penetrating the sensitive folds within, I cannot help opening my thighs and raising myself a little,' she smiled, 'so as to afford you a freer access to this most pleasurable spot.'

'Horby!' Arabella exclaimed in mock indignation. 'Your

prick is sticking out and pointed towards me, nodding its great red head as if in proud defiance.'

'Look at this poor fellow, Madam,' I replied. 'He craves your kind indulgence and only asks to hide his blushing head for a moment in your sweet nest ... won't you take him in your hand?'

'O, for shame!' Arabella blushed in mock horror. 'Put that horrid thing away. I won't look at it or touch it. I *won't* let you put it in. I *won't!*' She covered her cunt with her hand then, puzzlingly enough, used her other hand for a placing upon my prick, gripping her fingers around it. 'Mmm . . .' she sighed dreamily. 'This feels deliciously smooth and soft but, at the same time, firm and stiff.' I continued to caress her. 'Horby, let me up. What do you mean by your actions?'

'I mean that I am going to fuck you once again, Arabella. I am going to put my prick into your cunt and fuck you.'

'Ohh . . .' Arabella was being deliberately coy. 'I will not let you. This would harm me and hurt me.'

'No, my love, it will neither hurt you nor harm you. Let me put it in, do, my sweet pet.' I pushed the head of my prick in between the lips of her cunny and moving it up and down the furrow, said: '*There*! that does not hurt you, I'm sure.' I then stuck my cock at her inner opening and, with a sudden push, forced it in.

'Oh, Horby! Take it out! Oh! it is hurting me . . . ohh. You said you would not hurt me . . .' But I only pushed harder and something gave way inside and she felt my whole prick storm up into her belly. This had a visibly startling effect at first and took away her breath. When I went on to work my tool in and out and she felt it rubbing with a most delicious friction against the throbbing folds of her cunt, the feeling became one of overpowering delight, as she twisted about and heaved to meet my thrusts. We did not so much come together as explode.

'There, darling,' she sighed, 'don't you like that?'
'Yes . . . I like it now, that's very nice.'
'Now say the name of it.'
'Prick . . .' I whispered.
'Spell it out. Ugh!' she gasped.
'P-R-I-C-K. And yours?'
'Cunt. C-U-N-T.'
'And doing this?'
'Fucking. F-U-C-K-I-N-G.'
'Congratulations,' I said. 'But go on. Say what it is you like.'
'I like to feel your prick fucking my cunt. Oh . . . go on, it's just coming . . . PRICK! . . . CUNT! . . . FUCKING!' she screamed as I poured out a torrent of hot seed right deep within her belly.

I looked around after a time and noticed that absolutely everybody was engaged in the Noble Art of Fucking. In fact, it was some while before we all paused for breath.

'Ladies and Gentlemen!' Dashwood announced as we all recovered and composed ourselves, 'I now have an extra delight. Do you see this?' As Dashwood's divine milk punch was served by Paul Whitehead, we looked and saw a stone made of black obsidian. It was very beautiful. 'This is presently owned by Horace Walpole,' Dashwood declared, 'and it will be returned to him; meanwhile I am grateful to our Brother, Walpole's half-brother, dear Lord Orford here.' The Earl of Orford nodded and then slobbered at the mouth. 'This *Magick Mirror* was obtained from the Aztecs by a member of the Spanish expedition which colonized Mexico under Cortez. It subsequently passed into the hands of Dr John Dee, the great Elizabethean magus, renowned as being the most learned man of his era, and his assistant, Edward Kelley, saw spirits within this Stone.'

'Ah, yes.' Sandwich looked up from his hitherto quiet

fucking of Fanny. 'As Samuel Butler states in his *Hudibras* . . .' To my amazement, Sandwich burst into verse:

'Kelley did all his Feats upon
The Devil's Looking-glass, a stone
Where playing with him at *Bo-peep*
He solved all problems ne'er so deep.'

'Quite right, sir,' Dashwood responded warmly, 'but let us look at it for ourselves.' (*Editor's note:* Dr John Dee used a number of shewstones. The British Museum acquired what is claimed to be this particular one in October 1966.) 'Here! Take a look! And more punch for everybody!'

When it was my turn to look, I must confess that, initially, I saw nothing other than a black and shining stone. After a time, though, it was as if a grey mist descended to obscure my vision. I looked again as tears started to stream from my eyes and discerned a series of pictures as I heard voices. I saw Dashwood living to a ripe old age and influencing everyone within his orbit. I saw Sandwich relentlessly encouraging the exploration of the Globe by sea. I saw Whitehead living and dying for the ideals Dashwood espoused. I saw the Americans repelling the armed forces of the British Empire and founding their own nation. I saw France arising in Revolution to overthrow her ruling oligarchy amidst torrents of fire and blood. I saw riots in Great Britain, moving her more towards a marriage with Democracy. I saw the sun and the moon, the planets and the stars. I saw myself married to the gorgeous Arabella. I saw past, present and future and I saw you. I knew at that instant that there is the male and the female, energy, *energy*, ENERGY! That's IT!

'DO WHAT THOU WILT,' said Rabelais and Dashwood. This is the Law of Nature and of our own Natures. It bids carpenters to make tables, authors to write books, sheep to eat grass and wolves to eat sheep. Given the present wretched state of the World in our wars against Napoleon, it is high time that each and every one of us proceeds to realize that inmost Will within. On that night, which was a sacred occasion, we certainly did.